Operations Strategy in Action

Operations Strategy in Action

A Guide to the Theory and Practice of Implementation

Kim Hua Tan

Associate Professor of Operations Management, Nottingham University Business School, UK

Rupert L. Matthews

ESRC Case Researcher, Nottingham University Business School, UK

Edward Elgar

Cheltenham, UK • Northampton, MA, USA

Published by
Edward Elgar Publishing Limited
The Lypiatts
15 Lansdown Road
Cheltenham
Glos GL50 2JA
UK

Edward Elgar Publishing, Inc.
William Pratt House
9 Dewey Court
Northampton
Massachusetts 01060
USA

A catalogue record for this book
is available from the British Library

Library of Congress Control Number: 2009930867

Mixed Sources
Product group from well-managed
forests and other controlled sources
www.fsc.org Cert no. SA-COC-1565
© 1996 Forest Stewardship Council

ISBN 978 1 84720 777 7

Printed and bound by MPG Books Group, UK

Contents

Preface

Within recent times the explosion of the financial market, exponential increases in market volatility, uncertainty in investments and even the reduced security in the banking sector, mean it is likely there will be increased interest in the elements of an organisation that actually add value to society: operations. As interest increases, there will be a greater need to offer those with responsibility for managing and directing organisations from a high level to re-discover what their company actually does, rather than simply viewing it as a black box that produces profits. To reclaim the executives' interest in what the business does, there is a need for the operations sector to offer a more cohesive image of what it does to the executives, to wean them off their addiction to keeping their hands clean and managing by numbers. Unfortunately, with operations including almost all areas of business, creating such a coherent image is difficult, with some having difficulty moving away from operations as manufacturing or focusing on particular areas of operations, which does not help to gain the support of those in charge. From here it should be possible to begin thinking for the long term, and begin developing not simply to maximise profit but to give the organisation the best chance of survival in the future.

This book's aim is to offer a helpful insight into the subject by discussing the current state of the subject of operations strategy and why it is so important for an organisation. The first half of the book looks at this, moving on to discuss why the subject of implementation is so difficult, which may be a reason why executives have shied away from the subject. At this point in the book, the focus begins to move towards the development of the skills required for operations strategy implementation in general. Moving into the second half of the book, we offer specific tools and approaches to assist in the generation of a capability able to assist implementation. By focusing on the development of supporting skills, the book moves away from overly focusing on the work carried out by an organisation, as those involved are the experts. Moving away from such functional approaches to strategy, aiming for the development of capabilities for the implementation of an operations strategy, we have aimed to offer executives and managers alike a perspective that more closely matches their level. By directing this book at the level of those charged with organisational transformation, we hope to be able to build confidence in taking their organisation away from safe business-as-usual activities and give the customers consistent value, which financial markets seem unable to do.

1. Introduction to operations strategy

1.0 WHAT IS OPERATIONS AND WHY IS IT IMPORTANT?

The operations element of a business is effectively the part of the business that transforms the input into an organisation into the output that gives additional value to the end user than the sum of the inputs to the system. Drucker (1955) stated that it was not the ability to carry a more difficult activity or an activity more efficiently than a competitor that allowed operations to compete within the market place, but rather the ability to provide value for the customer. By appreciating this and continuing to develop the value an organisation has added to the inputs in line with the requirements of the market, the organisation should be able to remain competitive without the need to compete on price. What this means in regard to operations, is that it is the processes that take place within the operations function that allow an organisation to be present and compete within a market place. This is not to say that other functions within an organisation are any less important than operations; however, if an organisation is not carrying out or at least coordinating processes that meet these requirements, the organisation is effectively not contributing by adding value to society.

By focusing on the development of operations within an organisation it becomes possible for the organisation to effectively develop and define the value it creates for the end user to meet their needs in a way that other organisations are unable to do. Rather than focusing on the business functions that support operations, the developments translate directly to how the end user perceives the organisation by the elements that will ultimately relate to their satisfaction. Organisations that have focused on the development of the operations are the organisations that have been able to show long-term growth and success within the market place. Importantly, in these situations, success has not been dictated by a particular innovation, although innovation is important; instead it is their ability to continue to satisfy their customer that defines their performance. By focusing on operations, Toyota has been able to remain profitable where other firms have struggled and it has not had to offer products that redefine the market place. It is able to offer consistently satisfactory products that continue to change to match the needs of the market in a manner that uses resources in an efficient manner.

The operational element may be thought of as quite an aggregated element of analysis and difficult to focus specific improvements on, especially if a large range of products and processes are being carried out within an operations function. From a different lower-level perspective, individual processes could be thought of as too disaggregated to be able to develop in a way that will affect over-all performance. For this reason, a useful unit of analysis within the operations functions is that of capabilities, which are able to define how well an organisation is able to compete. A capability is a selection of processes and skills that can be effectively combined in a manner that directly contributes to the value the end user receives. Within the operations functions it is the coordinated development and deployment of capabilities that will be what determines if an operations function is able to perform in a manner that allows an organisation to compete. Particular capabilities that may give organisations competitive advantages may be elements that enable a number of business functions to focus their activities in a way that will be appreciated by the end user (Barney 1991).

1.1 THE CONCEPT OF STRATEGY

Before a suitable introduction to operations strategy is possible, it is first necessary to understand why there is a need for an operations strategy. Even before this, it is also necessary to understand why strategy is such a significant concept in business that warrants the amount of interest that it generates. For many years it has been considered necessary to be able to drive a company so that it is able to grow and continue making money for those that have money invested in the company. Unfortunately, this puts unnecessary focus on the results of business rather than focusing on the business means – can a business's success be gauged wholly on something that is simply a product of such a large number of elements? For this reason, it seems self-perpetuating for a company to review its own financial data to determine how it should operate in the future.

The definition of strategy seems to be heavily focused on its connotations in planning, but the subtle difference is that the planning is specifically long range in nature. Before discussing strategy in a business sense, the importance and effect of strategy will be discussed in other areas where long-range planning needs careful consideration. Sport and warfare are both examples of where suitable long-range planning can have significant effects on an outcome, and where focusing on the result alone may not be a suitable way to determine performance. With traditional, purer sports, the effects of natural ability are notable, with certain nations being more proficient at certain sports, where genes may assist in certain activities. However, due to people's almost infinite capacity to learn, the cognitive element becomes considerably more important. For athletes, the need to train could be considered a strategy to improve performance and build on natural ability, allowing a gradual improvement in performance over time. With the purer sports, although nature undoubtedly plays a big role in the performance of an athlete, techniques can allow step changes in the performance, with particularly successful ones being passed from one athlete to the next (e.g. Dick Fosbury).

As the complexity of activities increases, the importance of other aspects of ability becomes apparent: all too often athletes fail to perform at big events, even if their ability and technique put them on top on paper. In this case, it is another cognitive element that becomes important: the ability to use the correct ability and technique when required. To reflect this aspect, the use of sports psychologists has become more widespread to give athletes a mental edge, even in the purer disciplines. Performing well on a practice court or in a semi-finals will not allow someone to win – they have to be able to continue to perform in all situations. This aspect of sport seems to become even more significant when considered in regards to more complex sports, when deficiencies in physical, technical or mental ability will all affect overall performance. This is effectively another type of strategy that is employed to combine with the other types, where the athlete's ability in one area will neither determine success nor shape the following year's training plan.

When these ideas are developed and directed onto team sports, the mental elements are even more noticeable, especially in certain sports that rely on certain set plays. However, in other, less structured sports, developing such a capability is considerably more complex, as it requires the team as a whole to be able to adapt in an effective way without explicit direction from a coach or manager. This could be considered a team culture or dynamic where the importance of individual ability, technique and mental strength is second to how well the team functions as a whole. Here, it may be the presence of a managerial figure, who is able to create, develop or destroy this team element. A consistent element within the team could also potentially be as important as team make-up, where structure and culture are created around a particular element that may affect the team performance more than having a star player who does not complement elements already present within the team.

The final description of strategy in a non-business context is easily the earliest identified study, with writing from as early as 2000 BC. Although strategy in such a context is obviously very different from the above instances, there are similarities with the extinction of a species (within nature) or loss in a sports event effectively being another form of defeat. However, with the consequences of war being considerably more serious, the associated studies of past successful military strategies began much earlier than such thinking in the sports world. It has long been considered that effective military strategies are what are required for victory, but like the sporting analogy, focusing on a single component will seldom result in the required levels of performance. Such examples were demonstrated within the American civil war, where generals employed Napoleonic strategies without considering the effects of innovations such as long-range rifles on the situations.

Such an example is one of many where those in charge do not take account of how the situations have changed since the campaigns they studied took place. Military strategy could be considered in the same manner as the cognitive elements described above – that although they assist in overall performance they should not be focused upon to the exclusion of other information. An interesting example is Hannibal's defeat to the Romans, who were aware Hannibal's forces were considerably more able, but by employing a strategy of numerous controlled battles, they were able to consistently wear down morale. Even though a number of battles were lost, the overall aim of victory was achieved by understanding the importance of specific elements required for good performance. Although ability, technology, technique and morale are important in performance, through focusing on a specific element, the reduction in overall performance can be sufficient. Having said this, it may simply be specific abilities present in one's force compared to another that determine victory, or at least make defeat less likely.

In the military context, specific analogies to business become even more noticeable, where competing organisations do battle in the market place. The following sections will aim to outline how businesses approach strategy in different ways. With the consideration of this first section, the reason for its inclusion will be apparent, as although the fields and subject matter could not be more different, the common theme of strategy is relatively consistent throughout. This look at strategy also tries to outline the comment earlier that a single measurement, especially one that is a product of so many factors as profit, cannot be a suitable measure of performance. Would measuring a sports team's ability on a single performance be an appropriate way to prepare for the following year, or an army's future performance based on a single victory? Without taking account of many factors, it is simply not possible to gauge performance or prepare for the future. The next section describes how this is done when the primary element of information for the strategy process is financial data.

1.2 HISTORIC APPROACHES TO STRATEGY

In a traditional hierarchically structured company, the way strategy is approached in its most general way is by the collections of large amounts of business information for processing by the most intelligent people in the company. Situated within a headquarters, these highly intelligent people are charged with analysing the company data to determine the most appropriate course of action over the next planning period. Due to the processes required in large businesses, it is likely that the majority of this information will be financial but it is also likely that there will be some market-related data. The result of analysing this data will be an outline of how the company should look in the future, including what acquisitions and liquidations are necessary. Although assessing performance in this way, using financial data as the base unit of analysis, is inappropriate, it does allow the business to be assessed in a systematic way, using well-grounded Newtonian-based, economic principles.

The data and subsequent strategic plan, although fundamentally flawed, even if the financial data is accurate and unbiased, are considered a good foundation for this activity, as it means that the strategic process can be removed from actual business activities. This potentially gives investors confidence that if those in charge of the direction of the company are skilled at managing money, they should be able to make money for them. This creates a vicious circle, as shown in Figure 1.1, where those able to carry out this function require a grounding in finance rather than the

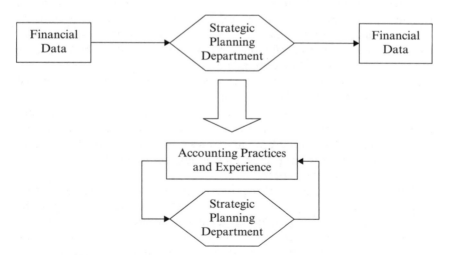

Figure 1.1   Purely financially driven development process

actual business function. However, is it possible to consider that a business makes money, simply because it makes money, or because it is able to create value in the business process that fulfils a customer requirement (Drucker 1955)? This is obviously not the case from an operations perspective, where the strategy needs to be based primarily around the business process while simultaneously considering the customer's needs. However, when the overall business strategy is based around financial data, with the overall aim of the activities based around profit maximisation, there is potential for difficulties.

Once the corporate strategy has been created that theoretically determines the best course of action for the company, it is then converted into a business strategy that is likely to be made up of a selection of business targets (see Figure 1.2). These may include the expansion of certain aspects of the business that have potential for greater profit and reductions in areas that are less profitable. The major problem with a process of this type is that apart from the lack of actual business information, there must be an extensive process of strategy dissemination, with the process being initiated from a single department. Not only does the planning department have to effectively communicate their work to the board, which may require considerable deliberations. The same process needs to be carried out when the corporate strategy is converted into a business strategy, where it needs to be approved and accepted by the business managers.

With the foundation of the strategy being financial, that is already looking backwards (Johnson and Kaplan 1987), combined with the time required to transfer such initiatives, once the information gets to the business processes, it will not be representative of the current business environment. This means that the targets that the business will be required to work towards may simply not be possible. Notwithstanding this, these are the targets that will determine if a particular function is successful in a particular year in the eyes of the board and the investors, which will in turn, determine the following year's plans. With such an approach to strategy, the long-term aspect of the work does not seem to be of particular importance, with the business functions doing whatever is necessary to meet financial targets. Figure 1.3 illustrates how this may affect an organisation's development over time, depending on functional dominances present within an organisation.

Although formulation of the overriding strategy is based around financial elements, the profitability of a particular business is likely to be defined by the operations that will realise the strategy. Taking a purely financial view of an organisation, there may even be a tendency for the operations to be considered a constraining factor or even a necessary evil. To convert the strategy into functional targets and aims, there are further

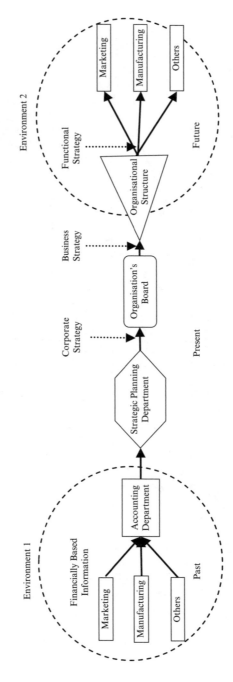

Figure 1.2   Corporate strategy process

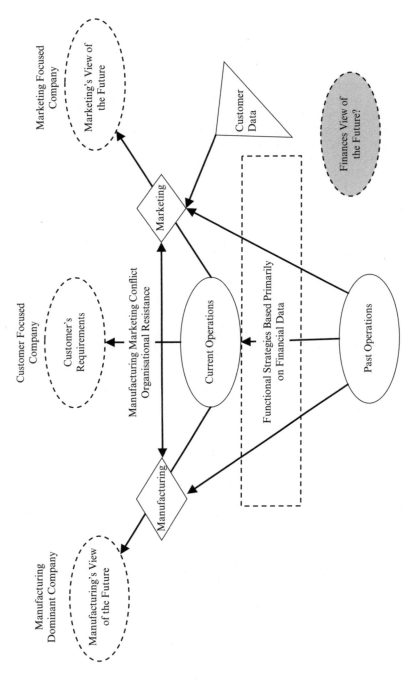

Figure 1.3 A financially driven strategy process

processes of dissemination, interpretation and conversion, to move from a corporate, to a business, and then to a functional strategy that aims to direct the functions in a way that achieves the higher-level business aims. However, due to the overall targets being based on financial data, the functional targets are unlikely to have guidance of how the targets are to be achieved. With a basis of profit maximisation derived from logic, rather than a more rounded understanding of the business functions, this may lead to business functions working towards business targets that do not consider the needs of the business. This is represented by the grey oval that illustrates how a financially driven organisation may develop itself out of business by not being able to meet the needs of the market.

1.3 FUNCTIONAL APPROACHES

In a traditional view of a company, all the different business functions have their own approaches and preconceptions of how to be successful in business. When business targets are based around the maximisation of profits, the functional approaches will all reflect this. Manufacturing will consider that the more time they are able to have their equipment producing, the more profit they will be able to make, meaning the primary aim must be to reduce unproductive time to a minimum and reduce associated costs to a minimum. A marketing view will be to sell as much as possible, by offering the customer what they want, when they want, so they are also able to maximise their volumes. However, if these are carried out in isolation, they will create considerable friction between the departments, due to aiming for different targets that are traditionally mutually exclusive.

The difficulty in both these situations is that the functions must achieve their targets to be considered successful, with no other constraints than a budget that is based on previous year's performances. Measuring performance in this simple way and driving developments in this way cannot be considered strategic, as there is no foundation for consistency. If companies give greater authority to marketing, this will lead manufacturing into inefficient ways of operating and companies directed by manufacturing will produce parts very efficiently but be unable to sell them. For this reason, over time business functions have begun to be considered more strategically, realising the introduction of consistency in functional developments is important for long-term company success. Considering the long-term impact of activities on the business, rather than basing all decisions on the financial information, has led the business functions to consider themselves in a more strategic manner.

For functions such as marketing, whose impact on the business is extremely difficult to quantify, with subtle aspects determining whether items sell, means this has greatly affected the approach of marketing. Rather than simply a selling function, they can act as customer representatives within the company to help develop long-term relationships. The traditional marketing activities such as advertising have also changed, by considering intangible elements that can build customer loyalty over time such as a brand that assists in reducing the need to determine a particular activity's contribution in a particular financial period. Other approaches include the focus on identifying specific markets that have potential for development into areas of future profit. Although here, the strategic aspect needs to consist of identifying future opportunities that are only possible by developing good working relations with the customers.

Although this development and the developments of the marketing function in general have improved strategic marketing, it is the development of manufacturing in a more strategic manner that is of more importance to operations strategy. Even so, as will also be outlined, both financially based high-level and customer-focused elements of the business are no less important within an effective operations strategy. By considering a company as a whole, rather than focusing on a number of different functions achieving their goals and creating a strategy that reflects this, there is potential for all areas to work together to achieve a single goal. Through understanding how all elements contribute to this goal, which is to create and satisfy a customer, this can be achieved without necessarily working against each other, where ideally the activity will result in profit. In this situation, even if there is not a profit, it may still be possible to consider the business a success by focusing on future developments that may not be at a stage where they are profitable but add intangible value to the company.

1.3.1 Manufacturing Strategy

Although the different business functions consist of very different jobs and activities, there is potential for each of them to have a dramatic effect on the business as a whole that can result in better financial performance. An area of early interest was manufacturing, once it began to be understood that measurements based on cost alone were not appropriate. Using a simplistic view of a manufacturing plant as simply making and selling functions, gaining a better understanding of how other functions could support the manufacturing element had potential to improve performance. This is possibly the reason why manufacturing strategy became a subject in its own right before other business functions but many years after corporate and business strategy (Hill 1985).

Historically, with such a fundamental view of a company, it was assumed that the more one was able to produce of any given product, the more profit it was possible to produce. If marketing was the function that determined if targets were met, the effect this had on the manufacturing department was to work to supply what marketing had sold in an appropriate way. With the amount of products that were sold seeming to have an obvious effect on profitability, marketing would be tempted to offer products in such a way as to increase sales. This may include such activities as volume discounts, low minimum order requirements or promising quick deliveries even though it may not have been possible for the manufacturing function to deliver. The result of this on manufacturing would have been many change-overs, short production runs and high inventory levels, all potentially strategic targets within the manufacturing portion of the business strategy.

With the marketing department potentially receiving more attention from upper management, the result of this would be manufacturing continual 'fire fighting' to meet orders that are received from marketing. This may lead them to spending a considerable portion of their time on business-as-usual activities, notwithstanding the fact that operating their function effectively required considerable time and effort. The addition of such disturbance from marketing, removes more of their time from being able to consider their business function in a strategic manner. However, an immediate effect of such activities on the business as a whole is great inefficiencies within the manufacturing function, which although translating to better figures for marketing, simultaneously reduce the profits for the company as a whole. In addition, requiring manufacturing to work against their strategic targets will introduce an element of conflict (Figure 1.3), which can further reduce the ability to operate effectively.

From the traditional marketing view of production as simply the source for the items that are going to be sold (Wheelwright and Hayes 1985), the above situation is almost inevitable and made even more likely if members of the board have more traditional views that consist of marketing determining profitability. However, with alternate views of the manufacturing capability as proposed by Hill (1985; 1993), manufacturing can gain the attention they deserve from upper management, as a way to improve the company's ability to compete. In the traditional model of manufacturing, it is thought that simply producing more will result in profit that in turn drives the marketing-driven view. However, as the understanding of the manufacturing function has developed, it can be appreciated that volume is not the only aspect that affects overall profit. By taking this perspective, it can be understood that focusing on different elements can improve profitability to a similar or even greater degree than volume.

Although it is true that producing more parts will reduce the unit contribution for amortisation of machines, machines generally have a fixed maximum capacity, meaning it is only possible to produce so many parts. Alternatively, by focusing on different elements that affect the cost to produce a particular item, it may be possible to achieve the same amounts of profit without having to manage the problems that can be associated with increasing volumes. This could be as simple as having to manage greater amounts of raw and finished materials or the knock-on effect of running machines for longer, such as the reduction in available time for maintenance. The problem is that the alternate approach to managing this element of the business would require considerable focus from the manufacturing function but also require appropriate support from the marketing function to be effective.

By focusing away from the volume approach of improving profit, possibly by identifying ways of reducing waste within the process through improving quality, changing design or even working with suppliers to reduce component part cost, profits can be greatly increased. What this requires from the business as a whole is an understanding that volume does not equal profit, and by possibly improving process technologies or other areas of manufacturing, profits can be increased. By focusing specifically on manufacturing strategy, Hill (1985; 1995) aimed to educate the marketing board members about alternate approaches to success. Even basing these arguments on profits, which, as mentioned above, is not the best measure of performance, is potentially a starting point to improve 'congruence of purpose and function' (Hill 1995, p. 55) by describing the effects in a suitable language.

As much as anything, the goal of Hill's work as a whole seems to be unifying the company, with concepts that transcend the organisational boundaries. With better understandings of the manufacturing function and by selling smarter rather than harder, it is possible to reduce the trade-offs where both departments seem to be working against each other, while simultaneously providing the company with better profits. However, unless the company's strategic plans are altered in an appropriate way to reflect this change in focus, there will still be a tendency to revert to the old way if they are continually directed towards meeting their traditional functional targets. The above approach to manufacturing strategy, although different from more traditional approaches to strategy, is still very much focused on profit maximisation, rather than being particularly focused on achieving a particular global strategy. However, this is just a potential approach to a manufacturing strategy and could be achieved with activities that are strategic, representing long-term consistency of aims.

An element of the above approach that does have potential for long-term improvement is the focus on marketing/manufacturing links, that could form the basis of improvements not based entirely on financial results. By improving relations between marketing and manufacturing there is potential for requirements of the customer to be considered when improvements are being made within manufacturing. Rather than marketing-driven manufacturing, there is a shift to 'customer-driven manufacturing' (Berry, Hill and Klompmaker 1995): by considering the customer during product and process developments they can be done to reflect the needs of the customer rather than the needs of a business function. In this situation, as with other elements of business, it is also important to consider the long-term implications of investment; even though investing in 'cash cow' products may make financial sense, decisions should not be made without considering other measures of performance.

Although the above approaches to manufacturing strategy consider developments in a slightly more strategic manner, they do not necessarily take account of the longer-range elements of strategy. This overall strategic vision is still required from the board so there can be consistency for the whole company or group of companies. However, the development of these approaches to other business areas allows for potentially better results that will keep the customer satisfied. Unlike the focus on marketing, within manufacturing, the need for new concepts is possibly less, as simply directing process improvements has the potential to return considerably more tangible benefits. Manufacturing is not without its own developments although it is considerably more practical and more likely to consist of getting the business-as-usual activities perfected. Even so, by combining a number of areas of development, more developed manufacturing strategy concepts can be created, that better reflect the needs of other business functions that promote lasting satisfaction for the customer (see Figure 1.4).

1.3.2   Transitions to a More Developed View of Operating

During the same period that the above approaches to developing manufacturing capabilities were presented, the competitive environment began to change with increasing competition in the western markets from eastern manufacturers. During the 1980s, with the appreciation of Japanese approaches to manufacturing, along with western alternatives, initiatives were introduced into manufacturing companies with the aim of improving quality to be able to remain competitive in global markets. The shift in focus required by upper management to understand the significance of focusing on manufacturing capabilities was actually only one aspect that needed to be considered when taking such a different approach to business. With the eastern businesses having a deep appreciation of the

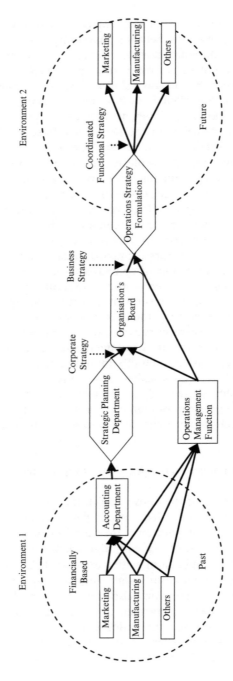

Figure 1.4 A more balanced approach to corporate strategy

systems they had developed, they were able to appreciate manufacturing's ability to meet customer needs by innovating as well as producing.

During the annual planning sessions of upper management, the reductions in market share and rise of companies offering improvements in all areas of business performance made such a change in approach seem necessary. The inherent problem in such a situation was its top-down, hierarchical nature, where ideas needed to be passed down and enforced. Altering approaches to manufacturing and marketing, although requiring a certain amount of change in culture to take place, did still fit in with the western way of business. Although management would have to change the way they carried out their strategic activities, it was at least possible to justify such activities from a financial perspective. The more difficult part of such a change in approach to strategy was not simply changing the aims and targets given to the company, but changing the approaches of the company to allow for generally better coordination. With the developing, but still traditional views of strategy, the introduction of such initiatives was still carried out in a functional way which would not help build the level of coordination that was well established in the east.

With the obvious financial benefits of the different approaches to manufacturing of lean (Bicheno 2004) or the Toyota Production System (TPS), choosing to adopt such an approach to running a business would, and for many companies did, seem like the right choice. Unfortunately, with the traditional, top-down, functional approaches, the total change required in the business was much greater than management understood, meaning that the support that may have been given with budgets was not matched with bottom-up training. Where the western approaches to more developed functional strategies required an amount of coordination, the eastern approaches required a business to be managed as a single business function. In these situations, if the upper management were introducing these initiatives with financially driven motives and only low levels of understanding about the approaches themselves, problems were almost inevitable.

Considering such initiatives as ways to increase profit and general performance instead of as a result of a deep understanding of the philosophies that allowed them to produce such benefits is a possible reason for so many failures in western business. The reason for their success in the east was due to a different approach of all staff and by considering management in a different way; this reduced the top-down nature of such initiatives, where management assist and facilitate rather than control and enforce. The new and fashionable approaches to business improvements required a 'bottom-up' approach to business that was grounded in business-wide understanding of what the total aims of the business were.

With a 'top-down' introduction, focusing on business results instead of customer-based strategic aims that should result from the initiative, other areas of the business were not developed in a suitable manner in order to promote and nurture a suitable culture.

The initiative, when viewed from a financial perspective without a deep understanding of concepts combined with a traditional functional view of business, would have considered the initiatives to be primarily manufacturing related. If this was reflected in how the approaches were implemented, the lack of support from other functions created may also have affected the approaches' effectiveness. The result of this may have been resistance to the initiatives that seemed to offer such obvious benefits when viewed in companies where these initiatives had been invented and the company-wide culture had been established. The problems were then magnified when considered from a financial point of view, such as return on investment, that would have been made worse by the resistance from other functions that may have seemed to have fallen out of favour with upper management. With a better understanding of the initiatives, it would have been apparent that the benefits from these new approaches to business resulted from the combination of all the areas of business, which may have been considerably more difficult to quantify in short-term financial measures. Many companies introducing such approaches would have soon realised that simply reducing the level of inventory in a warehouse did not reduce costs or improve performance, without other systems present that supported the needs of a low inventory system.

Unfortunately for many 'champions' of such initiatives, who may not have had such an understanding, when results did not noticeably improve following the introduction of new working practices, investment would have been reduced or even removed. What was probably not understood to a suitable degree was not the mechanics of such initiatives but their strategic nature with regards to the whole company. There needed to be a business/corporate strategy reason to introduce an approach that would have such a large effect on the way the business was run, rather than simply a cost reduction exercise. By understanding this, the strategic goals could be aligned with the introduction of the system, so that during the implementation, cost information was not the only gauge of performance. This would mean the performance of the initiative would not have just a single planning cycle to show a financial return, that if negative had potential to reduce support. Such targets could be to align business functions with a consistent approach to improvement, or could reflect the service that the customer was receiving.

Appreciating the reason for introducing such an initiative is not wholly internal and functional but that it should represent the needs of the whole company is very important. In a traditional western company, this could consist of all parts of the business strategy being consciously focused on achieving a specific business initiative (see Figure 1.5). If this is carried out successfully, all elements of the business will work in a way that is consistent with other areas of the business and help to achieve the business goals. The results of such a directed and synchronised strategy process could be consistent actions in all areas of the business, which has the potential to reduce the resistance mentioned earlier. The alignment and consistency between all departments (or business units) working towards a single goal could also mean that the financial effect of many coordinated improvements would be more noticeable, assisting in maintaining management's enthusiasm for the initiative. If the improvements also resulted in improvements that were directly noticeable by the customer, for example if marketing received positive feedback from an engineering activity, they may be more considerate to the needs of that area of the business.

Although initiating a western approach to process excellence, General Electric's (GE's) adoption of Six Sigma is one of the better examples of how such a change can be achieved while also demonstrating how very difficult it can be. Six Sigma is a statistically based approach to reducing process variation devised in the west to compete with eastern approaches such as Total Quality Management (TQM) whose heavy reliance on bottom-up activities created problems in some western implementations. The approach focused more on management's responsibility, an important element of Joseph Juran's teachings, but combined it with the ideas of W. Edward Deming, another very influential quality thinker; that reducing variation would result in reduced cost. The result was a fact-based, statistical approach that appealed to managers due to its structured nature but also to finance with its aim of reducing costs that resulted from the reduction of variation. Another reason for its appeal is that, unlike other approaches, it is specifically applicable to non production, administrative activities, which helped to expand the scope of the strategic initiative.

Even though Six Sigma westernised aspects of eastern approaches, it does not remove all of the difficulties faced during its introduction into a company, but assists in improving support. The problems that remain are achieving suitable understanding in enough members (a critical mass), while also converting this understanding into company-wide results. In GE this was possible due to the leadership of Jack Welch, who understood the potential benefits of the approach and had the ability to gain backing from all areas of business. However, on his own, leading from the front was unlikely to have been enough to guarantee success, which meant there was a need to introduce company measures that supported implementation, such as the alignment of the human resource function with the

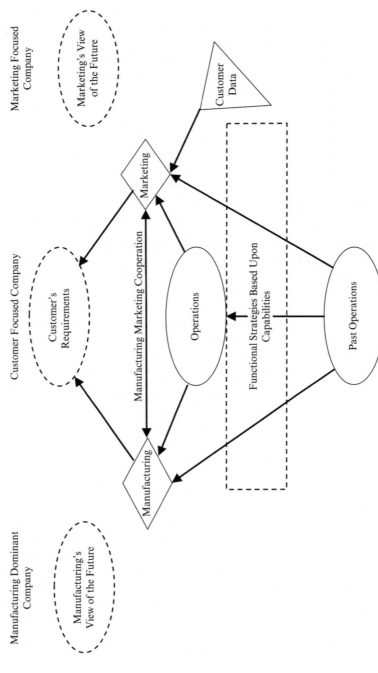

Figure 1.5 A coordinated, customer focused development strategy

18

initiative. Even though the approach could be fuelled by heavy investment in Six Sigma training of 'belts' (specially trained statistics experts), the support from other business functions to support the process champions also aided the initiative's success.

Understanding that successful adoption of the initiative offered an opportunity for GE to develop a sustainable competitive advantage, rather than simply reducing cost, was a reason Jack Welch managed to change company culture. Six Sigma, as a corporation-wide initiative, also represented a common strategic aim for such a diversified organisation, moving focus away from direct financial management, understanding financial success is the result not the driver of achieving the strategy (Drucker 1955). Altering the view of an improvement initiative from one focused within a particular area of the business to one that is relevant to the whole business is an important transition for both the subject and its use in practice. It reflects the need for cross-functional improvements that were mentioned in the functional, manufacturing approach to converting corporate strategy to business improvements.

1.3.3 Still Room for Improvement?

By reviewing approaches to improvement activities in relation to the overall business strategy, we have attempted to demonstrate the importance of considering these improvement activities strategically rather than simply financially or functionally. Even though the significance of such changes seems obvious enough to prevent conflict and build support, a change in how complex initiatives are approached has not been widespread. Demonstrations of how it is possible and that it is not necessarily the approach's fault for failure, such as GE, have also not assisted in changing the way organisational development is managed to improve effectiveness and general execution. Research outlines the need for a change in approach to such initiatives that helps to change and support the development of both cultural as well as more tangible changes.

This is reflected in the continued development of new production techniques that aim to remove the problems experienced with other, previously fashionable approaches to improvement. A highly regarded approach that is able to give results many times better than Six Sigma, lean and TQM is the Theory of Constraints (TOC) (Goldratt and Cox 1992). In a similar way to GE's implementation of Six Sigma, TOC works on the understanding that it is the whole system that determines success so it is not appropriate to introduce improvements to a single area of the business. Differently from Six Sigma, TOC understands that improvement made in areas that already have operational spare capacity (slack) cannot give improvements in performance to the system, so that the most efficient way to improve performance is to direct improvement to the system's bottleneck process.

The result of this is that by focusing improvements in a much more directed manner, the returns on investment should be improved significantly and, where successful, results are considerably more effective than similar implementations of other improvement initiatives. However, considering such an initiative from a more strategic perspective does bring up questions about whether it is as applicable as other approaches as a means of developing an effective company strategy. The reason for this is the basis on which TOC is established, which is that the purpose of a business is to make money now and in the future (Goldratt and Cox 1992). In regards to strategic activities, such a foundation has the potential to give additional weight to the financial approach to company management, even if it does promote the achievement of global rather than local goals.

Unfortunately, with the financial perspectives, such an approach also needs extremely careful strategic management to allow it to assist company operations as a whole, rather than just making it more profitable in the short term. Due to focusing on improving the company's ability to make profit, there seems a greater possibility to lose focus on a different aim of a company, that is to create and satisfy a customer. The effect of this could be the selling of one's future to succeed in the present, by maximising profit within the current market without looking forward and developing capability for the future. However, if in introducing such an approach to business a practitioner considers product and process development in the same context as the production system, the risks associated with such a system may be reduced.

With the development of an approach such as TOC to improve business performance, although the problem of improving business performance may have been solved, it is still the introduction and effective management that really determine if such an initiative is a success. This may be a reason for the subsequent developments of the TOC approach that enabled the ideas to be transferred from operational level-development to assist in specific strategic activities. As well as the continued fine-tuning of the TOC approach to take account of the need for strategic elements, there has been the development of a subject that aims to take account of these issues: operations strategy. Without focusing on a particular area, other than the operations element, operations strategy aims to introduce more practical aspects to the subject of strategy to assist in converting high-level strategic ideas into improved business activities without focusing on a specific business function.

The next section gives a brief outline and introduction to the subject of operations strategy to show how the above approaches to strategy have contributed to the current thinking of this approach to strategic activities. Within this subject the focus is away from a corporate, global vision of strategy and also away from the marketing elements; however, these still need considerable attention. Although the above approaches to these elements of strategy have a heavy financial bias it has been the aim to outline the need to move away from such a starting point. The reason for moving away from such an approach, apart from its potential irrelevance and self-perpetuating nature, is that strategic planning from a financial basis does not necessarily have a long-term element. Without an element that represents consistency from one year to the next, a strategic planning process based on such information cannot be considered strategic, as business targets can change from one planning period to the next. Although operations strategy does appreciate the need to consider financial aspects, the above outlines the need to consider it as one of a number of measures that drive developments and customer satisfaction.

1.4 THE NEED TO DEVELOP AN OPERATIONS STRATEGY

As outlined above, a single area of a business cannot be the focus of strategy and it is only when the scope of a particular type of strategy is expanded to include more elements of the business that it is able to reflect the needs of the business. Such thinking is in line with the view that it is also not a particular function that allows a business to be successful, but the way they all work together. Moving away from a functionally based approach to the management of a firm gives weight to the argument for the development of operations management capabilities that are able to coordinate functional capabilities more effectively. However, the focus of this type of work is at an operational level of business, concerned with the day-to-day running of a business rather than longer-range developments. For this reason, to reflect a broad view of a business, there should be a broad view of strategy that considers and integrates the different elements, rather than simply allowing for the needs of different areas of a business.

The foundation of such an idea of business and strategy is not new – along with proposing new ideas of business as a whole, Drucker (1955) proposed a different, more rounded approach to directing a business's development. As stated earlier, financial measures represent the result of efforts but should not be the only measure and cannot be used to drive improvements. For this reason, Drucker proposed a management-by-objectives approach to business that tracks business performance and development with seven distinct measures that although including financial measures understand the need for a more cohesive approach. Even though the ideas are very relevant today, such ideas were potentially ahead of their time but also, the business environment at that time did not require such approaches. In the 1950s, applying the technology that was available in a way that allowed profit maximisation was the major focus, and due to the stability of the environment in general, the risks associated with pure financial planning were fewer.

It was not until 1987 that such questions were raised again, to be heard by business professionals that management accounting alone was no longer an appropriate way of guiding a business (Johnson and Kaplan 1987). In a business environment that had many more examples of businesses that had been managed with the exclusion of other relevant business data to their detriment and demise, the need for a different way to manage a company was greater. This is potentially what formed the basis for a more operational view of business strategy and the development of operations strategy as a specific area of academic and professional interest. However, unlike Drucker's approach, the altered view of how to control a business was followed up by a relatively simple tool to integrate and present these old ideas in a new, manageable form. The Balanced Score Card (Kaplan and Norton 1992) measured the performance of a business in four areas that did not just show where the company had come from (financial) but also its current position and where it was going (see Figure 1.6).

With business operations being seen as an area with potential to offer a business a distinct competitive advantage through its effective management, a strategy that reflects such a coordinated business function also needs to include all relevant areas. In the above approaches to strategic management, the need to consider the business as a whole is outlined, to assist in reducing risk while also giving specific attention to long-term improvements. For this reason, operations strategy as defined by Slack and Lewis (2001) needs to represent four major areas of operations to aid consistent management of such an important aspect of the business entity. In the more traditional views of business, such an approach to strategy may seem like the manufacturing strategy approaches, although the operations that take place are not necessarily production. The operations could be any type of business, not necessarily manufacturing, but rather the element of the business where the transformation process takes place.

By considering operations as the transformation process rather than simply the manufacturing plant, which is the focus of manufacturing strategy, the scope of the strategy needs expanding in an appropriate way. As well as including the strategies involved within a given function, it

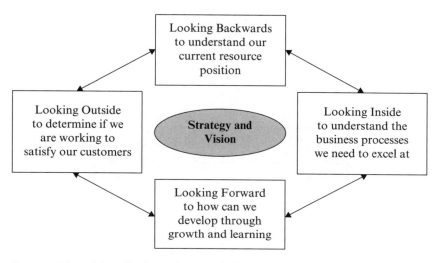

Source: Adapted from Kaplan and Norton (1996).

Figure 1.6   A balanced score card approach to performance measurement

must include higher-level transformation processes such as inter-business interactions within a supply network while also including low-level process improvement strategies. In addition to considering different levels of the transformation process, operations strategy also needs to be able to consider different types of transformation processes such as service and even charitable organisations, as the aims of them are all essentially the same. Within this setting, the need for operations managers is still present in order to improve performance, but operations strategy is required to direct their improvement activities in an appropriate way.

Slack and Lewis (2001) define operations strategy as 'the reconciliation between market requirements with process capabilities', reflecting both the need for marketing strategy and manufacturing/process-based strategy. This definition demonstrates the reason for already having touched upon both marketing and manufacturing strategies, showing the way both developed to reflect the needs of the business. Operations strategy also needs to reflect the overall corporate direction of the company, to prevent other business functions leading it away from the needs of the investors. In addition to these three areas, it is considered necessary to listen to the voice of the company, to enable the engagement of the company as a whole and learn from the experience they gain from carrying out the transformation process (see Figure 1.7).

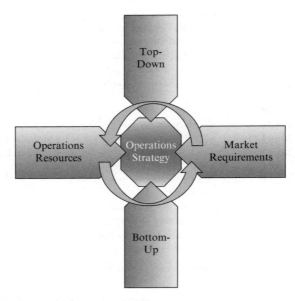

Source: Adapted from Slack and Lewis (2008).

Figure 1.7   Contents relations to operations strategy

1.4.1   Top-Down

The top-down approach to strategy reflects the traditional elements of corporate and business strategy, where the board or a strategic planning department determines the overall direction for the company such as divesting and acquiring certain business units. Unlike the traditional top-down approach, such information contributes to the operations strategy, rather than being the basis for other types of strategy. This ensures that the strategy that drives the development of operations is consistent with the requirements of the board and investors. In a diversified corporation this is particularly important, as it ensures business cohesion to maintain corporate identity. This may also be where a corporate initiative is formulated that forms the basis for further strategic activities across the business.

1.4.2   Bottom-Up

Not mentioned directly earlier, bottom-up approaches rely on the experience that is acquired from the day-to-day running of the business to contribute to strategic activities. Originally identified by Mintzberg in

1978 as 'emergent strategies', such a strategy is not implicitly formulated and then implemented; by learning and developing continually, strategy can be formed and realised (Mintzberg 1978). Learning in this way allows the business both to react quickly to localised situations without the constraints of a hierarchical system while continually developing capabilities to reflect the needs of the customer (Johnson and Medcof 2007). Unlike the other approaches to strategy already discussed, this specifically allows greater involvement of the company as a whole, as it is not reliant on top management or functional professionals to carry out strategic activities.

Such elements are particularly important within certain process improvement activities, such as TQM or TPS, as the responsibility for improvements is placed on this area of the business. Although Six Sigma involves similar type of activities, the presence of particular professionals or 'belts' to take responsibility means the emergent elements of this particular initiative are fewer, although a suitable culture is still important. Such an approach has been found to be, and still is, very successful in certain business environments, but it is considered difficult to initiate such bottom-up activities within a company that is able to maintain a 'consistency of actions'. 'Consistency of actions' is particularly important when pursuing a wholly 'bottom-up' approach, as without this there may result uncoordinated improvement activities. Development of a business culture that is focused upon improvements that relate to the customer's satisfaction is a possible solution to this, where all actions can be considered individually to determine whether they assist in reaching the organisational targets.

Including a bottom-up approach to strategy requires operations strategy to specifically consider the day-to-day learning process in the development of a strategy. This not only assists in improving involvement of the company as a whole, but it also enables strategic activities from more levels of the company that allow for a smoother and quicker transition between the formulation and implementation stages of a strategy. Bottom-up information also assists in giving those charged with working on operations strategy better process-based information. Not only does this have the potential to allow a more appropriate strategy to be formulated, but it also means that functional staff are involved in strategic activities, improving their commitment to the process. The reason for this is, as they have been consulted regarding their specific area of the process, the strategy should reflect their specific needs, in essence being partially their own strategy.

1.4.3 Market Requirements

From Drucker's (1955) definition of the aim of a business, the view of the client/customer must be carefully considered in any approach that aims to improve the performance of operations. As with more developed views of the marketing function (Thorpe and Morgan 2006; Ranchhod and Gurau 2007), the element within operations strategy that considers the market does not consider what can be sold, but instead what is required. As well as considering the types of products that are required by the market, it is the source of the information relating to what is required of these products. The marketing function could be considered a representative of the customer that determines how well the company is performing, by being the source of customer satisfaction, possibly in terms of standard performance metrics such as Quality, Speed, Dependability, Flexibility and Cost.

It is also the function's responsibility to determine how well the developments allow the organisation to perform in relation to the market as a whole, such as more traditional marketing measures that determine market positioning. By understanding the current position in relation to competitors, possibly in specific areas of performance, there is potential for improvement activities to be focused to make the biggest effect on overall customer satisfaction. The market is also the source of information relating to the actions of competitors that can potentially affect the competitive position of the company if the company is unable to react effectively. Fundamentally, the market function is present within the operations strategy definition to ensure that improvement and development activities that consume considerable resources are directed to result in better meeting market requirements.

By including the market requirements in the operations strategy, the other areas of the business are able to appreciate and obtain relatively direct information relating to who is widely regarded as the most important element in the organisation. The effect of this, as mentioned above with manufacturing strategy, is that process improvements can be directed to reflect the needs of the customer. The upper management are able to appreciate customer-specific requirements that will assist them in being able to formulate an appropriate high-level strategy. For the bottom-up perspective, understanding the market requirements at a relatively low level potentially represents the source of consistency that is required to make an emergent strategy possible. What is important when considering all these areas together is that all externally facing measures of performance will be relevant (Johnsen 2001). This helps to ensure that the result of the operations strategy process will be an operation able to satisfy the customer more effectively.

1.4.4   Operations Resources

Unlike the manufacturing strategy view of operational development, by taking the view of the transformation process, operations strategy's scope is considerably wider. Considering the transformation process as the unit of analysis means the content of operations strategy is much larger, both including the manufacturing elements as well as higher-level inter-business relations. By taking an operational resource-based view of a firm (Jenkins, Ambrosini and Collier 2007), it can be appreciated how it is the company's inherent ability to combine resources into capabilities that is the source of its intangible market value. It is an operation's ability, not only to add value, but also to develop the value it adds that is specific to the company that allows it to continue operating in a competitive market both now and in the future.

With a considerably wider view of the operations functions than manufacturing strategy, it is not possible simply to focus on a particular area of the business to improve operations. This means that the content of operations strategy is considerably larger than the functional approaches to strategy and it is specifically the operations resources portion that is expanded the most. When considering such initiatives as lean or TPS from an operations strategy perspective, it can be seen that these are not in fact simply manufacturing but operational initiatives, and, as mentioned before, unless the scope of the initiatives is expanded suitably to include all operations, they are less likely to be effective. Within TPS for example, operations strategy content, such as capacity management or supply network, plays significant roles in the initiative. If implementers simply focus on developments with the manufacturing elements by reducing inventory levels, it is not possible to realise the benefits of such an initiative that are enjoyed by those who developed the systems.

Where the operations strategy view of operations resources is fundamentally different from the previous descriptions of process and operational development activities is that it is essentially focused on the development of a company-specific strategy. By understanding that what defines a company's capabilities in business are the resources it has at its disposal, and through the consistent development of these specific resources, it will be able to meet its own objectives rather than those of a historically successful company. What also needs considering is the directed development of the company-specific intangible resources that when developed enable specific jobs or services to be provided that cannot simply be purchased (Barney 1991). The ability to offer a customer a company-specific product or service is effectively the manifestation of the capability to combine tangible and intangible resources in an effective way. Through the structured development and acquisition of appropriate tangible resources with the appreciation of their ability to provide the customer with what they require, the activities can be structured appropriately to develop capabilities that are required by the business.

The final element of consideration regarding the operations resources area of operations strategy is the operation processes. Although the resources represent the components of the business and the capabilities represent the systems, without an understanding of the processes that take place within the business, it is not possible to properly appreciate their relevance to the whole business. Understanding the processes present in a business also allows developments and improvements to be made with them. By carrying out such activities as business process visualisation, the relative importance or associated risk of certain processes can be identified for re-engineering to focus improvements in the elements present within a process (Pryor et al. 2007). For companies where specific activities are particularly important, the identification and optimisation of these processes are essentially similar to taking a Theory of Constraints approach to process improvement.

With the operations resources element of the business being where the majority of the transformation processes take place, its inclusion within operations strategy is obvious. Developing a strategy that gives specific attention to the area of business that carries out the important transformation process places focus upon the element of the business that will be responsible for the strategic changes. This approach also considers how the other elements of business can alter their approaches to support operational changes by learning from and directing further operational resource changes. Including the operations resource element in operations strategy allows the organisation to consider primarily what the company is capable of, such as what it can produce now and what it is potentially able to produce in the future. This means that when developing a company-wide vision, upper management will be able to do this in line with the specific capabilities of the operating function. Greater understanding of the operations function could even drive specific corporate strategy to direct particular investments into the further development of critical operations resources.

The operations resources elements are also very important for the other areas of operations strategy. It relies on the bottom-up approach to strategy so that the capabilities of the operation are able to adapt to in-process learning so that it can continually develop the process from the experience that is being accrued. The operations resource, as well as relying on the resources present to be able to realise developments, also requires input to take account of external factors that may need considering. The major benefit of including these two elements in operations strategy is that, while representing internal developments, they also carefully consider the views of those ultimately affected by developments. Without including these elements in strategy, it may become more difficult to realise innovations if they do not have greater appreciation of operational issues.

As mentioned earlier, understanding the links between the manufacturing function and the marketing function, when considering the overall strategy, has great potential to reduce conflict while simultaneously improving company performance. However, the operations strategy approach, as well as taking a broader view of the operations resource function, also has a broader view of the relationship between these two areas of business. In addition to marketing selling in line with the capabilities of the operations resources, it is also possible for there to be considerable two-way learning. The operations are able to develop in a manner that is consistent with the market requirements, while also being a source of information about further requirements of the customer and how operations should begin to prepare for these needs. Such interrelations can form the basis for particular elements of the operations strategy that direct the development of particular areas of the business to enable them to remain competitive in markets that are not yet present.

1.5 CONTENT OF OPERATIONS STRATEGY

Although an operations strategy that gives consideration to the above four areas is likely to be of more use than one that does not, it is however likely that the majority of attention will be paid to the operations resource element. Although the contribution of the other three areas is very important, it is likely that their input into the actual activities will be more of consideration rather than direct attention, with the actual work remaining within the different functions. This effectively means that paying specific attention to corporate strategy is still as important as with other approaches to strategy, although with an operations strategy approach corporate feeds into it, rather than being the sole driver. The same is also true of marketing strategy; although consideration is given to the marketing function, operations strategy is not concerned with traditional marketing functions such as advertising campaigns. Even so, the presence of a traditional marketing function with its own marketing strategy is just as important, if not more necessary today than historically, with the increase in the competitive environment. However, the marketing strategy does need to reflect the needs of the operations strategy, by developing approaches that assist in directing appropriate information into the operations function. The changes in corporate and marketing strategy when considered in relation to an operations strategy are to consider them both in a wider context, to effectively stop short-term measures, in effect, making them more strategic.

In this respect, the content element of these two aspects of operations strategy remains relatively unchanged from a more traditional view, simply including additional information. The fourth area of operations strategy, bottom-up, is, by its very nature, very different from the other two, being an observed phenomenon rather than an area of specific strategic attention. Even though focusing on developing this area can allow for important emergent elements of strategy, the way these strategies come about means it is not possible to study and direct them as that would mean they were deliberate rather than emergent. Without being able to study and direct such an approach to strategy, a different element of business becomes of interest, whose study and development help promote such emergent strategies. The concept of a learning organisation is very important in today's highly competitive market; without it, the learning may be restricted to particular professionals or functions. This effectively maintains elements of hierarchy within the organisation, which can resist change, reducing the organisation's ability to quickly identify and meet market requirements. Although this area of study affects the other three by effectively enabling the company as a whole, it is also not specifically studied within operations strategy, although its careful consideration is beneficial.

The remaining areas of operations strategy, operations resources, is the area where the majority of attention is directed when developing an operations strategy. This reflects the progression of manufacturing strategy into operations strategy, although as already mentioned the range of elements included within an operations strategy is considerably larger than the manufacturing function on its own. As with the three other areas of strategy, the most important change is not necessarily the increase in the amount of business elements it considers, but rather the way it considers them in relation to the other areas of business. However, even though it may be the interactions between the different elements that will determine excellent performance and offer sustainable competitive advantage, there still needs to be focus on the specific areas of operations, meaning within the study of operations strategy there must be substance and content.

As outlined above, focusing on almost any area of transformation and developing in a way that reflects the needs of the market are potential content. These areas include focusing on improvements at different levels of the business from introducing changes in a frontline activity to analysing the route products take along a value chain to identify and better understand the areas that require improvements. The following subsections will give a brief outline of some of the different elements that make up the content of an operations strategy, working from low-level processes such as directed performance improvements to high-level supply chain network strategy. Once these areas of operations strategy content have been discussed, there will be a section on operations strategy process, which is the activity of using the content to create meaningful strategy to be implemented within an organisation.

1.5.1 Process Improvement

Using the term 'low'-level improvements gives this area of operations strategy content relatively low importance, when it has anything but. The 'low' simply refers to the level in the business where these activities can (although not necessarily do) take place. The performance of an organisation is generally determined by its ability to carry out activities that are deemed important to the customer. These areas may be generic performance measures such as cost, quality and speed, although depending on the business in question, the generic measures of performance may be replaced by more company-specific measurements. This is to prevent ambiguity while helping to direct improvements, for example a measure such as speed will have very different meanings for a logistics company and a product development office. For this reason, more company-specific performance criteria may be more appropriate, such as order response, delivery lead time or time to market.

Using marketing information that is available to the process assists in directing improvements in a way that will affect customer satisfaction; combining this with a performance management system may further help to direct process improvements (see Figure 1.8). Such an approach to process improvement is particularly important when considered against traditional constraints in manufacturing such as trade-offs. Careful understanding of the acceptable levels of certain aspects of performance can

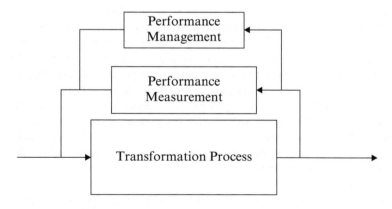

Figure 1.8   Performance measurement/management

allow improvements to be made that give the best overall improvement for the customer. Even though it has been possible to reduce the direct effects of manufacturing trade-offs with the use of more developed approaches to manufacturing, prioritisation of improvements is still important. Understanding how the resources available for improvements can be assigned to give the greatest improvements in customer satisfaction represents a way of maximising return on investments.

However, due to the constantly changing market place with new products, suppliers and even solutions to problems, the need to continually monitor performance criteria is established. Over time, even the performance criteria of a single product will change, and depending on the industry in question, may change very rapidly, such as consumer electronics. For this reason it is not simply adequate to focus on the process and products that are present in the market; it is essential to understand how different levels of process performance are able to change one's position in a market. As well as performance criteria changing over time, the product elements required by the market change over time, meaning a constant need to develop a product, but also a need to develop new products that reflect the need of the current and future market. The developments made in frontline activities are an important source of information that can affect a company's performance directly; they are also an important source of information that can be considered in the development of process technologies.

1.5.2 Process Technology

As mentioned earlier, although improvements can be made to an operating system to meet the needs of a customer, the processes used to make a product are likely to limit the extent to which these changes can affect performance. Not only is it that a particular process is unable to meet particular criteria in volume, quality or flexibility, it may simply not be able to produce a product. This means that an element of a product that is just as important as the product itself is the processes that produce it; without a match between the two, important market criteria will not be met. For example, a change in process technology, such as that witnessed in the automotive industry, can change the product entirely from a luxury item for transporting the elite to part of a basic existence. Although this example is one of the more extreme, the same can be true for much smaller changes, such as the development in robot laser welding improving car safety standards.

In certain industries, such as the oil industry in particular, the product and process are effectively interlinked, meaning that in certain instances it may be necessary to actually develop a market for a product. In other cases, such as the electronics industry, the importance of developing a manufacturing process as well as a product is extremely high. Without the ability to produce a product in such a way that there is a market for it, there will be no process for recouping the costs associated with the design and development activities. However, with the possibility of licensing developments, for others to develop a process there are alternate way to recoup research and development (R&D) costs, but unless the focus of the business is R&D rather than production, this is likely to be considered the exception as opposed to the rule. Although product and process development seem quite closely interlinked, history has shown that it is still possible to be extremely successful in business by developing the process technology capability. On many occasions, Japanese companies have been able to take developments from elsewhere in the world and apply their abilities in process technology, allowing them to redefine the market in such sectors as automobiles and consumer electronics.

In certain industries where the coordination of particular manufacturing processes offers potential for improvements in performance, there becomes a need for a different type of technology to support coordination. Where the coordination of two co-located departments can be very difficult, the scope of such technology can be appreciated, and so can the potential benefits. Enterprise Resource Planning (ERP) is an example of a type of indirect process technology which, although working alongside the transformation process, allows better operation-wide understanding that can promote coordination. When it becomes possible to observe, analyse and control operations, the knowledge associated with the process can increase, helping to further direct improvement activities. Indirect process technologies do not necessarily need to be as high tech or as capitally intensive as an ERP system, although what is understood is that they should support and assist, rather than detracting from the direct process so the supporting activities do not become the main focus of operations (Drucker 1955).

Examples of this type of activity are statistical process control (SPC) and the development of management procedures, but could consist of the appliance of science to almost any business activity. SPC uses another type of indirect technology (metrology) to measure business processes to gain a better understanding of the way a process varies. By combining quality, production and process engineering functions, its correct use can develop more consistent and capable processes while developing coordination between functions. The construction of management procedures for certain management activities can help remove or support the judgment of those within the process that can effectively act as a decision support tool for management, automating regularly repeated activities. To prevent their maintenance and operations detracting from the primary business process, it is important to view the activities from the perspective of the end user, to assess how the activities contribute to the value that they realise.

Both indirect and direct types of technologies have an important role to play within the operations resource area of operations strategy because they represent the current and future capabilities of a company to perform the transformation process. They also determine the company's ability to continue operating, as they define the rules and systems that maintain control within the operation as well as the specific transformation process. The inclusion of process technology within operations strategy gives specific focus to both the direct and supporting capabilities required in the system to analyse, control and develop operations to achieve the operations strategy. In addition to this, it is the systems that make up a company that have the potential to create, develop or destroy culture, meaning that appreciating the need for consistency when altering them is extremely important. With business processes having direct effects on business culture, there can be a shift away from the view that culture is difficult to define and create, due to the ease with which business processes can be changed (Bossidy and Charan 2002).

1.5.3 Capacity Strategy

Out of the different areas of operations resources, capacity planning is probably the area that receives the most attention from traditional practitioners, although the scope of these views is likely to be immediate operations management issues rather than operations strategy. Determining the number of staff that are required to meet the customer demand in the following month to ensure orders can be met is an operational issue rather than a strategic one, although expanding the range of the view makes it strategic. By concentrating on better forecasting or how much inventory should be held, the manager is potentially able to reduce variation in production requirements, which greatly helps improve traditional measures of operating efficiency. However, the effect of this can be to overlook operating issues that are present in the system that may be considerably more costly than the cost of orders that were not met or machines that were not utilised, such as the need to manage large amounts of inventory. Appreciating that a particular system is able to produce certain quantities and respond to certain requirements allows the capacity strategy to be matched to the market's requirements and process's capability.

Through the development of certain approaches to manufacturing, it has been possible to reduce many of the traditional trade-offs, such as low inventory with quick response times. Systems such as just-in-time help to control the capacity squeeze that can restrict efficiencies when demand begins to reach capacity. However, what such systems gain in control they potentially lose in flexibility and ultimate efficiency. There still needs to be consideration given to how total demand will change over time. Rather than simply considering how to allocate staff to meet demand, decisions need to be made on the point at which machines need duplicating or replacing to meet demand. This decision can only be made after careful consideration of the long-term market conditions with reference to product and process technologies. Where staffing issues could be thought of as relatively flexible, investing in a new technology not only needs justifying financially, but also has the potential to dramatically alter the market within which it is present.

As stated in the process technology section, the technology available can potentially determine the presence of a market and also define the competitive criteria present in a market. The presence of these two issues relating to the effect of the introduction of a new process technology places additional importance on the decision of whether to invest and, if so, when to invest. The actions of competitors and the market conditions will determine how a company should proceed in its capacity strategy: whether to lead, follow demand, follow the competitor, anticipate or prepare when resources are available. These all have different associated risks and benefits, while also having different effects on the market themselves; as has been said, there are no non-passive actors in an organisation (where the organisation in this case is the whole market) (Callon 1993). The decisions are made considerably more difficult when their results can take a considerable amount of time to realise, such as the construction of a new plant.

Although focusing on the levels of staffing required to meet an order and the introduction of a new process technology in an existing facility can allow demand to be met, there is a time when the squeeze is too great and additional plants are required. The way this situation is addressed can have considerable effects on the organisation's abilities, as there is potential for these decisions to be made on a purely financial basis. In this situation, the case for keeping an old plant is strong, due to the low book value; however, as noted in facilities planning literature, the costs associated with operating can be considerably higher due to many inherent issues (Tompkins et al. 2003). The financial-based argument is also present if the decision has been made to invest in a new plant: to minimise the cost per unit produced, it may be beneficial to build a plant that is able to produce what is required by the market in the most efficient manner possible. With a traditional view of mass production, the way of achieving this is to build a large plant that may have flexibility considered by allowing future expansion.

Although this approach may again seem the most logical from a financial perspective of being able to produce the parts in the most cost effective manner possible while considering the future, it does not consider a number of additional factors. Although promoting economies of scale through efficient manufacture of parts, when plants increase in size there are also the associated diseconomies of scale, such as communication, hierarchy and bureaucracy overheads. Such a decision also effectively locks the company into a particular investment for a considerable period of time, which is a considerable risk when markets are so changeable. For this reason choosing the smallest size of facility that meets current demand will fulfil both requirements, while leaving future decisions unconstrained. Without such constraints, future bases of operations can be selected to reflect the market needs, rather than available capacity enabling choices that reflect current market conditions. As well as reducing the diseconomies of scale, such an approach could reflect the needs of the customer with reduced lead times, but also offer economies of scope in plants that specialise in particular areas of operations.

The decisions related to capacity need careful consideration with regards to the other areas of operations strategy; however, unlike the other areas, the risks associated with achieving a capacity strategy can be considerably larger. The reason for this is that it is likely to require considerable investment based on current market conditions, process technology and product technology when the decisions are for the future. Unlike the other areas where it may be possible to develop organisational capabilities that are developed in parallel and complement the transformation process, capacity strategy is significantly more tangible. For this reason, an approach to capacity strategy that builds flexibility and promotes the establishment of other capabilities could be considered a way to add intangible aspects to a capacity strategy. Building up capacity through a number of small steps allows for the creation of an organisational network, assisting in developing customer-specific capabilities or promoting the development of focused factories that pursue process excellence across the network. This is effectively how a single company could apply supply network thinking to the way they work to meet their customer demands for capacity, which is the next topic to be discussed.

1.5.4 Supply Network Strategy

The transformation process that takes place within a firm can almost never be considered a single activity and is generally made up of a number of components that represent the different elements that make up the product's cost. In defining the value chain, Porter (1985) identified the main elements that contribute to part cost and how each part of the business needs to be considered when determining the final selling price. Without considering each particular element, it would not be possible for the part to be supplied, meaning that if an element were missing there would be no selling price.

Figure 1.9 is an example of a value chain for a single company, but it is well documented and understood that a product is not generally created in its entirety within a single firm and passes through a number of stages on its way to the customer. In the same way that is it unlikely that a single company can entirely process and distribute a product, it is also unlikely that the series of companies that produce a product will be arranged sequentially to make a simple chain. Due to end products generally being made up of numerous component parts from different suppliers and being distributed through numerous channels, the companies that work together to supply a product are arranged into networks, as in Figure 1.10. For this reason, the effective management and associated strategy relating to the network will have a considerable effect on a company's ability to supply a product in the required form, while adding value in the most effective way.

Historically, if the strategic processes were carried out on manufacturing

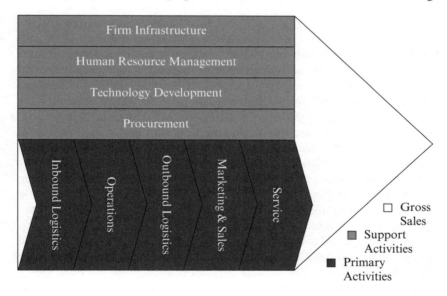

Source: Porter (1985).

Figure 1.9   The value chain

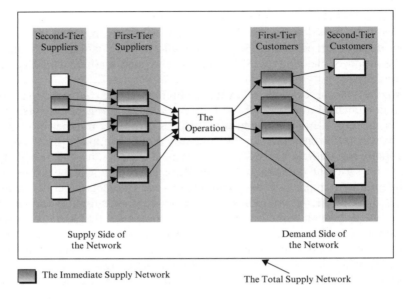

Source: Slack, Chambers and Johnston (2007).

Figure 1.10   A single organisation's supply network

facilities using financially based data, the figures tended to suggest that if
supplied parts were made in house, purchasing costs would be reduced and
profits could be increased. However, what the financial view did not take
into account was that the capabilities required to produce and develop the
parts and process also needed considering within the investment argument.
Unless all processes were specifically produced for the system, there would
also be a difficulty balancing capacity if there was only to be one customer,
which may result in less efficient supply or the need to run the suppliers as
separate companies, removing some of the benefits of vertical integration.
In terms of an organisation, vertical integration is similar in nature to a
hierarchically organised company, where the structure slows the movement of information and reduces the company's ability to change. In a
vertically integrated company, the problem is considerably more 'plumbed
in', with the company only able to supply parts that require the supply
chain that is in place. The Raleigh bicycles company and the Ford motor
company are both examples of this. Without being able to quickly and
effectively alter products and their cost structures in a manner that reflects
the needs of the market, there may be significant repercussions for the
health of the business.

The developments in the east of networks of supplying companies working together demonstrated that vertical integration benefits were possible without the associated restrictions. With the breaking down of traditional supplier–customer barriers, combined with developing abilities to supply effectively through supplier development activities, this could greatly increase the ease with which two companies could work together. When it became possible to realistically choose between internally and externally made parts, both with consistent quality and supplier performance, the choices for purchasers increased, increasing the significance of developing a suitable supply network. With a single company being both supplier and customer to many firms, the hierarchy is reduced and the effect of a single company's actions on other companies within the network is also reduced. Companies with a significant number of supply links or spokes are able to reduce the effect of disturbances within the network, reducing network shock (which is caused when a company within a network stops functioning). Such a network can also allow companies to more effectively tailor their supplier network to take account of the requirements of a market at a particular time.

Flexibility and security are not the only benefits of working effective within a supply network: making the choice of whether to make or buy allows companies to focus their operations on specific capabilities that define their operations. When a company has the choice of what it makes, it is able to make a choice that reflects the needs of its customer but also one that is in line with what the company considers important. The company no longer has to produce everything it needs or only outsource commodity products, but can outsource products that may not fit with its specific development strategy or core competences (Hamel and Prahalad 1990). This increases a company's ability to specialise and excel in particular areas, by developing capabilities it considers to be particularly critical to adding value for its customer. This can also allow organisations to source particular elements of the products that are able to benefit from low-cost labour or particular capabilities that may not be present locally.

Presence within a network allows further benefits; rather than simply outsourcing the supply of pre-designed parts, there is potential for greater levels of collaboration within networks. Enabled by the use of indirect process technologies, geographically disparate collaborations can be coordinated, allowing complex new products to be developed using knowledge present across a network that prevents a single organisation being responsible for the associated financial risk. Taking this idea further, virtual enterprises are possible that can be initiated by a single entrepreneur's idea, with all elements being outsourced. Such approaches being so heavily reliant on distributing risk and establishing trust, that may not have been present within traditionally run organisations, increases the importance of developing an appropriate supply network strategy. Television programmes and Hollywood films are both examples of how complex activities can be undertaken outside a traditional organisational structure. These activities do show the need for additional elements that require consideration to facilitate activities, such as personal networks and latent organisation, that are alternate structures to base activities upon (Robins 1993; Starkey, Barnatt and Tempest 2000).

1.6   PROCESS OF OPERATIONS STRATEGY

As outlined above, there is a great need to consider many areas of business to be able to create an appropriate operations strategy. Even specific areas have numerous sub-topics that need taking into account, specifically operations resources. Focusing on any of the areas has both the potential to create an effective strategy and improved business results, while simultaneously leading an organisation in the wrong direction. In this introduction, it has been the aim to illustrate how in all areas of operations strategy it is not only possible but important to consider the other elements; however, there is still the problem of how to reconcile market requirements with operations resources. Rather than solve this issue, it has been thought that focusing on the improvement of operations may be a substitute for a carefully formulated operations strategy. This is potentially why companies choose prescriptive approaches to operations improvement, such as Six Sigma or TQM, as they consider both market requirements and the development of operations resources. Although such approaches may consider the necessary elements, it is unlikely they will be suitable unless alterations are made to meet the needs of a specific business's requirements.

Specific situations require that there is a degree of 'fit' between the market requirements and the operations capability, which the more prescriptive approaches may not take into account. GE demonstrates that to be successful, it may be necessary to exert pressure on a system through incentives and authority to make a company change so that it fits a particular operations management approach. Unfortunately, this can be expensive and time consuming, meaning the need to develop an appropriate operations strategy becomes important, when companies may not have the necessary financial reserves or time requirements. A strategy should be formulated that reflects both the needs of the market and operations capability, otherwise additional attention needs to be focused on developing the market or the operations so that a particular strategy can be achieved. This is likely to include allowances for time, effort and investment to understand how to move from the content to create an appropriate strategy that reflects a company's needs. The operations strategy process uses the elements of content with market requirement data to develop the strategy, that systematically account for the requirements of the system. The result is that the strategy reflects the needs of the organisation to enable introduction, to reduce time and cost but simultaneously improve the results of the activity. Approaches to operations strategy process will be discussed in the next chapter.

1.7 SUMMARY

The aim of this chapter has been to introduce the reader to the subject of strategy and, in particular, operations strategy. The theme throughout has been to stress the importance of each aspect, and the reasons for considering multiple areas in the development of a strategy but also how to use it within an organisation. In the global business arena, 'business as usual' no longer exists as the world is constantly changing and competing is becoming more difficult. Companies can no longer formulate general strategies that result in slight changes in performance; investments need to be directed to add maximum value to the operations. This means an operations strategy should be formulated that is specific to the needs of the organisation, to allow for the directed improvements the market requires while also building capabilities that define the company against its competitors. Capability development has also been a theme of the introduction that reflects the need for a strategic capability to be able to combine and consider numerous elements of strategic information to convert strategic ideas into organisational activities.

The capabilities that have been mentioned, that are necessary and are developed within the specific areas of operations strategy, represent intangible strategic resources that are not necessarily dependent on the details of a specific strategy. Through the development of capabilities that assist in strategy realisation, a company could develop a sustainable competitive advantage, being able to apply these abilities to the most appropriate strategy. It is the presence of specific company-specific capabilities that allow the coordination that is required for the implementation of a strategy that is often considered more important than formulation. Without the implementation of a strategy, there will be no change in a company's operations, meaning the time and effort spent on the process represent a very poor use of resources. Even with substantial resources and good strategic fit, the implementation process of a new strategy can still be a very complex process. For this reason, the importance of having a good understanding of the content and process of operations strategy is no less than having good skills in the implementation of strategy.

2.   The practice of operations strategy implementation

2.0   THE CASE FOR IMPLEMENTATION: WHY IMPLEMENTATION IS AN APPROPRIATE FOCUS FOR THE OPERATIONS MANAGER

The introduction touched upon a number of approaches to implementing an operations strategy once formulated and one in particular cannot be thought of as a tool specifically for strategy implementation. Although GE used the Six Sigma approach effectively to achieve its strategy and significantly reduce its operating costs, the main reason was likely to be the fit that was present with the strategy, the approach and what the market required of GE. If GE's aim had not been to reduce total operating costs through improved process control, it is unlikely Six Sigma would have been as able to assist in pursuing its strategy. It would have also been a considerably less successful exercise if, once achieved, the improvements were not appreciated by the market to justify the investment required in the development and maintenance of the system.

Although within the GE example, particular focus was given to the statistical professionals or 'belts', the position of these professionals was likely to be very similar to that of an operations manager. Operations managers are located in a position within an organisation that is similar to a capability, where they may straddle a number of functional elements to coordinate particular developments. As stated in Chapter 1, the importance of these capabilities for an organisation working on the implementation of an operations strategy is significant. Without capabilities that are able to provide value that is of importance to the end user, an organisation will have difficulty remaining in business. For this reason, it is the function of the operations management to implement the operations strategy. Possibly by focusing their efforts upon supply network planning, process improvement or process mapping, the results of individual activities may be focused on localised improvements in performance, with the result of all operations management over time representing the implementation of the operations strategy. Slack and Lewis (2008) commented that it was likely that those charged with integrating development activities would be the operations managers, and the development of an operations management capability was important if not essential before beginning specific operations strategy activities.

With the operations management function representing an inherently strategic capability, it is important for upper management to appreciate this. Although an operations management function is an important resource within a firm, unless the global aims are effectively defined in terms of the organisation's operations strategy, there may be potential for developments to be uncoordinated. The result of this, as with functionally dominant organisations, may be the pursuit of localised operational goals that may overlook the global requirements of the organisation. Although the position of the operations management allows the effective coordination of different functions, within a traditionally structured organisation, their role and relation to the rest of the organisation may be difficult to define. If operations management pursue their own goals, the value of the function may be more difficult to justify in relation to the traditional, established elements of the business such as manufacturing and marketing. Defining the primary role of the operations management function as the implementation of operations strategy allows all functions and upper management to be able to understand their role, and how their work relates to their own goals.

2.1 EXISTING FRAMEWORKS AND APPROACHES TO OPERATIONS STRATEGY IMPLEMENTATION

Over the past 30 years, there has been the realisation that if a strategy is not implemented, there will be few, if any, positive business results associated with the whole strategic process. For this reason, there has been increased focus on developing ways of implementing strategy and also how the careful consideration of the organisation during formulation is likely to improve the organisation's ability to implement it. One of the earliest areas considered important to the implementation of a strategy was structure, with Chandler (1962) introducing the idea of 'fit' between strategy and structure. Galbraith and Nathanson (1978) took this a step further by stating that structure tends to follow strategy or, as Pryor et al. (2007) stated, strategy should drive structure rather than be changed only once a structure has become so inefficient that it is not possible to continue in its current state. During the past three decades, additional areas have been added to structure that have been focused upon to assess their effect on the strategy implementation process (Bourgeois and Brodwin 1984; Guth and Macmillan 1986; Floyd and Wooldridge 1992). Following this, there began the introduction of approaches that assist in problem articulation and definition, that were able to allow those involved to create strategies that account for the areas that are affected by the strategy. These specific areas of attention then developed into specific frameworks that aim to convert complex, company-specific activities into step-wise processes attempting to include all areas needing consideration.

By outlining and discussing a selection of different approaches to operations strategy implementation, the aim of this chapter is to build on the introduction by adding to the concepts of operations strategy content and process. Demonstrating how both content and process relate to the strategy implementation process, this chapter also aims to build appreciation for the complexity of the subject of operations strategy implementation and the difficulty of applying it to a business situation. The different approaches will be grouped into different categories that reflect the different perspectives taken to implementation. Beginning with the people-oriented approach of Hoshin Kanri, the manufacturing-focused approaches will then be discussed. The chapter will conclude with two approaches that aim to introduce more structure into the process of strategy implementation, in an effort to assist progress and develop confidence in achieving the aims of the activity.

2.2   HOSHIN KANRI

Sometimes referred to as policy deployment, Hoshin Kanri's true meaning is much deeper than simply being a process of educating all within the company about the operating procedures. The essence of the approach is not simply to educate those within a company who will be carrying out strategic activities, but to work towards ensuring their goals are shared with those of the company. It is also an approach to developing targets that reflect the needs of the business and directing improvement activities towards achieving them. Forming a large part of the quality movement in Japan, acting as one of the pillars of TQM, Hoshin Kanri represents an important element of the Japanese approach to developing a company that is often overlooked when implemented in the west. Although Hoshin Kanri has been present since the introduction of Statistical Quality Control (SQC) to Japan, its specific relevance and significance to organisational development were not appreciated until much later (Akao 1991).

2.2.1   Culture

One of the most significant elements of a Japanese company compared to western companies is their commitment to continually improving the processes for which they are responsible. Such ground-up focus and commitment to the business functions have often meant it has been difficult to implement such approaches in western business in their original forms. The basis for the argument of why such activities failed to produce the results that had been achieved in Japan was the culture present within the Japanese companies, with a ground-up understanding and commitment to performance excellence. Such an argument was likely to have received further fuel from reference to Miyamoto Musashi (1584–1645), whose books act as guides for Samurai Warriors. With such a long heritage of appreciating the need for 'Heiho' or strategy, expecting western companies to be able to approach such a way of working could be considered unrealistic.

What the formalisation/articulation of Hoshin Kanri did was demonstrate that such deep seated understanding and appreciation of the company's strategy was not necessarily bred into all those born within a country, but could be learnt. Pfeffer and Sutton (2000) identified that in Japanese companies, the knowing–doing gap simply did not exist, which they considered to be a major reason for the number of unsuccessful strategy implementation activities in western business. Identifying Hoshin Kanri as what was present within the Japanese firms that allowed the gap to be reduced had potential for being the missing link in western implementation of processes such as TQM. In a similar way to the points raised by Bossidy and Charan (2002), Hoshin Kanri allows those within a company to effectively integrate their specific abilities into the system, allowing upper management to tailor their goals to the abilities present in the system.

2.2.2 Foundations

The processes involved in Hoshin Kanri strongly reflect its origins and importance within the implementation of Total Quality Management, where one of the key elements is the Plan, Do, Check, Act (PDCA) cycle proposed by W. Edward Deming. Within Deming's teachings, the continual development of shop floor activities is central, and without a high level of commitment, it is difficult to drive the company towards overall quality improvements. Another contribution from a major quality guru, which is actually the primary focus of Hoshin Kanri, is determining and implementing breakthrough activities, which was an approach originally proposed by Joseph Juran. Although the primary focus of the initiative, the breakthrough initiatives are heavily reliant on the continued feedback that is available from the PDCA cycles, which allows continual and adaptive review of the breakthrough development activities.

2.2.3 Process

The foundation of a Hoshin, or direction, is developed at the board level, where analysis of current market conditions and the operating environment is carried out. Then through an open dialogue, possibly similar in style to Beer's and Eisenstat's (2004) Honest Conversation or Bossidy's and Charan's (2002) robust dialogue, all members can build a fact-based understanding of the business as a whole that is not founded on functional perceptions. Due to the frankness of the process, the outcome of the activity should be more representative of the needs of the whole company, creating a stronger plan that results from a group dialogue, which helps to capture and concretise strategic goals (Akao 1991). These visions and objectives are then passed down to lower levels of the company for further discussions. Understanding that the objectives and aims are representative of the company as a whole, group consensus of the general aims will be improved. However, this is not simply a one-way flow of information, and further strategic consensus can be created through the modification of the aims that takes account of conditions that may not have been known or suitably presented in the data available to upper management.

The nature of the next level of discussions is likely to be very different from the dialogues discussing the company as a whole. Whereas the company-wide aims were likely to be data based, the next level down will require understanding of how these aims can be achieved in relation to the specific processes that are present in the firm. The discussion's aim is to establish how to achieve the company strategy in a way that best reflects the needs of the different business functions involved in the improvement processes. To determine the processes and projects that will be necessary to meet upper management aims requires careful consideration of actual conditions that reflect all areas of the business. For this reason, there needs to be further open discussions regarding proposed approaches to meeting aims agreed upon with upper management.

The result of such a discussion will generally be between three and five major strategic change initiatives, representing breakthrough improvements in performance. At this stage, these approaches are then the focus of the improvement activities, using process and quality improvement tools to work towards achieving the aims and accomplishing the initiatives. These activities are the major responsibility of senior management, who will spend as much as 80 per cent of their time on them, to ensure they are progressing in an appropriate way. However, it is not only the responsibility of management to implement these activities, which further assists in preventing such activities being seen as top-down or forced initiatives. During the implementation, there are consistent, open discussions between all levels of the organisation, backed up by a continual flow of fact-based information that is available from the frontline PDCA activities.

2.2.4 Catchball

The 'catchball' element is extremely important throughout the process of Hoshin Kanri; this is represented in Figure 2.1 by the double-ended arrows. The three elements are openly discussed between the different levels of the organisation, passing back and forth until both parties are able to agree they are appropriate. Of particular importance is the 'catch-ball' between the implementation team and senior management, which effectively represents a process of strategic review to assess whether the effects of previous initiatives have been appropriate. Carrying out such reviews relatively frequently also allows the overall company aims to be continually reviewed in regards to the company's capabilities and market requirements. Although it is important to ensure that targets are appropriate for current conditions, consistency is also important which is reflected in the long-range targets focused on moving towards a visionary future state of the company a number of years in the future. The longer-term plans reduce the organisation's ability to change planes wholly on current conditions, but focus on building long-term capabilities. This also offers an opportunity for management to review previous plans critically in an effort to improve overall consistency between planning activities.

Although the process may be considered relatively straightforward and

Source: Akao (1991).

Figure 2.1   Hoshin model

unrelated to a particular strategy, the details of such activities would be tailored to the needs of a particular strategy being carried out by a particular organisation. For example, if the process was involved in implementing a total quality system, the elements included would consist of quality tools and if it was an operations strategy, there could be elements of content included. Where the Hoshin Kanri approach is significant is in the way that it involves the different levels of staff in the strategy process. By creating a system of communication and connection between the different levels of staff, all levels are able to take specific responsibilities for company strategy and overall company direction. Although the majority of the Hoshin Kanri activities for the frontline staff will consist of process improvements, the connection they have into business-wide, long-term strategies has potential for them to appreciate how their work directly affects the direction and success of the company as a whole.

Without introducing a system such as Hoshin Kanri alongside a company's operating system such as TQM, which specifically relies upon the input from all levels of staff, it may be more difficult to develop buy-in to the approach. Bossidy and Charan (2002) suggested a similar approach that can be supported by procedures to create a culture where staff are able to appreciate how their activities directly affect company strategy. The easily visualised interactions involved in Hoshin Kanri, along with suggested tools to aid communication, mean that its introduction into a more traditional company may be relatively simple. Compared with that described by Bossidy and Charan (2002), Hoshin Kanri's visible structure could assist in promoting bottom-up support that may be more difficult in a procedure-based system.

2.2.5 Limitations

The potential applicability of Hoshin Kanri may be reduced slightly in western companies if their organisational structure is excessively hierarchical or excessive amounts of tension are present between the organisational levels in the company. In these two situations the ability for the frontline to appreciate their input into the strategy process would be reduced, due to the extra time required to transfer the organisational vision into frontline improvements. With an excessive number of 'catchball' activities, or each taking too long to reach an agreement, the senior management may have to consider interim aims that have not yet been implemented when altering their plans. It may also be difficult to implement in a divisionalised company, although the problem of an excessively long strategy deployment would be reduced if the overriding company aims reflected the group rather than particular units. Although this may affect the total effectiveness of the Hoshin Kanri approach, it could still aid in creating a divisional strategic consensus, which could assist in improving divisional performance.

2.3   THE FERDOWS AND DE MEYER APPROACH

One of the most established assumptions in operations is the concept of trade-offs between operational performance metrics. Skinner (1966) stated that two performance metrics could not be improved simultaneously unless there was slack in the system, meaning an improvement in one would result in the degradation of the other. In traditional manufacturing companies, such constraints were likely to be batch size and lead time or part quality and part cost. The traditional way to meet new performance levels was to invest in the system to increase the amount of slack available; what this resulted in was simply the movement from one performance frontier to another (Figure 2.2). These assumptions began to be questioned when during the 1970s and 80s, Japanese manufacturers were able to compete on numerous aspects of performance without the same problems experienced by western companies. Ferdows and De Meyer (1990) also commented that there were some western companies able to perform in this way, meaning the specifics of the operating system may not have been the only reason for the performance advantage.

Ferdows and De Meyer (1990) proposed that there should be a particular way to develop capabilities that, rather than requiring trade-offs,

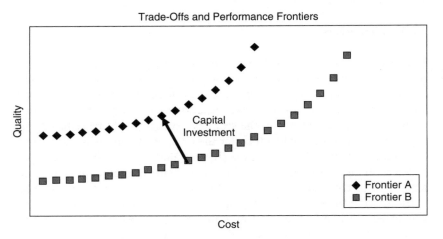

Figure 2.2   Performance criteria trade-offs

could complement previously developed capabilities. By determining an approach to developing performance capabilities that enhance previously developed capabilities, there seemed potential to promote longer lasting, less fragile developments. From an operational point of view, this approach would assist in gaining company-wide backing for the initiative through the different developments acting cumulatively and complementarily. The resulting positive effect this could have on financial results could assist in maintaining or even increasing upper management support for the activities, while removing the need to effectively juggle different performance initiatives. This effectively removes the need for specific areas of improvement that would aversely affect other areas of the organisation and ultimately return to their original level after a period of time. Such a 'management by drive' would not result in a net gain for the system and reduce support for new initiatives (Drucker 1955, pp. 110–11).

2.3.1 Ferdows's and De Meyer's (1990) Research

The form of Ferdows's and De Meyer's investigation was a study regarding the manufacturing performance of a range of companies in relation to the main performance metrics, Quality, Dependability, Speed and Cost. By determining how the company's performance varied in relation to metric-specific criteria over a period of time, the order in which capabilities were added within companies could be determined to confirm the sand cone hypothesis that capabilities can be built upon one another (Figure 2.3). Although the study was unable to prove the hypothesis that there was a specific order for developing capabilities or that it was more difficult to develop more than a single capability, the importance of operational control was noticeable in all of the performance metrics. This confirmed that the base of the sand cone should be quality, as without being able to

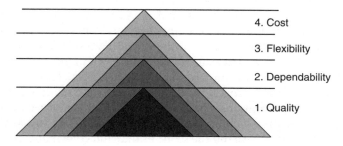

Source: Ferdows and De Meyer (1990).

Figure 2.3   Development of lasting manufacturing capabilities

exercise greater levels of control on the operations, it was not possible to consistently perform in regards to the other performance metrics.

Additional questions could be raised such as what activities directly contribute to dependability, other than determining what the customer requirements are and establishing whether they are being met. The other levels of the sand cone, as determined by the study, can all have elements attributed to the quality of the operating process, and performance in each is likely to require a different type of quality. Slack and Lewis (2001) explained how it was not necessarily quality that was important in allowing high levels of performance, but in fact the amount of process knowledge those interacting with the system had. Such knowledge allowed them to effectively control, understand and influence variation, ensuring unknowns could be removed from the system. If Ferdows and De Meyer are defining quality as simply conformance, the sand cone may be slightly less ambiguous and offer greater direction. With the number of different ways the word 'quality' relates to such an organisation, a different terminology, such as process control, may possibly be more appropriate for the base level of the sand cone.

2.3.2   Different Types of Control

From the relatively early days of mass production, it has been the companies which have been able to produce most consistently that have been able to define the market, whether it was Ford in the 1900s or Toyota in the 1980s. The use of the word 'consistency' could be thought of in terms of quality, but during these two periods quality had a very different meaning. In the early days of the automobile industry, cost was the drive and being able to produce cars as cheaply as possible transformed the market, with the quality perception pertaining to the type of good that could be purchased for such a low price. More recently the defining factor has been reliability or innovation and it is the manufacturing systems best able to supply these consistently that currently define the market. As time progresses, the presence of the lowest level of the sand cone, as conformance, becomes increasingly established as a prerequisite, with the higher levels defining a company's ability to perform. However, unlike historically, where the processes being analysed were relatively compact in nature, as the operations expand so do the number of elements that affect an organisation's ability to maintain control. For this reason, it may be appropriate to expand the scope of the sand cone model to include more elements of the larger organisation, such as the supply network that requires system-wide knowledge to be controlled effectively.

Expanding the scope of the operations from simply a manufacturing process to a supply network situation has the potential to offer slightly more specific directions in improvements. Within a manufacturing process, Slack and Lewis (2001) explained that developing process-related knowledge to a high level could enable a company to perform well in many areas, even those not initially considered directly related to process performance, such as marketing. Such relatively low-level process improvements could act as a base for improvements allowing higher-level activities to benefit from the control. However, rather than considering these as dependability activities, if they were also considered quality improvement activities, the tools and skills required to carry these out would already be available within the system. The level of activities would be those that support and supply the lower-level processes whose consistency is likely to be just as important as the processes they support, but due to these processes not resulting in non conforming products their control may not be considered a quality control activity. Improving process control of supporting business functions adds dependability to the process, by reducing the possibility of parts not arriving at a process when required.

By continuing this process upwards through the organisation, improvements in the additional performance criteria are possible. Japanese firms have shown that greater understanding of suppliers and development of suppliers are important components that can positively affect numerous performance criteria. Although such developments could be classed as dependability, supplier development or improvements in flexibility, the basis for these and other elements is the development of supplier quality, but also quality of the operating system. Using such process technologies as ERP to give process information about other entities in the system could allow decisions to be altered to take account of current conditions. Such systems, although extremely capitally intensive, offer large potential cost savings, although as with the sand cone, it is necessary that all the lower levels of the system are operating under a suitable level of control. Where this may disagree with Ferdows's and De Meyer's conclusion is that although it is important to have a suitable level of control at all levels of the business, to operate effectively on a supply network level does not necessarily mean that total process knowledge is required (Slack and Lewis 2001).

2.4 HILL'S APPROACH

Terry Hill (1985) developed a number of interesting concepts that began to increase the scope of manufacturing-related developments through understanding that manufacturing capabilities that reflected the business strategy were able to offer an organisation long-term performance advantages. Unfortunately, it was likely that understanding at a corporate level was that other functions offered more potential for achieving their competitive aims than manufacturing. This effectively meant that manufacturing were required to adapt to the requests of other business functions, even though their abilities to perform had some of the most tangible effects on customer satisfaction. The situation was then exacerbated by the tenure of managers falling, fuelling the pursuit of activities that would maintain the status quo. For this reason, Hill proposed that the scope of the strategic process should increase to take account of more areas of the operations, allowing for a 'congruence of purpose and function' (Hill 1995, p. 55).

The aim of such an approach to strategy was first and foremost to aid company-wide 'commitment through understanding' (Hill 1995, p. 56), meaning that through familiarisation with problems caused by previous strategic decisions, future decisions could take account and learn from the past. Hill suggested that such commitment and understanding could be developed by focusing activities on a single strategic goal, to create a common purpose, similar in some respects to a management-by-objective approach to business (Drucker 1955). In this way, the overall strategic vision and the results of day-to-day activities all work to move the company in the same direction towards a single goal. Once this is achieved, Hill stated it was then important for there to be a process of regular measurement of appropriate, unambiguous metrics to track the performance of the company, which could also be used for the allocation of resources and rewards to further promote strategic change.

2.4.1 Developing a Company-Wide Goal

Establishing company-wide goal congruence, although relatively simple in theory, can result in a considerable amount of debate between the different functions to determine which of the many elements of the business should be the focus. Hill (1985) proposed the concept of order winners, which was later joined by order qualifiers (Hill 1995), to express product features and process capabilities in terms of customer requirements. An order winner is an element of a product or service that will determine whether a potential customer will choose that item over another item. An order qualifier is an element of a product or service that must be present for a customer to consider purchasing an item. In terms of specific products these two factors can be specific features or a level of performance in a generic performance metric, such as the length of time a product is expected to function without causing the owner a problem. Due to the continuous scale of these metrics it is likely that different levels of performance will result in different types of satisfaction for the customer, where a single metric can offer both order qualifying and order winning capabilities (Figure 2.4). Although both have different effects on a potential customer, neither should be forfeited in favour of the other, as both are required for success in the market place.

As with Ferdows's and De Meyer's proposed sand cone, there is a similar relationship between order winners and order qualifiers as there was between the different performance metrics. As quality needs to be the base of improvements with regard to the development of operational functions, order qualifiers form the base of the customer selection criteria, as without meeting these requirements an organisation is unable to compete. For this reason, although order winning criteria have the potential for increased customer satisfaction and market share, resources should not be allocated to their development until the order qualifiers have been satisfied. Unless this is done, it is likely that customers who may have been attracted by particular criteria may be dissatisfied with the overall performance. Such a situation could lead to good sales performance, that is short lived, until the true performance of the item is established. Such a situation is comparable to marketing parts with a short lead time, but unless the parts conform in a suitable manner and the short delivery time is dependable, there will be no long-term benefits to the organisation.

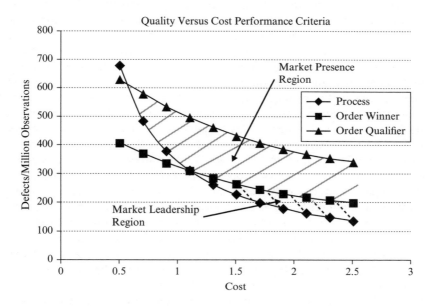

Figure 2.4   Quality and price as competitive criteria

2.4.2   Customer-Focused Manufacturing (Berry, Hill and Klompmaker 1995)

As mentioned in the introduction, the aim of a business is not to sell more or produce more efficiently, even though some traditional functional strategies may incentivise such aims: it is to satisfy customer requirements. The more proficient a company is at satisfying a customer, the better a company is likely to perform in the market place. By aligning the strategy, goals and control systems to meeting the customer needs, it should be possible to drive a company towards the development of processes and products that are customer focused. Developing in this way will mean that the company's activities in all areas of the business will consider and identify the needs of the customer. Being able to continually develop and innovate what is being offered to the customer in a way that is in line with their requirements has the potential to reduce the effects of competition. Learning about the customer combined with relevant information detailing manufacturing's capabilities allows the development of long-term customers.

2.4.3   Capability Development

Although the use of order winners and order qualifiers can help an organisation identify what specific elements are important to its customer, a weakness of the approach has been identified. Due to the dynamic nature of a competitive market, the competitive criteria of even a relatively stable item will change over time. As products and processes develop, the costs and value associated with specific elements of an item will change; the effect of this is that as improvements are being made, what was once an order winner may over time become simply an order qualifier. This effectively means that although it may be possible to identify how customers will relate to different features in the future, it does not give direction to what will be required in the future. What it does guide is the need to develop processes that achieve today's order winner ever more efficiently. As companies should only begin allocating resources to order winners once order qualifiers have been met, so being able to achieve basic requirements more efficiently should leave more resources available for identification, development or even invention of the order winners of tomorrow.

Although it may be possible to criticise order winners and order qualifiers for being current measures of performance, their use to create company-wide focus on the customer and assist process development and resource allocation means the approach is not without merits. Using company-wide measures and understanding to develop strong connections with the customer, the research and development activities can be aligned with the customer's needs and the manufacturing capabilities. The development capabilities could form the basis of an order winner themselves, such as design capabilities and the development of a brand image (Hill 1995). Although not associated with particular product features or characteristics, building an image that is synonymous with innovation or quality can be an important element for improving market performance.

With the understanding that it is likely that today's order winners will become tomorrow's order qualifiers, and order qualifiers should be met before resources are allocated elsewhere, this could form the basis for process development. By understanding that order winners will need to be delivered as standard in the future, the process can be designed to allow for these to be delivered as efficiently as possible. The more efficiently order qualifiers can be met, the greater will be the resource allocation to order winning criteria development, possibly with specific allocation allowed for the innovation of process technology. With such an approach to process development it could be possible to maximise long-term resource allocation to order winner developments. Although Hill (1995) mentioned using competitive benchmarking as a potential approach, the approach is more likely to be of use to 'catch up' with competitors, rather than as a means of developing new order winning elements.

The criticism of the order winning criteria not offering enough direction in development could be considered misguided. It is very clear that it is backwards looking in its approach and it is unable to prepare for what a competitor will offer in the next generation of products or services. However, what it does do is outline the need for better company-wide alignment of purpose that understands the need to internally sell capabilities so the product's development forms the best fit between the customer needs and manufacturing capabilities. Using this as a basis, the Hill approach aims to bring the customer into the company to improve long-term learning to enable the development of customer-specific capabilities. Combining this with how the approach can assist in the efficient allocation of resources to focus upon the development of future order winning criteria, it becomes quite a powerful approach. The approach may look inwards on the company but, importantly, due to the customer empathy of those developing the capabilities, they should be able to see the situation from the customer's perspective.

2.5 THE HAYES/HARVARD APPROACH

Wheelwright and Hayes (1985) identified four different approaches to viewing the manufacturing function within an organisation in regards to the organisation's overall business strategy. The Ferdows and De Meyer (1990) and Hill (1995) approaches both take a manufacturing perspective of developing a well-rounded business strategy, whereas Wheelwright and Hayes (1985) address the function as one of a number of strategic capabilities and identifying relationships between the functions. Although the focus of the approach may be different, the overall targets are relatively similar, and it benefits from presenting specific stages of development that allow organisations to assess their current stage. This allows those carrying out the strategy process to compare current positioning with business and market needs, assisting in the transition from a concept to a suitable development plan.

Companies aiming to develop their manufacturing capabilities generally need to progress from one level to the next, as the understanding of one level forms the footings for the level above. Unless capabilities are developed in this way, and a company attempts to 'leap frog' a level (Wheelwright and Hayes 1985, p. 100), as with the Ferdows and De Meyer (1990) approach, improvements may be difficult and resource intensive to maintain. Below, the four stages will be discussed in turn from the lowest stage representing a traditional firm's approach to manufacturing to stage four, that represents a world-class approach to manufacturing capabilities.

2.5.1   Stage 1: Internally Neutral

Although not always, this is often the stage at which new companies begin operating but it can also be the stage at which very traditionally organised firms reside. At this stage, the manufacturing function is almost considered a necessary evil required to produce items and is considered the constraining factor on the other elements of the company. In a newly formed company, it is likely there will be an entrepreneurial development that is geared at meeting the requirements of a particular market segment. Without competition in the new sector, the abilities and processes of the function that produce the items are of little concern. It is the different business functions' abilities to initially develop the idea and sell the items that are the primary focus, with business strategy targets that are set for manufacturing consisting of meeting the demands of the other functions. Manufacturing's strategic targets are likely to be based around efficiency, but have lower priority than other functional targets. In this situation, the market or company's competitive advantage may have a short lifespan, resulting in manufacturing investments being withheld to prevent investment in equipment that may soon be obsolete.

Traditionally organised companies which may reside in stable markets, which on the surface couldn't seem more different from newly formed ones, may have surprisingly similar approaches to manufacturing-related developments. As with the dilemma of investing in soon to be obsolete technology, established companies may also balk at the thought of investing in new technology. If satisfactory parts are being produced on equipment, the tendency may be to continue to aim for small improvements that allow them to meet sales requirements. With a stable market and product, the need to change is almost removed, with any changes being the choice of those controlling the company who may only introduce changes when the product requires it. Taking a view that does not consider manufacturing to be able to offer constructive input to the business strategy, the justification to develop to a level higher than the minimum will not be present.

In addition to minimising the negative effects manufacturing has on business performance, managers who have little knowledge of the processes involved aim to minimise the business risks associated with any decision. When changes are required, it will be necessary to invest in external capabilities to advise, develop and manufacture new equipment. Without an appropriate appreciation of manufacturing, the managers are likely to choose technologies that are general and flexible or keep processes manual where possible. Through keeping the equipment non product specific, manufacturing's learning capacity can be actively suppressed to maintain their position within the company as a function that does not affect the company's competitive position. Although this could be thought of as maintaining a level of top-down control on manufacturing that enables flexibility in the processes, it is likely to be a very inefficient approach when compared with 'focused' manufacturing facilities.

2.5.2   Stage 2: Externally Neutral

Stage 2 is also a relatively common stage within traditional companies and marks where stage 1 companies must develop to when they are unable to continue operating with their current approach. Such a change may happen when competition within a market increases or process developments begin that result in general purpose equipment no longer being competitive. Management appreciate their current approach cannot continue if they are to stay within the market. However, they still do not consider manufacturing as a function that offers them a competitive advantage, resulting in only a small amount of manufacturing process developments in-house. To allow for change and improve their manufacturing capabilities they must look outside the company, often to the companies which are their competitors, to identify and copy manufacturing approaches that will make them more competitive.

Investments in manufacturing process technology are considered a way to regain a company's competitive advantage, with production efficiency remaining the key to achieving its business strategy. Similar to stage 1-type companies, they are also generally located in relatively slow moving industries or controlled industries. Within highly competitive environments, the effect of continually following the leader would result in substantial competitive ground being forfeited due to the continuous loss of first mover advantage. When taking this approach, it is important for there to be considerable continuity between the different processes, due to the low levels of process knowledge within the system. Without continuity, considerable additional effort will be needed to deploy the new technology (see Section 2.8.5). An example of this would be the problems associated with introducing computers into a 1930s typing pool; even though the technology is vastly superior, without considerable training, the typing pool's output may fall considerably. To prevent such a situation, it may be necessary for R&D to develop products that can be produced on processes similar to existing ones, enabling a process of gradual change. However, it is likely within a stage 2 organisation that R&D would be heavily product oriented and the involvement with the process development would be aimed at maximising economies of scale, with the primary aim being to minimise the negative impact of the manufacturing function. Although there may be some positive input, the main aim of the interactions with process development would still be to minimise the negative impact of the manufacturing function and maximise process efficiency.

2.5.3   Stage 3: Internally Supporting

An internally supportive manufacturing function no longer considers the operations of their processes their primary concern and, importantly, general management do not consider them in this way either. The development of the process and product technologies is actively aligned with the overall business strategy working to strengthen the organisation's competitive position. To promote the approach, the manufacturing managers need to have a board view of the business and be able to command a suitable position within the management team to allow all within the team to appreciate how different elements of the business relate to manufacturing. Understanding how manufacturing's capabilities can be used to promote specific elements of the business strategy can assist in coordinating strategic activities across the business. Manufacturing must in turn be able to effectively convert elements from other areas of the business into appropriate manufacturing objectives that are meaningful and relevant to manufacturing personnel.

Managers of an internally supportive manufacturing function need to appreciate overall business conditions and long-term trends within the industry. Through greater understanding of how developments are progressing, product and process development activities can be focused to ensure that when the overall business strategy requires certain capabilities that may take considerable time to develop, they will be present to be efficiently integrated into the business strategy. To assist in the integration of these technologies into the day-to-day business, the operating system must be able to actively promote an integrative approach to business function management. Careful developments in infrastructure as well as structure are required to create a common purpose of all levels of staff that can be maintained over a long period of time.

The benefits of moving from stage 2 to stage 3 are significant, due to the company's ability to develop better internal relationships that make use of all the abilities that are present within the firm. The transition also allows companies to more effectively manage developments within their industry without over-reliance on their direct competitors over which they have no control. Whereas the change in stages from 1 to 2 is relatively simple, consisting of mainly appreciating external conditions and employing suitable contractors, the change to an internally supportive organisation requires developments of integrated capabilities within the firm.

Although the benefits of the stage are realised through better coordination, the importance of initiating this within the management team is significant; without suitable involvement of the manufacturing capability at this level, getting the lower levels of the organisation involved will be difficult. If this capability is not present, a change in stage may only be present temporarily, possibly while a difficult marketing situation is navigated, then quickly revert to the previous state. Wheelwright and Hayes (1985) also identified a potential condition that is almost inherent in the approach. Due to the manufacturing manager requiring a broad understanding of operations by effectively moving the company to stage 3, they may receive a promotion to general management. If the replacement is unable to continue working at an appropriate level, the company may revert back to its previous level when operations begin to return to a functional way of operating.

Drucker (1955) gave an interesting example of the important aspects required in the movement from stage 2 to stage 3, describing IBM in the 1930s. Unlike much later introductions of lean techniques in western business, it was appreciated how important other, infrastructural elements were to the operation of a different operating system. Through a process to 'make jobs big' (p. 223), the shop floor workers stopped being employed as muscle, but were recognised as cognitive beings, responsible for all aspects of their jobs, with employment security and wages reflecting these changes. Empowering the workers to take responsibility for quality and quantity produced, the role of the supervisor was removed. This role was replaced by that of a senior machine operator responsible for developing staff, who also took the role of project manager for the introduction of new processes. This allowed new processes to take account of the requirements of those who would be operating the process, assisting in improving the introduction of the new processes as well as their performance. The development required changes in numerous departments that built an effective manufacturing capability rather than developments taking place in a particular area of the organisation. Instead of considering the process as one that develops a manufacturing capability, it was introduced as a customer (being end user and employee) satisfaction delivery capability.

2.5.4   Stage 4: Externally Supportive

Although stage 3 has the potential to promote better company-wide coordination through careful consideration of all areas of the business strategy, the capability is still acting in a reactive manner. The business is able to effectively match the developments in product and process technology to the requirements of the other elements of the business, but the manufacturing capabilities are essentially being led by other elements of the business which in turn may be led by the market itself. The result is that the manufacturing elements may not be developing as effectively as they could and not offering the end user as much as they may be able to. The next stage accounts for this by pursuing the development of processes and products in tandem, while considering information from the market. By considering the market directly, the manufacturing function can determine how best to apply their capabilities to the opportunities present in the market, allowing it to redefine the market through product innovations that are led by manufacturing capabilities. Unlike all previous uses of the manufacturing function, the approach becomes increasingly difficult to imitate, due to both product and process technology having been developed together, reducing competition and potentially improving profitability.

The organisation must understand that manufacturing is the capability within the organisation that is able to offer them a sustainable competitive advantage in the market place. Manufacturing needs to take a lead role, while not dictating but continuing to coordinate the different business functions. However, rather than a reactive role as in stage 3, manufacturing now works proactively to identify new opportunities their capabilities can exploit. The company appreciates that the continued, focused development of both product and process technologies will allow it to establish a lead role in its business field. However, understanding that the business field is likely to continually change, the supportive role of externally facing business functions allows special consideration of ways to meet additional customer needs. Through deep understanding of the manufacturing capabilities, combined with customer-focused learning, the other functions may be able to identify opportunities to which the capabilities can be applied, that are outside the organisation's traditionally targeted market.

Managing a transition from stage 3 to stage 4 requires the careful development of all areas of the business; unlike stages 1–3 that can effectively continue operating within a traditionally run company, stage 4 requires deeper developments at all levels of the company. An externally supportive company requires the integral support of the human resources function to promote the development of appropriate skills that are necessary for the development of the manufacturing capability. All manufacturing staff need to be able to contribute to the aims of the company, with management promoting an 'experimental and organisational learning' (Wheelwright and Hayes 1985, p. 104). Both structural and infrastructural elements of the business are important to assist in continually promoting the stage, meaning they require equal attention and require directed activities from business elements other than manufacturing. The move from stage 3 to stage 4 requires much greater effort than all the other transitions that include continuing effort that develops a suitable culture throughout the company. Although requiring more effort, when achieved companies are able to class themselves as 'world-class manufacturers' and should be able to remain competitive irrespective of market and environmental conditions.

2.5.5 Forces and Effects

The first two stages, that have almost always been present in business, are still relevant today, but only where there is a considerable level of stability or control of stability. Without a need to consider the development of manufacturing capabilities, especially the development of producing manufacturing equipment in-house, diverting resources to their pursuit could be considered by management as using them in a non strategic manner. In such a company, to meet the business strategy, the manufacturing capability's aim is to produce the products as quickly and as cost effectively as the marketing or R&D departments require. In this situation, as the product or market requirements alter over time, it is likely there will be little disadvantage to those companies which follow the initial movers in the industry. However, in today's open and highly competitive global market, unless there is specific intervention from external forces, the approach may be inefficient. Such forces could include government legislation, a strong union presence or a carefully controlled competitor network where it is preferable to maintain the status quo.

Moving to the higher levels of manufacturing capability allows a company to be less dependent on external forces present within the market place to allow for a lack of ability to react or cope with changes. If such changes are relatively infrequent, it may be possible to progress to a higher level to allow for the change, but if efficiency quickly returns as the main aim of manufacturing, the need to remain at the higher level will decrease and the company may revert. However, if the market is constantly changing, to continually progress to and revert from higher stages will become inefficient, forfeiting important profit making opportunities as new approaches are being introduced. The higher levels described by Hayes and Wheelwright allow the company as a whole to become more integrated, where the customer begins to be considered in all areas of the company. This increases manufacturing's ability to develop themselves in line with the business's needs, allowing the company to more effectively meet the market needs and maintain a stronger position within the market place, developing in line with the corporate aims.

Many companies consider that achieving stage 3 is all that is required for them to maintain a strong position within a market, with the risks associated with aiming for stage 4 not being justified by the benefits. However, it is only at stage 4 that it is possible to consider manufacturing as a source of competitive advantage. Manufacturing assists in the development of the business strategy, making the most of its capabilities; at this stage, manufacturing is truly a strategic capability that ensures all activities work to complement and utilise capabilities present within the function. The stage 4 company is better able to proactively manage change in the business environment and direct it in a way that stage 3 companies are unable to do. Being able to influence and potentially direct market developments, stage 4 companies are less affected by direct competition and developments over time, meaning the manufacturing capability offers a sustainable competitive advantage for the company as a whole.

The Wheelwright and Hayes approach focuses around the manufacturing capability's ability to assist in achieving an overall business strategy, rather than being the main focus of strategic activity. Understanding the role manufacturing can play within an effective company, while appreciating the supporting roles required from the rest of the business, has potential for developing a more balanced business development plan. Establishing the four stages allows companies to effectively understand their current position on the scale to determine what structural and infrastructural changes are required to help move them to the position they require. The approach, by considering the firm as a whole at every stage of development, helps senior management appreciate the benefits of developing the manufacturing function. The approach also demonstrates the need of all business capabilities to understand the importance of considering the effects of actions within one department upon other departments. This assists in reducing departmental myopia, where functional goals and developments are pursued at the expense of other departments that can result in the overall business performance suffering.

2.6 HILL'S FRAMEWORK AND THE PLATTS AND GREGORY PROCEDURE

Although these two approaches are different in many respects, they have a common theme, where the different levels of an operations strategy are considered as a whole, so that formulation effectively reflects the needs of the different levels. Hill (1995) aims to link operational activities to high-level corporate objectives though five steps, with the 'order winner' concept forming an important link between marketing strategy and manufacturing-based elements. Through open discussions between the different operational levels, the different components of the operations strategy reflect the needs of the business functions involved in the process. Although not implicitly mentioned, the use of a 'catchball' approach to strategy formulation is likely to assist this approach to develop strategies that reflect all needs of the business. As shown in Table 2.1, by understanding how the infrastructural elements also make an important contribution to an operations strategy, they can be considered to support the process-focused improvements.

Although this approach to developing an operations strategy assists in creating one that considers the relevant elements of the business, it does not direct those involved in the process to the specific activities necessary to achieve the strategy. The framework, although likely to aid implementation, cannot specifically be considered an operations strategy framework for implementation. The process assists in giving a structure to the formulation of the strategy, ensuring that all of the important elements of the process have been considered during the formulation process. Hill's framework could possibly be complemented with quantitative data to assist in demonstrating the relative importance of all the areas under discussion. However, with such aggregated topics of discussion as 'brand image', determining specific figures would be extremely difficult. Including such information within Table 2.1, with how elements relate to each other,

Table 2.1   Hill's framework

Step 1	Step 2	Step 3	Step 4	Step 5
Corporate Strategy	Marketing Strategy	How do Products or Services Win Orders?	Operations Strategy	
			Process Choice	Infrastructure
– Growth	– Product/ service marks and segments	– Price	– Process technology	– Functional support
– Profit		– Quality		– Operations planning and control system
– Return on investment	– Range	– Delivery speed	– Trade-offs embodied in process	
– Other 'financial' measures	– Mix – Volumes – Standardisation or customisation – Innovation – Leader or follower	– Delivery dependability – Product/ service range – Product/ service design – Brand image – Technical service	– Role of inventory – Capacity, size, timing, location	– Work structuring – Payment systems – Organisational structure

Source: Hill (1995).

may assist in understanding how particular elements should be prioritised but may make the table undecipherable.

The Platts–Gregory procedure (Platts and Gregory 1989) attempts to address these problems by reducing the scope of the activity to the operations only (Figure 2.5). The procedure is able to focus on specific quantifiable metrics that are important to the customer. All questions that are asked early in the formulation process are directed outwards to establish market needs and inwards to establish current performance. Unlike the Hill approach, that may be reliant on the information being filtered through other functions before review, market-relevant information is less aggregated. This means that once reviewed against the current levels of performance present within the operations, rather than the strategy requiring general increases in performance, it is possible to determine the specific amount of improvement required to change the company's

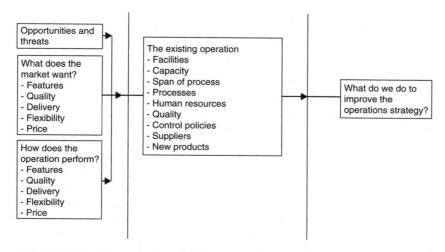

Source: Adapted from Platts and Gregory (1989).

Figure 2.5   The Platts–Gregory procedure

competitive position. Although this information will assist in giving the company's strategic improvement activities a scale to work towards, this information is not sufficient to build an operations strategy. For this reason the approach has two further steps where this information is used as a basis for broader strategic activities.

When the information relating to the organisation's current performance within the market has been determined and the different areas of improvement have been prioritised, the particular focus of the operations strategy can be determined. Although understanding current and future position is important for the strategic process, they do not assist in creating a plan for progressing from one to the other. For this reason, the second stage of the process critically assesses the current performance against the current operations resources to determine the capabilities present within the system. Through a process of analysis, it is possible to create a plan that allocates resources for capability development of the current system in a way that will most effectively meet the requirements of the market. The resulting plan can then be compared with the overall operations strategy to assess if the developments are not only taking the company where the market requires it, but also where the corporate strategy is directing it. Through further reconciliation of the two, the result can produce an effective operations strategy that uses resources in a way that reflects both internal and external requirements.

2.7   THE SLACK/WARWICK APPROACH: THE OPERATIONS STRATEGY MATRIX

The two approaches above, while aiming to introduce structure to the strategy formulation process to allow for broader consideration of what can assist implementation, could both be thought of as being directed towards the manufacturing function. This is not to say that they would not be used for an operations strategy; however, the process for conversion into a strategy is likely to be very complicated to ensure all elements that can affect operations are considered in regard to how they contribute to the strategy. It is also likely to be difficult and time consuming to consider all the elements of operations against market requirements to create a coherent strategy. This is likely to be why Slack and Lewis (2001) aggregated the elements into four main areas that, unlike performance metrics that may cause ambiguity (Garvin 1993), give cohesion and focus to the different elements of operations (Figure 2.6). By grouping resources together into areas that can be the focus of operations management study in their own right, an understanding of these specific areas can develop that can offer a range of benefits to the customer.

Each of the four areas – Capacity, Supply Network, Process Technology, and Development and Organisation – is able to affect a company's ability to perform in each of the main performance metrics. For this reason, it is appropriate for the approach to formulating an operations strategy to

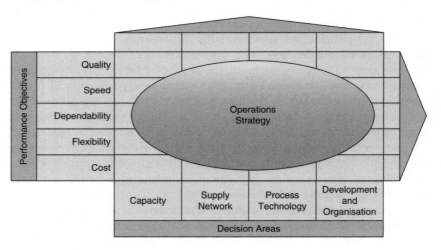

Source: Slack and Lewis (2001).

Figure 2.6   Operations strategy matrix

be arranged as a matrix. The proposed capability developments to the main areas can then be critically analysed against each outwards-facing performance metric. Once this has been carried out, the overall change in performance resulting from the planned activities should be compared with the overall operations strategy to ensure that the sum of the developments is moving the organisation in the correct direction. Slack and Lewis (2008) demonstrated how the effects on the different performance metrics could be prioritised to reflect the elements of the improvement activities that were most critical to the overall strategy and the organisation's success.

Although each of the four areas of operations strategy has the potential to dramatically improve the performance of an organisation, it is likely that certain areas will be more critical for achieving particular organisational goals. The operations strategy may be structured around the improvement of a specific area that is essential for achieving the targets. For a global company, this may be the supply network or for an innovative design company process technology and development. Where this particular approach assists in effective formulation is that the process continues to take account of the organisation as a whole and does not overlook the other areas of operations. Where there may be a need for particular focus on a particular area, the other areas can also be considered and, through careful analysis, the development of the other capabilities can be structured to complement the critical capability. Through the use of the matrix, focus is possible while simultaneously creating an operations strategy that aims for global improvements in performance.

2.7.1 Marketing Influence

An important element of this approach is the consideration of the operations strategy definition of 'the strategic reconciliation of market requirements with operations resources', meaning there should be a significant market contribution. The overall aim of the operations strategy is to improve market competitiveness, meaning, as with the Platts–Gregory procedure, that the performance objectives need to be determined from the market. However, this approach may not be sufficient to drive organisational development and performance improvement if targets are based on traditionally sourced marketing information. As mentioned above, the approach begins to more fully address the operational needs when the marketing function is integrated into the manufacturing development process, which is further assisted by 'catchball' discussions between marketing and operations. This can allow the performance objective to consider customer-specific learning while marketing can develop the customers to utilise capabilities that are present within the organisation.

2.8 PLATTS'S 5P APPROACH

The above approaches focus heavily on the process of operations strategy, which essentially consists of how to move from operations strategy content to a formulated strategy. Although the processes are likely to create strategies that are appropriate for the organisation in regards to their corporate aims, operational resources and also the markets they are serving, they still need implementing in the company. If they are not implemented, and there is no change in post implementation operations, the time and effort put into strategy formulation are wasted. For this reason, Platts developed an approach to strategy implementation that considers the main areas of an organisation that need to be considered to implement a strategy effectively. These are Point of Entry, Procedure, Project Management and Participation, all of which have their own content and need to be considered throughout the implementation process to assist the activity. Following this, the fifth P, Purpose, was added by Mills, Platts and Gregory 1995. When discussed by Slack and Lewis (2008), Procedure was replaced by Process, which may cause ambiguity with 'content and process' but will be one of the Ps in the following sections.

2.8.1 Purpose: The Strategic Context

Similarly to the corporate strategy, it is important for those initiating the operations strategy to create a clear organisational target and vision of which the whole organisation can be made aware. Using concepts such as strategic fit is important to demonstrate the need to change the company's abilities to reflect the changing needs of the market; this helps to put the change into perspective for those who will be affected by the activity. Through the careful guidance and support of the dissemination of the vision, unease with the current activities can be introduced that can foster support for the strategy. Continued guidance throughout the operations strategy is important to maintain commitment and motivation when strategic fit may not be present. Active involvement and support can also facilitate the upward flow of information that can allow emergent strategies that are better able to account for new conditions to be considered in reference to the vision. The 'purpose' element sets the stage for the other elements of the 5P approach, determining how they will be carried out, the reason for carrying them out and how success will be gauged.

2.8.2 Point of Entry: The Organisational Context

The structure of an organisation will greatly assist in the types of strategy that it is able to implement; however, changing the whole organisational structure is unlikely to be possible with anything other than a 'green-field' site. For this reason, the way in which the implementation team is structured should reflect the needs of the strategy while assisting with the integration of the team with the organisational structure that is already present. The position of the implementation team within the organisation is also likely to be important, as this will affect how the team interacts with those who are affected by the strategic activities. Although Drucker (1955) considered the terms 'line' and 'staff workers' only to be relevant within the armed forces, where the team members originate is likely to affect their perspective of strategic activities. Staff operatives tend to be focused further into the future while line operatives concentrate on internal developments, meaning the balance within the team should reflect the important areas of the strategy. Combined with this, Slack and Lewis (2008) also consider the appreciation of more subtle, informal relationships present within the organisation important when developing an implementation team.

2.8.3 Process: The Methodological Context

Although strategy implementation is considered to have the greater effect on operational performance, the attention that has been given to the above approaches demonstrates that formulation of the operations strategy should not be overlooked. Slack and Lewis (2008) stated that both academics and consultants recommend the use of a 'stage model' approach to formulation, such as those outlined earlier. By consisting of stages, the approach will offer a methodical process for formulation that progressively builds a strategy reflecting all the information that is considered relevant. At this stage it is important to continually consider information originating within the firm so that formulation can account for current conditions and allow for emergent strategies that are able to contribute to the formulation process. The use of such a model ensures that during the strategy formulation, all important areas of the business are considered to assist in developing a strategy that while meeting the needs of the business environment is also realistic and attainable.

Using a stage approach to strategy formulation also means that the strategy can be presented visually, demonstrating the analysis and thought processes that went into its creation. This assists effective communication of the reasoning behind the strategy, assisting in building strategic consensus while also introducing people to the process and allowing them to contribute, further promoting the upwards flow of information. It demonstrates how the work that would be required of them directly related to the overall strategy is considered important for achieving acceptance and commitment to a new strategy. Unfortunately, as organisations increase in size, the use of such an approach to developing understanding of a new strategy is likely to become increasingly difficult and time consuming. For this reason, careful consideration of the strategy's 'point of entry' into the organisation is necessary, to assist in the deployment and acceptance of a new strategic direction.

2.8.4   Project Management: The Delivery Perspective

Once formulated, the strategy needs to be translated into changes in operations that result in developments that are in line with the company's strategic aims. Unlike the regular transformation processes that take place within the operations functions, the activities required are likely to be very complex and unique, and may be carried out by a group of individuals that have not worked together before. In other fields of business where there are requirements of this sort, the activities are managed as projects, which is the means taken in this approach. This means that to implement an operations strategy effectively, although not specifically mentioned, may require the presence of an in-house project management capability to assist in the management of the activity. Taking such an approach allows the management of all elements of the strategy to be coordinated by a single resource. With the tools available within project management combined with suitable experience, they should be able to coordinate and control the resources required for the implementation effectively. With suitable experience there should also be experience present to interact effectively with the numerous stakeholders involved with an implementation project. Through effective communication upwards, downwards and horizontally, the project management function should be able to develop strong personal networks that assist with implementation (Noble 1999).

Due to the nature of projects, they have distinctive starting and ending points, which may not be appropriate for some types of strategy that require continual attention or are too large to be able to be managed easily as a single project. For this reason, it may be preferable to approach certain strategies as a sum of a number of smaller projects or a programme of projects. The benefit of this is that as the projects are smaller, they are easier to manage and complete, but also there are fewer opportunities for the environment to change over the course of the project. The result of this is that the need to carry out mid project planning activities can be reduced, although not necessarily removed, as the need to learn from a live project is still important for producing a suitable end result. Slack and Lewis (2008) commented that although such an approach does allow more complex implementations, the resource management of the projects becomes a significantly more complex activity. Rather than simply managing the resources for one project, it is necessary to manage many projects simultaneously, which may require effective coordination if there are some resources that are used on numerous projects. Fortunately, due to this being a common problem within project management, there are tools present within the subject that assist in the management of such problems.

2.8.5 Participation: The Operational Context

The participation element of a strategy implementation activity has been a theme throughout the other four areas; from creating a company vision to integrating the activities, communicating the strategy to creating an effective team, all areas rely heavily on participation. The reason for this is that without effective participation of the company, expecting a suitable amount of development may be unrealistic if the majority of the organisation is acting as organisational ballast. Although some consider that a hierarchical, rigid organisational structure with an appropriate rewards system assists in the implementation of a strategy (Hrebiniak 2006), this is as likely to be from reassurance of what is correct rather than actual commitment to a strategy (Guth and Macmillan 1986). However, if the aim of the organisation is to become world class, the approach may not be appropriate for the change or simply too capital intensive to achieve the buy-in and commitment of all those involved in the system. Hrebiniak (2006, p. 17) mentioned that getting the 'right people on the bus, in the right seats' was important, reflecting the need to carefully select team members rather than relying solely on authority to develop involvement. In addition, establishing organisational goals that are in line with the personal goals of those involved with the strategic process will mean rather than simply humouring the boss, they will be personally committed to achieving the goals.

Slack and Lewis (2008) spoke of a number of different ways in which participation could be improved, that although they are considered by the other areas, are particularly relevant to improving participation in an implementation project. The way in which the implementation team interacts with the rest of the organisation will have a significant effect on the results of the project as well as how much participation there will be. Unless there is a suitable amount of interaction between the team and business functions, ownership of the resulting strategy and associated learning opportunities that allow the tailoring of solutions to specific conditions will be reduced. Accounting for this type of participation can allow functional staff to develop their understanding of the high-level strategy while feeding important functional information to the implementation team to assist the formulation of subsequent plans. The greatest level of participation described by Slack and Lewis was where the whole learning process took place with the functional staff, so that the results of the learning process could truly be considered the result of functional work. Although the time and resources required to develop a solution with an 'apprenticeship mode' may be large, once formulated implementation could take place much more quickly (Bourgeois and Brodwin 1984). The other levels have similar levels of interaction as the Wheelwright and Hayes approach, with the least amount of participation taking place with the delivered approach, which has almost no interaction. Although such an approach may result in poor levels of acceptance and only be suitable with relatively simple, incremental changes, it is likely to be the quickest and cheapest way if what is required is relatively standard. However, if implementation of the solution is not possible, the resources that are saved by taking the approach will be irrelevant: 'buy cheap, buy twice'.

In the approach outlined by Slack and Lewis (2008), there is no explicit direction to the interactions that take place within the different stages and where one should begin the approach to implementing a strategy. Figure 2.7 shows the likely contributions and interactions (where there is a two-way flow of information) each has with the other elements; from this it is likely the starting point will be 'Purpose', potentially concluding with the project management element. Unfortunately, due to the actual scope of each element being so broad, the overlap between the different elements is likely to be significant, which may make focusing on activities more difficult. If it is not possible to focus, the development of broad and deep knowledge of the different areas will not take place, reducing the ability to create an appropriate implementation plan. Although the approach is focused on strategy implementation, apart from the inclusion of project management, a number of the other elements focus on formulation or are additional operations strategy content. Without suitable direction into how to integrate these elements into the operations strategy implementation process, it may be difficult to make effective use of the additional information.

2.9 PRYOR'S 5P APPROACH TO STRATEGY IMPLEMENTATION

Initially proposed in 1998 as a process for strategic quality management (Pryor, Anderson and Toombs 1998), Pryor's 5P approach was later expan-

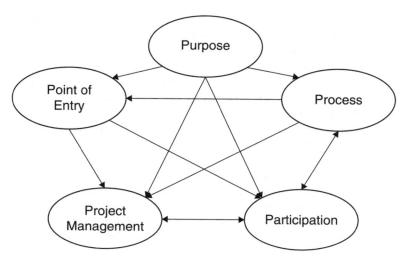

Figure 2.7   Interactions between elements of Slack's and Lewis's 5Ps

ded to assist in the implementation of other strategic activities (Pryor et al. 2007). As previous examples touch upon, introducing system-wide control into an organisation has the potential to improve organisational performance in more areas than those directly affected by traditional quality concerns. The 5P approach aims to give more structure to the introduction of such control into an organisation, enabling it to form the basis for the implementation of other strategic activities. With the appreciation of the complexity of strategy implementation and the general lack of focus on creating suitable frameworks, the benefits of one are likely to be significant (Pryor et al. 2007). Pryor et al. (2007) commented on the large number of areas of academic study that were involved in strategy implementation, such as organisational development, behaviour theory and operations research among others. However, unless an approach gave suitable consideration to all these areas, it would be difficult to benefit from excellent implementation that can give world-class results even when used with a generic strategy.

Although it is almost universally appreciated that effective implementation of an average strategy is vastly preferable to poor implementation of a brilliant strategy, there is still a need for a more integrated implementation methodology. Pryor et al. (2007) proposed that the creation and use of such a framework would allow the whole strategy process to be moved into the organisation, to enable effective, autonomous formulation at a lower level (Braganza and Korak-Kakabadse 2000).

The promotion of such levels of empowerment would allow companies to remain competitive in the 'hypercompetitive environment of today' (Pryor et al. 2007, p. 3), while simultaneously developing a core competence in strategy implementation. Through effective integration and coordination of all areas requiring appreciation within a framework, the conceptual confusion associated with strategy implementation could be reduced (Cravens 1998). Once all areas are considered as a whole, the specific alignment of the elements involved in strategy implementation can be carried out to further promote and enable the activity (Figure 2.8).

Although bearing a resemblance to Slack's 5P approach, Pryor et al. (2007) aim to offer greater structure to the process, offering specific areas of focus for each stage while also suggesting their interconnection. The connections along with the expansion of each of the areas allow those charged with implementation to appreciate important areas of consideration and the impact they are likely to have on the other elements of the model. Although the two approaches are quite different, it is likely that they can each assist in the use of the other; however, it seems that the Pryor approach is aimed at developing the idea of a management by objectives approach (Drucker 1955), rather than identifying additional elements of operations strategy content that allow implementation.

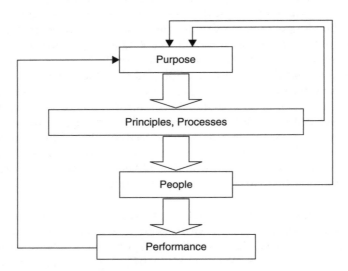

Source: Pryor, Anderson and Toombs (1998).

Figure 2.8   The 5Ps paradigm

2.9.1 Model Components

Pryor's model aims to allow such activities to be initiated at a corporate level, while understanding that they should not be totally based on financial performance of the company. The 'purpose' is similar to the 'purpose' and 'process' elements in the Slack approach, both setting broad operations goals. In addition to setting broad operational goals and targets, the Purpose defines the boundaries the organisation will operate within to achieve the corporate goals including values to reflect that financial goals are not the only aim of the business. The Purpose sets the 'strategic direction' by setting a broad range of organisational objectives to guide all levels of operations, which is similar to Drucker's 'management by objective' (Drucker 1955). The stage effectively sets the overall strategy for the organisation, as the Chandler (1962) and Galbraith and Nathanson (1978) strategies should drive structure, which is the next element of the model.

The structural element of the Pryor approach is notably different from that of Slack and Lewis (2008): Pryor considers structure to consist of the internal and external elements that affect the way those implementing the strategy operate. The internal elements are the Principles that determine the way the individuals in the system conduct themselves on a personal level, consisting of such elements as ethics, core values and philosophies. By setting the tone of operations and establishing these operating parameters at all levels of the organisation, top management can be confident that decisions will be made that are consistent with the organisational aims. Without promoting such understanding within the company, there may be a need to continually monitor and control elements of the organisation to ensure all decisions are consistent (Hart 1992).

The external structure is that which affects how those within the system conduct themselves with respect to the operations as a whole. These include areas such as responsibility, authority, accountability and control, as well as the processes that directly contribute to the products or services produced in the transformation process. Through systematic analysis of these processes, they can be effectively improved to assist in achieving the organisational goals while simultaneously improving the level of control in the system. Carrying out activities such as process visualisation was an example given in their work that could help create a culture that continually develops processes in a way that maximises the benefit to the customer, who may not necessarily be the end user. Effectively communicating these processes as well as Principles throughout the organisation can help to drive behaviour towards achieving performance excellence (Pryor et al. 2007). A very similar point was raised by Bossidy and Charan (2002), where by focusing specific attention on the operating system of an organisation, it was possible to develop an appropriate organisational culture showing that this may not be predefined by the country of origin.

The Processes and Principles affect the way the people within the system conduct their activities, and this needs to feed into an element that defines how the people conduct themselves, individually and as part of the organisation. The Process and Principle elements, although greatly affecting the way those in the system will conduct themselves, do not pay specific attention to how those within the system interact. The People element considers them as elements of the whole system, and it is how they interact with the system and each other that is not only important for implementing strategy but also organisational performance as a whole. Building on the Process element, it is important that those involved with the processes become owners and stakeholders, appreciative of how their actions and performance affect other elements in the system. The attention of the Pryor approach to the People element establishes their view of the key role they have to play to link different elements of the system together, such as customer and supplier. Even with the obvious importance of the People element within the strategy implementation process, Pryor et al. (2007) commented on how human resource attention in the subject has been 'feeble or missing' (p. 12). Combining this with the traditional top-down views of strategy, it may be difficult for those formulating to accept the organisation's contribution; however, overlooking this essentially squanders their significant contribution.

Within an organisation, determining the current level of performance is essential, as it is a means for the company to understand where it currently is, which may simply be something as simple as bottom line profit. However, in a company implementing an operations strategy, understanding the effect of its efforts in more detail is likely to be important for continuing the development process. Without an appropriate means of measurement, determining the effects of the activities during the implementation process is impossible. However, Pryor et al. (2007) stated these should not be overly complex, as it is essential for managers to understand all measurements, allowing them to maintain improvement initiatives to help ensure long-term survival and profitability.

Although not shown in Figure 2.8, as well as providing important information for managers, information relating to the development of the system is very important for the People and Process elements. Appropriate feedback from Process alterations can assist in giving the system owners better understanding of the process which will assist in further improvements. Establishing the elements of business performance that directly contribute to customer satisfaction and linking such information to the processes that affect those within the system can help further develop commitment to the strategy (Kaplan and Norton 1996). Figure 2.8 does show the Performance feeding back into Purpose, which allows the process to receive appropriate information about the effects of the overall strategic direction. Rather than simply relying on financial data, the information that feeds into the strategy formulation process is specifically tailored to the development activities that are taking place within the operations resources.

2.9.2   Pryor's 5Ps Aims

Although potentially lacking in operations strategy content, Pryor's 5P approach considers elements that promote effective implementation in general. In a very similar way to Pfeffer and Sutton (2000) and Bossidy and Charan (2002), the importance of creating a culture that is focused on strategy implementation is as important for improving organisational performance as the strategies that are actually being implemented. An important feature of the approach is the conscious move away from high-level strategy formulation, which although the Platts and Gregory 5P approach tries to move away from is still present, with two of the five Ps still effectively assigned to formulation. In Pryor's 5P approach, although the corporate level is important to initially setting broad targets and operating values, they could possibly be left outside the operational activities due to them not being directly involved. The other elements of the Purpose stage, that consider how to achieve these goals, could effectively be carried out by operational staff, only involving board-level members to discuss activities in the implementation team, similar to the Hoshin Kanri approach (Akao 1991).

Due to this approach assigning the majority of activities to operational staff, possibly operations managers, it should be much easier for them to meet regularly to discuss progress and respond to feedback than higher-level staff. With greater direct involvement in the processes, the operational staff will be much better placed to effectively revise plans and resource allocation that account for local requirements. Through the development of an operational team responsible for such activities, those involved are able to take direct responsibility for the company's strategic direction. With appropriate, effective collaboration, lower levels of staff are able to direct organisational development in line with corporate aims and upper management should be able to appreciate the importance of the capability that has been developed among those involved. Understanding the variety of elements involved in strategy implementation, the capability could begin to be managed as a function in its own right, rather than focusing on the separate elements that contribute to the activity (Braganza and Korac-Kakabadse 2000).

Compared with the Platts and Gregory 5P approach, as already mentioned, Pryor's is much less focused on content, although content could be included in the Process and Purpose elements. However, by ensuring there is appropriate focus on the development of strategy-specific capabilities within the Purpose element, Pryor's 5P approach could integrate these elements of operations strategy. As it was presented, the 5P approach seems more concerned with the creation of a strategy implementation core competence that assists in developing an organisational culture that promotes operational excellence rather than implementing a particular strategy. This reflects the approach's origins in quality management, and would be likely to assist greatly in the introduction of a system such as Total Quality Management or just-in-time, where small, continual developments are important. However, the approach may be less able in its current state to be able to drive towards and implement complex activities, due to lack of attention to the introduction of completely new developments. For this reason, the inclusion of 'point of entry' and 'project management' may assist if the approach was required to implement more challenging strategies. The approach could also be used as a way of developing the system in preparation for the use of Slack's 5P approach, with the systematic developments of a culture and operating systems that actively promote the strategic developments.

2.10   CONCLUSION

The above approaches, although aimed at operations strategy implementation, take very different approaches to the activity. Even though operations strategy as a whole aims to move away from a purely top-down approach to strategy, most of the approaches continue to maintain focus on top management to formulate before passing down. Even though the approaches consider the input of the frontline staff, the process of actually introducing different approaches to working and different areas of focus seems to be lacking. The Platts–Gregory procedure, although taking considerable care in considering the main elements of the business, does not give specific tools for determining links between the different areas. Without such information it is likely that these decisions will be left to upper management to make assumptions from experience, about the areas that are important for improving performance. Out of the above approaches it is only Pryor's approach that pays specific attention to performance measurement of the strategy implementation process, appreciating that through the use of an appropriate system it is possible to make decisions based on facts.

Without such continual and consistent feedback it is almost impossible to determine the effects of an operations strategy (Humphreys 2004) and simply relying on financial measures is not appropriate, even though it is one performance measure that will almost always be present. Although not included in this review of the literature in its own right, performance measurement can be an important tool in the implementation of strategy as well as a means of improving overall business performance. As mentioned in the introduction, approaches such as the Balanced Score Card carefully select a number of performance measures, whose performance directly contributes to achieving a strategy, which is included within the Performance element of Pryor's approach. However, without effective understanding of the operations function, combined with the many elements that make up operations strategy content, determining which elements are critical can be a time consuming process. To account for this, Kaplan and Norton (1996; 2001; 2004) continued to develop their approach to give organisations a more structured approach to implementing their strategy. Unfortunately, what this may improve with regards to the time required for implementation it is likely to degrade in terms of organisation-specific learning that is important if not essential for continued development. Without such understanding, the formulation may be inappropriate and implementation may not build the cultural aspects that are important for long-term sustainable success.

3. Why is operations strategy implementation not easy?

3.0 INTRODUCTION: OPERATIONS STRATEGY IS NOT EASY

As outlined in the previous two chapters, as a subject operations strategy is not a simple area of operations to conceptualise. With an extremely large amount of content, combined with the number of elements within a particular organisation, simply defining what an operations strategy consists of is a complex activity. This means that the formulation of an operations strategy that is relevant for an organisation, not necessarily a good one, is likely to be an elaborate process. Reconciling the amount of relevant information from the market with the relevant information from the operations elements will inevitably consist of the consideration of an enormous amount of information. Although a number of the approaches described in the last chapter begin to develop stepwise processes for formulation that aim to take account of all relevant data, they still require those involved in the process to take a large cognitive leap from having all the information available to them to producing something of use to the organisation.

In addition to the reconciliation of present information that requires careful choices to best use available resources and opportunities, the process also needs to direct the organisation in the future. Although operations strategy pays specific attention to moving away from the more fanciful approaches to strategy of the past, there must still be an element of creativity and uncertainty, to develop and select options that will maximise an organisation's chances of success. Even with the effective use of simple strategies as described by Pryor et al. (2007), the decision still needs to be made to pursue the development of capabilities that allow the company to meet specific market requirements. If such a decision is not made, the operations strategy may tend to maintain a status quo between the market and operations that may result if a purely objective approach is taken to the analytical process. This shows the importance of combining the relevant content with additional information from within the system about the organisation in general, promoting the effective combination of data with ideas, possibly making use of an entrepreneurial flair. Such a statement is not to refute the evidence proposed for emergent elements of strategy (Mintzberg 1978; Wheelwright and Hayes 1985; Beckman and Rosenfield 2008; Slack and Lewis 2008), but before such activities took place, it is likely decisions were made that created a structure that allowed management to deal in more general terms.

With the complexity and importance of the process, even though such activities may not be carried out within a strategic planning department, it is likely to require extensive experience, abilities and responsibility among those entrusted with the formulation process. Unfortunately, what this may potentially lead to is formulation being carried out by managers who have extensive portfolios of experience, who, although able to make decisions that can draw from considerable knowledge, may potentially be hampered by a lack of vision or willingness to experiment. When both the organisation and environment are constantly changing, the importance of such experience may even decrease, trapping those involved in the process within past failures, unable to see they are operating within a different setting. In such cases, it becomes important to use the experience as a tool to analyse past errors to develop new approaches that effectively resolve the problems of the past through processes of fact-based analysis. If this is not appreciated, although experience may assist in the effective analysis of data, creativity may not be actively promoted and embraced, resulting in business-as-usual strategies prevailing. Without such creativity, it may be unlikely that questions will be asked about how developments should be promoted to allow the organisation to effectively develop its capabilities to remain competitive in markets that may not yet exist.

Although this process is likely to be very complex, requiring careful discussions to assess the importance of all relevant information, the most important element of this is that it is an open discussion forum, which is considered important by many (Akao 1991; Beer and Eisenstat 2004; Kaplan and Norton 2004). As with marketing and corporate strategy, the process does not necessarily need to be fully based in the realities of the operating company, with creativity playing an important role in the process. Even though inappropriate strategies may not make up the final strategy, a range of potential strategies allows those within the process to understand why particular strategies may not be appropriate. Such elements further promote discussions, allowing those involved to apply their experienced-based knowledge to develop solutions that represent all those involved in the process, which can improve solution ownership (Kaplan and Norton 2004). From long-term commitment to the process goals rather than focusing on the details of the discussion, the process should not be bound by the decisions that have been made. With the understanding and appreciation that the activities are the result of everyone's ideas, it is possible to select and discard ideas quickly, even after the discussion process has ended. With consensus being focused around the ends rather than means, changes in how it is to be achieved, if required by the environment or in light of new information, should not reflect on a particular participant in the discussion process, assisting in a process of continued learning.

Where operations strategy implementation becomes much more difficult than formulation is that it needs to take the elements of the discussion and convert these into tangible changes in the operating process. By careful consideration of current operations during the formulation stage, the product of the process should be appropriate for current operations, meaning it should be possible to implement. What this means is that formulation and implementation are interdependent (Hrebiniak 2006), and considering the implementation process carefully during formulation is likely to greatly assist implementation. As highlighted in Wheelwright and Hayes (1985), the situation is particularly relevant within a 'stage 2' manufacturing company; in such companies, unless process technology developments are similar to the current processes, it is unlikely it will be possible to introduce them. For this reason it may be important for the formulation process to consider if it is realistically possible to implement a particular strategy considering the amount of time, resources and abilities available for the implementation process. This important constraint within the formulation process is likely to make implementation easier; however, if focused on it may also lead to the selection of business-as-usual strategies. For this reason, there is likely to be another important consideration during the formulation process: not only is it possible to implement the strategy, but also does the strategy develop the organisation in the correct way to meet market requirements, stretching current capabilities (Hamel and Prahalad 1994) (Figure 3.1).

Although heavily dependent on formulation, operations strategy implementation is not predetermined by formulation; it requires its own specific attention, consideration, planning and abilities for it to be successful. Importantly, where success in formulation may mean the creation of an appropriate plan of action, success in implementation exposes those involved to considerably more risk, with failure being considerably easier and more tangible. As Drucker (1955), when discussing the important but missing link between scientific management and process development, stated, if one plans without consideration of doing, 'one dreams rather than performs' (p. 245). For this reason, implementation should possibly be considered more important than formulation due to the more tangible results. If formulation requires the consideration of the implementation process to improve the tangible output, and the improvement of tangible results is the aim of the strategy process as a whole, the importance of

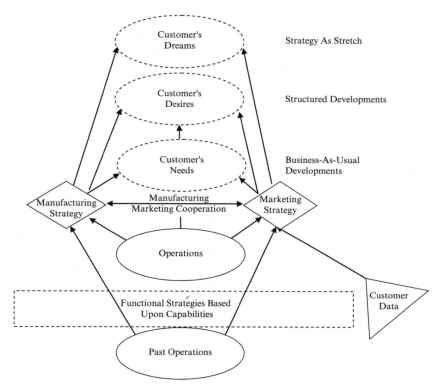

Figure 3.1   Operations strategy as stretch

implementation for success increases. However, unlike the formulation process that needs to consider large amounts of complex information to create a relatively condensed action plan, the implementation process must take this information and expand it to the whole organisation. Implementation also requires activities that are focused around integrating ideas into the organisation, to develop it in line with the strategic vision, compared with the formulation process that is based around discussions, giving it fewer constraints.

3.1   THE PROCESS OF STRATEGY IMPLEMENTATION

Strategy implementation could be thought of as the reverse of the formulation process. Instead of aggregating a large array of information from all areas of the organisation to create a suitably focused vision, the vision needs translating back into information that is relevant to all the areas that originally supplied the information. Problems begin to arise when those involved in the process need to add information to the strategic vision to create an action plan for the particular implementation activities. Although the creation of an appropriate strategy will determine the overall changes required, it is unlikely to define specific actions that are required to realise the strategy. Even if the formulation process was in depth enough to define specific requirements, there is still a need for development activities that account for the local conditions during implementation of which the formulation may have been unaware. These conditions may be environmentally based, although they may also relate to in-depth process knowledge that will determine whether particular process developments are possible. Where decisions are made and information added to expand a strategic vision for implementation, it is important to return to the idea of strategy as consistency of actions (Mintzberg 1978). Although the idea is important with the overall strategy promoting business consistency, the information added to the vision also needs to be consistent to ensure after implementation the result is appropriate and operations have been developed to consistently work towards the strategic vision.

Analogies made between the high-level corporate performance and process control are not as difficult to comprehend as one may think. Although the scale of the corporate- and business unit-level controls may have more elements feeding into them, they are also affected by internal and external forces. Business units are affected by environmental conditions, such as competitor activity and economic conditions; so are internal processes, being affected by environmental 'common cause variation' (Dale 2003, p. 407). The process of developing performance at a process level is relatively easy in comparison to higher levels of the system due to both the direct connections between different elements and the ease and speed of data collection and process adjustment. As mentioned in the previous chapter, the higher levels of the process will be affected by variations at the lower levels which may allow a fact-based approach to strategy at the higher levels during formulation. Approaches that assist in developing capabilities that produce lower-level control will allow information to be fed into the formulation and implementation process, where higher-level interrelations can be identified and based on more than experience and 'gut feeling'.

The significance of the development of process control in an organisation's ability to achieve a strategy is appreciated by Slack and Lewis (2001), where through developing process knowledge, different elements of the operations strategy can be implemented. The approach taken by Pryor et al. (2007) has begun to look deeper into the issue of developing a quality organisation that is focused and aligned at all levels to the achievement of quality goals. Using the development of a strategic quality management system as a basis, it was appreciated that quality, control and strategy implementation were closely connected, with the capabilities that supported quality-focused operations assisting strategy implementation. To develop from a system developed for quality management, the scope of the activities needed expanding from the process level, to appreciate the importance of system control at all levels of the business. In both Pryor's 5Ps and SPC, it is not the specific processes that are important, but the knowledge, capability and understanding that are associated with the process that can be applied across an organisation to enable controlled changes to take place.

Here, as with statistical process control, it is not necessarily the quality improvement that represents the major change; instead it is the capabilities that are developed alongside the processes or systems that are gaining control or reducing non-conformance. Pryor, Anderson and Toombs (1998), while developing an approach to establishing a quality management system, later identified this as a capability for implementing strategy. In a similar way to statistical process control, it is not the specific processes that are important, but the knowledge, capability and understanding that are associated with the process that allow it to be controlled and developed in an appropriate way.

For an organisation embarking on the process of a development strategy, formulating a strategy and assigning considerable resources, it may be difficult to appreciate that the main aim is not actually to meet a number of specific performance targets. In this situation it is also going to be considerably more difficult to gain backing from upper management if this is how the activity is defined, as their focus may be on what returns the activity will give on the resources invested in the process. For this reason, they may focus specifically on the processes rather than the development of capabilities that should take place in parallel, meaning they may focus on process capability figures (that reflect the amount of variation in reference to design specifications) and process development rather than the abilities associated with the activity. In more general activities, this may consist of the development of capabilities within the implementation team being monitored and developed rather than just monitoring the processes with which they are involved. As Mintzberg, Ahlstrand and Lampel (1998, pp. 209–10) discussed, it is the double loop learning that is of more importance; the knowledge developed from a specific process is of only limited importance, compared with understanding related to the application of analytical skills (Figure 3.2). The development of the non-application-specific skills means their versatility will be increased, allowing them to be

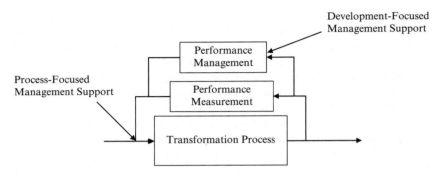

Figure 3.2   Performance measurement/management

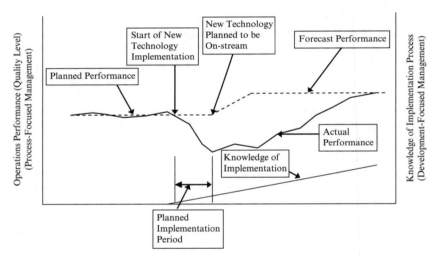

Source: Based on Slack and Lewis (2001).

Figure 3.3   Technology implementation from two management
perspectives

applied in other areas that may not necessarily be related to the original area of investigation. However, a balance is still necessary to ensure that time and resources invested in the development process contribute to the end user, otherwise an organisation may be extremely proficient but have no customers.

This missed focus of the process of strategy implementation could be one of the reasons for the number of failures in implementation (Thorpe and Morgan 2006) (Figure 3.3), but could also be a major loss in opportunity for the firms carrying out the activities. Slack and Lewis (2008), while outlining the 5Ps approach, touched on this, with the participation within the process being an important element for implementation, but also the importance of the learning opportunities that are present. With the 'apprentice' style of implementation, although the focus of Slack and Lewis was on how well the process developments would be accepted, this could be seen as missing an important point. The time required for the development of the strategy was considered a drawback but it was not mentioned that this time spent could create a strategic capability within a business function. If this capability was suitably developed during the initial implementation, it could be applied to subsequent activities, taking account of local requirements, reducing the need for external support during future implementation activities (Johnson and Medcof 2007) (Figure 3.4).

Within its present form, Platts's and Gregory's 5P approach remains noticeably finite in nature with the process having distinct starting and ending activities, with no obvious feedback systems present that could assist in creating an implementation capability. With a finite approach, the apprenticeship approach will always be seen as suboptimal, where the best approaches are likely to be seen as those that are able to implement a particular strategy with fewest resources that are able to produce the expected results. However, if a long-term capability building perspective is taken to the apprentice approach, the results begin to have considerably more value within the organisation, even when comparing the extra resources that may need to be spent to pursue the approach. By taking a long-term approach to operations strategy, considering the measures of performance as the development of specific capabilities that allow the organisation to meet future requirements, the priorities may begin to alter. Rather than measuring the resources and time spent on a particular implementation activity, but also considering the capabilities developed during the activity, the individual activity is not considered a destination, but a point on a strategic trajectory. Where collaboration is actively promoted (Figure 3.4(b)), the organisation is considerably better equipped for future implementation activities, even though the return on an individual activity may be less.

3.2 A BUSINESS SCHOOL APPROACH TO THE PROBLEM

Johnson and Kaplan (1987) were not the first by a long stretch to comment on the irrelevance of financial data as the only source of information on which to base the development of a company. Although similar ideas were

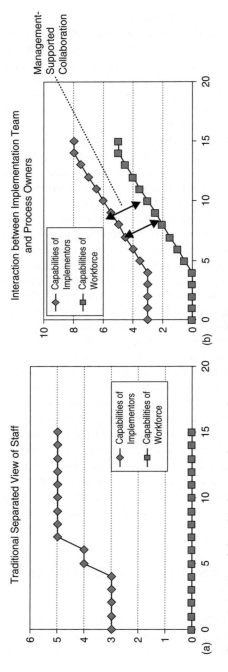

Figure 3.4   Capability development from implementation process

outlined by Drucker (1955), Kaplan and Norton (1992) presented their work in a form that was more easily digestible for traditionally minded executives. By identifying the specific elements of a company that are important for its long-term success and control, the approach soon became accepted as an effective way for companies to monitor their own development. The system also provided sufficient information about the company for those directing developments to understand how specific developments at low levels of the organisation contributed to the organisation's corporate aims. The structured approach to performance measurement allowed those responsible for the allocation of resources to make decisions based on relatively accurate company process-specific information, rather than relying on experience or a hunch. The effect of this was that driven and directed investments were more likely to have the desired effect on overall business performance than those based on assumed connections between metrics.

Following the introduction of the system, organisations found they were able to control their development and with the inclusion of a learning and development aspect, important operations strategy content helped drive performance. The approach allowed the operations strategy to be represented visually, which assisted the whole organisation as everyone could appreciate how their activities contributed to overall performance, while also helping them appreciate the reasons for high-level strategic elements, promoting bottom-up commitment within the organisation. A likely reason for the approach's success was that it was not initially devised as a tool for strategy – it was an operational approach to controlling an organisation that built a strategic capability in parallel to the focus of the activity. Implementing the process as a form of control rather than expecting a specific return allowed all additional benefits from the approach to further add to the commitment for the system. When the strategic significance of the approach was identified, there would already be the capability present within the system to specifically direct and control strategic developments.

Taking the process of strategy implementation from a business school perspective, the aims are likely to be focused squarely on improving operational profitability, possibly following the work of a consultancy. The above situation lends itself relatively well to a consultancy, being able to develop an appropriate Balanced Score Card (BSC) for an organisation relatively quickly and easily, utilising its abilities to analyse an organisation to allow it to effectively monitor and drive its performance. The shift in perception of the BSC was reflected with the subsequent work on the approach (Kaplan and Norton 1996; 2001), which assisted in implementing a BSC from the outset as a tool for strategy implementation. Although on the surface, from a perspective similar to Slack and Lewis (2008) where the amount of time invested in the implementation is considered a gauge of performance, a deeper understanding of both the process and the system that is being implemented is forsaken. Without the ability to appreciate why the system works, there is unlikely to be a suitable level of knowledge within the system to tailor the approach to meet new requirements. Without giving those within the system the abilities to control development, they may see the BSC as a form of top-down control (Lewy and Du Mee 1998), potentially reducing their commitment to the implementation process.

The progression of the BSC to strategy maps (Kaplan and Norton 2004) aims to fill in the gaps that may seem to have been created in developing an approach that implements BSC as a means of strategy implementation from the outset (Figure 3.5). By visualising the strategy process, the development of a strategy map assists all those involved in articulating how different elements of the organisation contribute and affect the

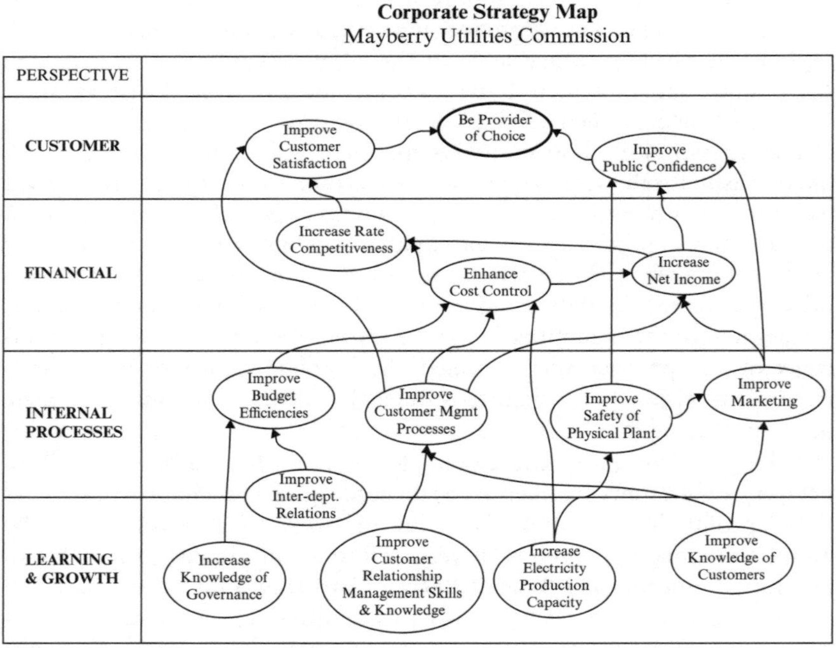

Corporate Strategy Map
Mayberry Utilities Commission

Source: Balanced Scorecard Institute.

Figure 3.5 Example strategy map

achievement of a particular strategy. The approach also sets out a number of specific maps that assist an organisation in pursuing particular types of strategy, such as 'customer lock-in' or 'product leadership' (Kaplan and Norton 2004, p. 10). These assist those involved in participating in open conversations about an organisational issue using a template that assists in promoting discussion while simultaneously acting as an important starting point. However, as with the potential problems of the BSC although the approach helps develop consensus at a high level, it does not specifically involve those within the organisation, which may also affect bottom-up commitment to the activity.

Without specific focus on involving all levels of the organisation, the strategy map approach may be less effective at driving organisation-wide developments than the BSC. The approach may also lead organisations to pursue specific strategies that may not be appropriate for the operations resources present in the system and also what the customer requires. There must also be specific consideration of developing an understanding of the processes within the organisation, otherwise the results may be based on assumptions, making the process outputs potentially inappropriate. Combining these potential issues with the approach being initiated from a high level of the organisation may result in an action plan that creates high-level consensus, but is neither tailored to the organisation nor has the commitment of those charged with implementation. Even if those carrying out the activity have a good understanding of strategy maps, it could still be considered similar to a consultancy or delivered approach (Slack and Lewis 2008) that has potential to be rejected once deployed into an organisation. As with the original application of the BSC, to develop understanding within the organisation before pursuing specific strategic activities is likely to be important, to allow the strategy map to be developed from fact-based understanding of the system.

Out of the different approaches to strategy implementation it is only Pryor's 5Ps (Pryor et al. 2007) that gives specific consideration to the development of a capability that is focused on strategy implementation. However, if the implementation of a strategy is considered predetermined by formulation, investing in the long-term development of a capability that is not directed towards a specific strategy is probably less likely to gain full backing from those allocating resources. Taking an approach that is specifically focused on achieving particular strategies and organisational goals is likely to gain more backing from top management; unfortunately, if a consultancy is employed for the activities, it will mean the important capabilities will remain with them. This allows them to continue to implement strategies for other companies that management may consider an effective use of resources to achieve their organisational vision, but in the long term they are forfeiting important learning opportunities. However, when the return of the investment is required within a particular time frame, the approach is much more likely to gain further support than a system that requires the critical review of all business processes to promote the development of a suitable culture. Assigning resources to such a process is likely to require considerable long-term commitment from those allocating resources; without a defined target the process may even be considered to have no driving element to maintain long-term support for the initiative. In this respect, implementing such an approach is similar to that taken by GE implementing Six Sigma, where it was the sustained support of Jack Welch with the alignment of appropriate human resources elements that meant the activity continued until the capability was established and financial returns were observed.

3.3 OTHER APPROACHES TO DEVELOPING A STRATEGY IMPLEMENTATION CAPABILITY

The above may be a reason for Pryor's 5Ps (Pryor et al. 2007) approach not having received greater acceptance as an approach for strategy implementation, being seen as the new way to do TQM. This may also be a reason why consultancies have also continued to develop their own firm-specific approaches to strategy development and deployment within firms. Through the development of their own knowledge about the process, it becomes advantageous for them to have specific tools that represent their own core competences (Hamel and Prahalad 1990) that may even limit the learning opportunities available to the client's organisation. Although a different field, a similar situation may be present within accounting that is reflected by the relatively small amount of literature on its use in a strategic nature (Bhimani and Langfield-Smith 2007). Rather than defining themselves with organisation-specific approaches that set them apart from the competition, accountancies are more often employed to carry out more standard activities. Unless they are specifically employed to determine how to finance an organisation in the most effective way, they are unlikely to spend considerable time and effort on the activity. It is only once those within the organisation move to different positions that they are able to apply their understanding of how an organisation functions and use the processes they have experienced to improve business functions. It is only when the capability's strategic potential is appreciated and is applied appropriately that it begins to be more than simply a commodity resource.

This appreciation, although not reflected in the research in the area, helps to explain accounting firms' moves to the more profitable industry of consultancy, through the promotion of management accounting services. As with the more traditional consultancy approaches, the development of the in-house capability does not require reporting in literature as it is simply something that has been developed and applied at the point of use. However, as Bhimani and Langfield-Smith (2007) stated, financial measurements should not be the only measurement, showing that developing an internal accounting capability specifically for the implementation of strategy may be inappropriate for an organisation. This may not have been reported in operations strategy literature, but when working with numerous organisations, accountants may be better positioned to understand the accounting processes as part of the firm as a whole, which may not be possible when working within an accounting department. They are also likely to have very different relationships with the other functions than an external firm, which may very noticeably have the specific backing of the top management team promoting the development of cross-functional business understanding.

Taking an approach that develops a specific capability to be strategic and using it to effectively implement a strategy is an approach that has been touched upon on numerous occasions. The specific capability that has been demonstrated as a capability is quality, which is likely to be why Pryor et al. (2007) developed their approach from its foundations in the implementation of a strategic quality management system. However, with other occasions of developing this specific capability, it seems that the capability's development was as a by product of simply improving the organisation's ability to control processes. Although examples given show that this is the case, the focus in the last chapter was always to emphasise the importance of integration of the different operational functions. Unless there is the specific development of an operations system that is specifically focused on functional integration, the significance of the capability is likely to be reduced. Without integrating elements of quality-related thinking into all areas of the business, those specifically charged with the task of 'improving quality' are likely to have greater difficulty in creating an overall change. For this reason such an approach will require considerable support from top management to develop cross-functional support, driving the initiative while developing appreciation, knowledge and ability of the initiative's core aims to be successful.

This is by no means a criticism of the approach of consultancies to developing and implementing strategies for their clients but aims to consider the process from a different angle that aims to take a longer, more strategic view of the process of implementation. This is not to say that strategy implementation needs to take a long time; rather, it is a journey without a destination and the capabilities that aid progress will mean organisations are able to take more difficult routes or survive difficult terrain. For this reason, the aim of consultancies could be more focused on innovative ways of developing these skills and assisting the client to effectively alter organisational processes to promote the activities that are considered important, such as Pryor et al.'s (2007) Processes element. Rather than carrying out analysis themselves, by educating those within the system to use so called 'meta-tools' (Bicheno 2004) they will be able to analyse the systems themselves to continue developing after the consultant's support has been removed. The approach does not necessarily mean the earning capabilities of the consultant are reduced, but as with the approach to strategy, they take a long-term approach to customer relations, where they may be continually employed to maintain the system, introducing innovations to strategy tools as they become available. They could also be the port of call for operational systems issues, if managers within the system feel concern that the system requires further development to assist operational system integration.

3.4   ELEMENTS REQUIRED FOR IMPLEMENTATION

Although the above approach tries to expand Slack's and Lewis's (2008) approach to the employment of a consultancy to implement a strategy, it is by no means an ideal approach, merely suggesting how organisations could more effectively utilise capabilities present within their own and other firms. For an organisation aiming to carry out the strategy formulation and implementation effectively without involving external capabilities there needs to be a number of steps but also specific tools to assist the process. Organisations cannot be expected to develop innovative strategies immediately and effectively implement them without support, whether it is in the form of a specific capability or an implementation framework. However, as with the above descriptions, placing too much expectation on a particular capability or operations system is unlikely to result in the best outcome; instead strategy should become more consensual (Maylor 2005). Not only should formulation and implementation be interlinked (Hrebiniak 2006), so should the initial system analysis and process control to allow them to focus away from optimising specific elements of the process. Unless there is an understanding that all elements of the process are carried out with consideration of the other stages, making use of all information within the system, the process has the potential to be inappropriate.

The presence of numerous feedback loops within the Pryor 5Ps strategy process begins to address this issue but, as mentioned, there does not seem to be suitable focus on creativity or innovation. Although the fluid movement from the different areas is a considerable benefit of the system and could be beneficial in other approaches, there may still be room for a more traditional approach that considers areas requiring specific study. If these are not carried out, the development of suitable skills for later in the process may not be identified, but also maintaining a high-level view that appreciates specific strategic aims should form an important driving element of the process. If the Pryor 5Ps approach were to become too operational, developments may take place that focus on short-range goals or development that are not in line with higher-level targets. The Purpose element may carefully define how the operation should develop, but the elements included within this do not seem to effectively promote the inclusion of elements that drive operations in a suitable manner. Instead, the elements seem to pay more attention to ensuring that operations conform, reflecting the approach's origins in quality where conforming to specification is a driving principle.

An alternative approach needs to be based on the elements discussed already, including the development of a suitably integrated strategic capability, an understanding of the organisation and an understanding of environmental requirements. These elements need to be used together to develop an appropriate overall strategy that focuses specifically on driving the organisation, whether it is back into a competitive position or into uncontested market space (Kim and Maubourgne 2005). Following this stage, through the effective use of the strategic capability, well-grounded strategies can be implemented. However, as outlined above, embarking on such an approach requires a 'leap of faith' into the unknown as well as requiring considerable assistance, especially when, at the beginning of the process, there may not be suitable knowledge within the system to conceptualise the whole process. To develop confidence within the organisation for such a process, there needs to be specific 'meta-tools' available to those who have identified the need for the whole process to be initiated. These conceptual, cognitive tools need to be able to assist in the early stages of the process to develop ideas and begin to add body around the initiative as a whole to transfer the process from the board (or drawing board) to the organisation.

Out of these different elements that should make up a successful strategy process, the most difficult to actively promote with specific tools is the development of a broad understanding of the organisation. Unless this is present, it is likely to be difficult to initiate the process from the top of the organisation. For this reason, a traditional consultancy may still be able to play an important role in analysing the organisation's current processes to assist in the development of a realistic operational understanding of the organisation, possibly providing it with appropriate motivation. This is by no means saying that there may be a lack of functional, process-based information within the corporate planning elements of an organisation, but unless it is possible to create discomfort in current approaches, the perceived need to change will be less. Drucker (1955) spoke of the particular types of board members who have moved through the ranks of an organisation, which is likely to be important to maintain consistency and stability within an organisation but may simultaneously stifle innovation. The whole idea of someone working their way through an organisation to the board is potentially inappropriate for an operations strategy, unless they have been developed specifically as general or operations managers, allowing them to take a broader view of the operations. However, this does not necessarily solve the problem; as Akao (1991) stated, these managers should be spending a considerable amount of time on strategic activities, meaning they may still lose their broad process knowledge that aided their corporate ascension.

For this reason, employing an external element to assist in building a fact-based picture of the organisation should not be considered a failure on the part of the top management team, but simply a process of continual learning in which they participate. From an operations strategy perspective, this activity contributes to the 'bottom-up' up element (Slack and Lewis 2008); however, the sheer volume of information is likely to require careful control, analysis and manipulation for it to be of use to the company at higher levels. As with the aforementioned capabilities, an element that was able to carry out such a complex activity would require considerable development. Unless it was necessary for other business elements to develop such an internal auditing or due diligence function, justification for creating such a function may be difficult. It may also be relatively easy for those within such a function to carry out activities as administrative requirements, that Drucker (1955) states may not be a valid business function unless it contributes directly to the primary business function, enforcing his staff/line stance.

The risk of such an in-house function becoming a paperwork function rather than a function for effective process analysis maintains the argument for employing an external organisation to assist in operations analysis. Through the effective articulation of the requirements of the activity from the board to the business functions in an effort to assist support for the external contractors, a picture of current processes could be efficiently mapped, assisting management in making decisions based on up to date relevant information. The approach could also be assisted by alternating the consultancies used for the activity to allow the top management team to develop a 'true' picture of the operations, created from multiple perspectives that discount the effects of approaches taken by particular auditing teams. The result of spending time and resources on such a preparatory stage of the strategic process is likely to be very important for the process as a whole, as it forms a strong basis upon which the top management team can build subsequent processes. The activity will also assist in engaging those within the organisation in the strategy process, and, as with Hoshin Kanri (Akao 1991), forming a direct link between the process levels of operations and top management. The effect of this should be increased commitment to later strategic activities and, as with Hoshin Kanri, there will be appreciation that lower-level information will be considered during formulation, assisting commitment to subsequent strategic activities. Although the consultancy will be an external entity, it will be important to establish how it is to interact with the operational functions to aid the development of the understanding and trust to promote an effective working relationship, even if it is only for a short period of time.

3.5   THE TRANSITION TO THE OPERATIONS STRATEGY PROCESS

The above is a potential way of creating a sense of purpose within an organisation, but it is important to stress that these can only be considered preparatory activities for the strategy process, to form a solid foundation of knowledge. At this stage, the need for a specific purpose may not be necessary; it may even be beneficial for there to be no preconceptions of what the aim of the process is. With a clean slate at the beginning of the process, it will be possible to develop activities that reflect the organisation and market conditions rather than being constrained by experience that will only ever assist in maintaining a business-as-usual approach. Unfortunately, the promotion of creativity can be difficult within a forum of experienced individuals; for this reason the following chapter will investigate what is really meant by creativity. From this, the chapter will move to how creativity can be approached in a more systematic, rigorous way, with the aim of reducing the need for or improving the chances of flashes of inspiration (Figure 3.6). Through the application of these ideas upon the base of process knowledge and understanding, the results of purpose developing processes will have greater certainty of producing effective, innovative plans. Introducing a level of certainty and increasing confidence into this process will also develop confidence in that element of strategy,

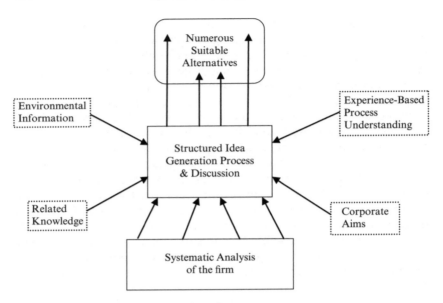

Figure 3.6   Creative problem identification process

reducing the risk associated with allocating resources to the process. This may lead to potentially larger allocations of resources to this stage, allowing greater levels of understanding to be built and more effective plans to be produced as the luck involved with idea creation can be removed.

The next stage has considerable attention paid to it within operations strategy: it is the conversion of an overall strategic aim to an operations strategy, or operations strategy process. As touched upon in the last chapter, although there are a number of approaches that assist in developing well-rounded plans, important elements remain missing that either require considerable creativity for a new plan, or accommodate preconceived ideas to minimise negative effects (Hill's framework and Slack's operations strategy matrix respectively). Chapter 5 introduces an approach that is able to systematically develop appropriate action plans from initial elements that are not present within other approaches. Importantly, the approach promotes the creation of numerous alternative plans while simultaneously engaging the organisation in their creation, stimulating and promoting contributions to the process from all organisational levels. The result of this stage of the process is a number of systematically generated action plans that those involved with can use to investigate and build understanding of the reasons behind the introduction of specific working practices (Figure 3.7). The basis of the approach is empirical research that helps to build confidence

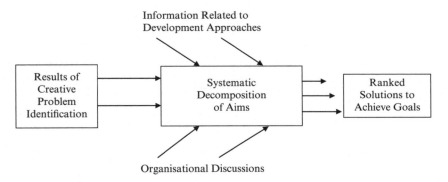

Figure 3.7   Action plan development process

in those using the process that they are introducing appropriate plans but also confidence in those implementing the activities as they will not be perceived as a particular manager's 'sacred cow' (Meredith and Mantel 2006), miracle cure or the current fashionable approach.

The final chapter aims to take a different approach to an element that has already been considered by Platts and Gregory in their 1994 approach. The project management approach to effectively carrying out difficult activities has a number of important characteristics that allow a different approach to be taken to strategy implementation that was not given particular emphasis by Slack and Lewis (2008). For this reason, the chapter will outline what the subject of project management has to offer the process of operations strategy implementation and how it can be integrated into an organisation to help the development of a culture and an alternative organisational form. An important element of the book so far has been the importance of developing a suitable strategy capability to allow the entire organisation to implement an operations strategy. The important difference between project management and the other capabilities mentioned is that although not developed as a primary business function, it has the ability to assist all direct business functions to improve their ability to develop in a strategic manner (Figure 3.8). The chapter will then conclude by outlining how the effective development of a project management capability has the potential to engage an organisation in driving the strategy processes. Through the effective development and consideration of particular business functions, there is potential for such a business function to consider and answer important questions that have been raised by other approaches to operations strategy implementation.

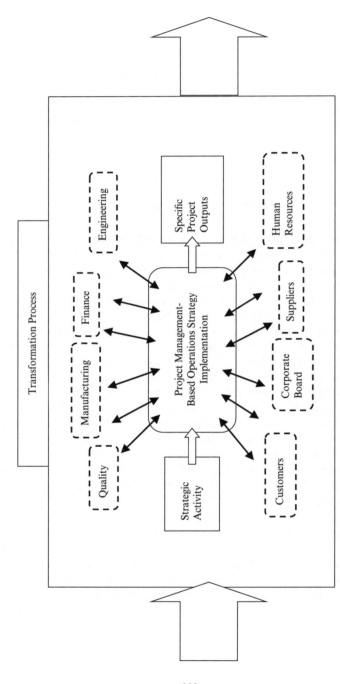

Figure 3.8   Project team interaction with transformation process during implementation

4. Guiding implementation: creative alternative generation

4.0 INTRODUCTION

How can a manager generate and choose a set of actions to implement a business strategy effectively?

With strategy sometimes being considered a plan of action to achieving desired business goals, effective strategy formulation should include the setting of objectives and the identification and evaluation of alternative actions. Following this and the consideration of current environmental conditions, the selected choice needs to be implemented. However, a review of the literature shows that there may be over-emphasis upon the setting of strategic objectives as the primary focus of the formulation process. Current strategy frameworks and processes (Hill 1985; Platts 1993; Mills et al. 2002) seem to focus on broad directions and the establishment of strategic objectives, but seem to be weak in translating these into specific actions for implementation. Garvin (1993) points out that strategic objectives (cost, quality, delivery and flexibility) are too highly aggregated to direct decision making. Being broad, ambiguous, generic categories with a multitude of possible interpretations they cannot suitably direct developments. For example, quality alone can mean reliability, durability or aesthetic appeal among many others, and each of these is very subjective in its nature. Possibly for this reason, many researchers (Anderson, Cleveland and Schroeder 1989; Swink and Way 1995; Kim and Arnold 1996, Tan and Platts 2003a and b) have indicated that the process of linking strategic objectives to actions is often overlooked, resulting in subsequent implementation activities performing poorly.

The ability to generate many alternatives is an important part of managerial problem solving and decision making (MacCrimmon and Wagner 1994). However, many managers approach decision making in a way that neither puts sufficient options on the table nor permits sufficient evaluation to ensure that they can make the best choice (Garvin and Roberto 2001). Decisions made without considering suitable alternatives may have devastating consequences. Drucker (1967, p. 147) succinctly remarks: 'Whenever one has to judge, one must have alternatives among which one can choose. A judgement in which one can only say "yes" or "no" is no judgement at all. Only if there are alternatives can one hope to get insight into what is truly at stake.' However, the search for alternatives is often restricted or biased by managerial values, human perceptions and psychological acceptance or simply in an effort to avoid risk (Harrison 1999).

Alternative generation is a complex, yet essential part of a decision making process, especially for decisions involving strategic issues. The process might involve managers' experience and intuition, the use of idea generation techniques, and qualitative and quantitative modelling approaches. However, there are some shortcomings in existing techniques in terms of providing managers with a structured approach to identifying the range of feasible alternatives even before the decision making process begins. Goodwin and Wright (1998) argue that existing decision making techniques are, in general, likely to be mechanistic and unable to make appropriate use of the judgement of those involved. They also point out that the potentially more critical element of developing options for the decision making process is relatively under-emphasised in decision analysis.

Intuitively, it would seem sensible to spend time looking for alternative courses of action before using decision analysis to evaluate them. Thus, the question that we address is: 'How can multiple perspectives of a decision problem be addressed, that allow feasible decision options to be recognised?' In this chapter, we focus on how creative thinking can be promoted through the visual representation of scenarios to assist managers in identifying and generating potential actions that meet requirements of the strategic objectives. The chapter begins by describing the characteristics of the creative problem solving, and explains the blocks to creative thinking. We then explain how diagrams and problem visualisation can be used to enhance managers' capacity in the generation and evaluation of actions. Finally, we describe and compare various common causal diagrams used by managers. The chapter concludes by discussing the implications of using diagrams to better link action plans to operational objectives.

4.1   WHAT IS CREATIVE THINKING?

Wertheimer ([1945] 1959) argued that creative thinking was about breaking down and restructuring our knowledge about something, in order to gain new insights into its nature. Understanding how we see the world may therefore be an important instrument in our ability to think creatively, which was supported by Kelly (1955) and Rogers (1954). These arguments indicate that creativity occurs when we are able to arrange our thoughts in such a way that readily leads to a different and better understanding of the subject or situation that we are considering. Rickards (1985, p. 5) defines creativity as: 'the personal discovery process, partially unconscious, which leads to new and relevant insights'. Rickards (1988) also advocates a view of creativity as a universal human process resulting in the escape from assumptions, and discovery of new and meaningful perspectives or as an 'escape from mental stuckness'. In broad terms he believed creativity is to do with personal, internal restructuring.

Taking a different view, Weinman (1991) considered that creativity was the ability to go beyond the mundane and obvious and reject the traps of repetition and pre-set categories. Similarly, Gilliam (1993) defined creativity as a process of discovering what has not been considered – the act of making new connections. More simply, creativity can be thought of 'as the production of novel and useful ideas in any domain' (Amabile et al. 1996, p. 1155). Effectively, creativity requires the use of imagination; while language is a way of expressing creative feelings, creativity often results from images and sensations that can be more difficult to express in words. As Koestler (1964, p. 177) said: 'True creativity often starts where language ends', which will have some significance when we come to look at ways of finding new paradigms to deal with problems.

These various definitions seem to agree that creativity involves an in-depth thought about a subject and an ability to come up with new and different viewpoints. Immersing oneself within a situation to be able to see the situation from a different perspective and identify new ways of applying existing knowledge can be a central part of this.

4.1.1 The Benefits of Creative Thinking

Creative thinking benefits all areas and activities of management. It can help to find new and better ways of marketing goods, to devise new production methods, to find new ways to motivate people, among others (Proctor 1995). Creativity helps to improve the probability that things can be done in a more efficient and effective business-like manner. As new situations arise, managers need novel solutions for dealing with problems, since it is often difficult to find solutions by thinking simply in a conventional fashion; but why do companies need to be brought to the brink before reinventing themselves? Logical thinking takes our existing knowledge, uses rules of inference to produce new knowledge and can prevent repetition, maintaining systematic learning and development. However, because logical thinking progresses in a series of steps, each one dependent on the last, this new knowledge is merely an extension of what we know already, rather than being truly new. Logical thinking has only a limited role to play in helping managers and executives to be creative. The need for creative problem solving has arisen from the inadequacies of logical thinking. As a method of using imagination along with techniques employing analogies, associations and other mechanisms help produce insights into problems, and identify solutions that are less reliant on current activities.

Adapting to change and creating change are necessities for a company that wishes to perform well in the long term. Sticking to traditional ways of doing things can lead to difficulties, especially within modern business environments that experience rapid cultural, economic or technological changes. Change is an ever present phenomenon to which businesses of all kinds are forced to respond just to ensure survival and not necessarily to prosper. With the rapid growth of competition currently taking place in the business world there are additional reasons for wanting to understand more about the creative process (Van Gundy 1988; Rickards 1988). Firms need to maintain a competitive edge over their rivals and this requires creative thinking and creative problem solving. Growth or just survival reflects an organisation's ability to develop (or adopt) and implement new processes able to provide new products and services consistently (Van Gundy 1988). For this reason, 21st century businesses require new problem solving and decision making strategies to be able to offer what is required by the market.

These changes in an organisation's operating environment are not always gradual and can even be sudden and dramatic. These rapid changes are often associated with the phenomenon of paradigm shift, which represents that completely new approach to solving an existing problem.

4.1.2 Paradigm Shifts

A paradigm is a set of rules and regulations that defines boundaries and helps organisations to be successful within those boundaries. In these circumstances, success is measured by the problems solved using these rules and regulations. Being successful often means achieving improvements in products, services or methods of production and marketing, such improvements may be associated with incremental advancements in technology. Paradigm shifts, on the other hand, are different from continuous improvement. Examples of paradigm shifts include major changes in transportation methods, for example travelling long distances by air instead of by land or sea. Within the world of telecommunications, paradigm shifts have made it possible to send complex, accurate messages over great distances, facilitated by the introduction of highly sophisticated mechanisms such as telegraph, telephone, fax, live video by wire, optical fibre and satellite communication.

Paradigm shifts demand a change in perspective, without which thinking can become blinkered because people stick too rigorously to a particular paradigm and this can lead to overlooking opportunities and threats which may have a critical impact on a business. It is quite possible that two competitors may see the same opportunity or threat in different ways and the one that is able to make the best response may be able to gain a sustainable competitive advantage over its rival. By appreciating how existing capabilities can be applied to solve new problems, organisations may be able to remain competitive within rapidly changing markets.

The process of paradigm shift can be encouraged and become effective early using creative thinking, which introduces new ways of viewing a situation. Creative problem solving methods make extensive use of techniques and approaches that help to find solutions to recalcitrant open-ended problems.

4.2   THE APPROPRIATENESS OF TECHNIQUES

Arguably established techniques of creative problem solving do not always produce desired insights into problems (see Manor 2002). In brainstorming, for instance, participants gravitate towards a state of groupthink and do not always obtain creative insights into problems. Moreover, more elaborate methods, such as the use of random analogies, may not produce original or relevant ideas. Research into how particularly creative people get ideas shows that they progress systematically in their thoughts (Proctor 1995). They examine only a small number of possible options and ascertain the general direction in which a solution is to be found based on their prior knowledge and experience. However, the power of creative problem solving tools should not be underestimated and their usefulness in providing new insights into problems needs to be understood, that can allow the establishment of such relevant problem solving knowledge and experience.

McFadzean (1998a, b) maintains that creative problem solving techniques can be categorised in three ways, namely paradigm preserving techniques, paradigm stretching techniques and paradigm breaking techniques. All three of these approaches facilitate creative thinking. Paradigm preserving techniques involve searching for a solution very close to the source of the problem. Brainstorming is a technique which falls into this category (McFadzean 1998c). Participants in brainstorming are encouraged to build on each others' ideas and as a result ideas are developed, but not significantly changed. By contrast, paradigm stretching techniques can encourage the generation of more creative insights. Among these techniques are the use of metaphors, object stimulation and the heuristic ideation technique (McFadzean 1998c). Paradigm stretching techniques use unrelated stimuli and forced association to encourage the production

---

EXERCISE 1

Tank Refurbishers

Tank Refurbishers clean out and reline industrial storage tanks. In an increasingly competitive market margins are becoming tighter and profitable business ventures more difficult to find. Nearly all the tanks the firm refurbishes are cylindrical and vary considerably in terms of the volume of liquids that they contain. The procedure is to remove the ends, clean and repaint the inside of the cylinder, clean and repaint the end sections and re-weld the pieces after the repainting. How might the firm seek to be more competitive in the pricing of its jobs?

Question:

Does your solution depend upon applying an existing paradigm, stretching an existing paradigm or using a paradigm shift?

---

of novel insights (McFadzean 1998b). For example, the heuristic ideation technique encourages participants to force fit ideas together to create solutions that although potentially irrelevant can give different positions from which to start idea generation. Paradigm breaking techniques are able to produce very novel, creative ideas that may be less likely with the other two categories. In this case, searching for ideas and insights is not confined to the vicinity of any previous solutions or approaches that have been adopted, such as Rolls Royce applying its customer service skills to the manufacture of Aero engines. Paradigm breaking techniques include wishful thinking, rich pictures and imagining (McFadzean 1998c), possibly based within group activities that immerse those involved within potential scenarios. These methods use unrelated stimuli and forced association to encourage creativity. In addition, they help participants to use all their senses and to express themselves using other modes of communication such as drawing, dreaming and role playing.

4.2.1 Blocks to Creativity

The need for techniques to stimulate creative thoughts comes about because as individuals we can have physiological and psychological blocks that impair our ability to think in a creative manner. Terms such as 'tunnel vision' and 'negative mindset' prevent us from thinking beyond applying existing paradigms to solve problems. In other words, those involved may tend towards using tried and trusted, previously learned and applied ways of doing things (Morgan 1989).

Managers and executives tend to stick with familiar ways of doing things. This is because there is risk associated with trying something new. This viewpoint is reflected by comments such as 'we have always done things in this way and they have always proved successful in the past so why change?' However, it is important to realise that because paradigms have life cycles there is a need to look for new ways of doing things before they become obsolete, ineffective or inefficient.

Sticking with existing paradigms too long, possibly due to them being previously successful, may even produce blocks to the creative thinking process. Although there are other blocks to creativity, the following mentions some of the major ones.

Arnold (1962) suggested a number of blocks to creative thinking:

1. *Perceptual blocks*, which prevent a person receiving a true, relevant picture of the outside world. For example, managers always operating an organisation based wholly on financial information.
2. *Cultural blocks*, which result from influences of society. For example, union-based resistance to new approaches to working.
3. *Emotional blocks*, such as fear, anxiety and jealousy. For example, moving to an unknown business sector.

Adams (1986) added a fourth category: intellectual and expressive blocks. These may be summarised as:

1. *Perceptual blocks*: Concentrating on a particular aspect may be of detriment to the system by not seeing the situation within a wider context. This can be due to the physical limitations of the viewer's senses, but can also be caused by past experiences affecting the perception of the situation.
2. *Value blocks*: Similar to perceptual, but of a softer nature where personal values can affect how the decision process is conducted; if irreconcilable values and situations coexist, there can be difficult organisational and personal dilemmas restricting someone from making suitably objective decisions.
3. *Self-image blocks*: At a personal level individual creativity is restricted by the person's position within the process. Concern for how ideas will be received may even mean they only produce ideas that are expected rather than ideas that are right.

EXERCISE 2

The following illustrates perceptual blocks. Try it for yourself:
How many times does 'f' occur?

'Following the sinking of the old frigate "Ferdinand", Nelson fought his way carefully around the cape in foul weather in the hope of meeting his foe again off the far side of the island. By close of the day he found his adversary adrift and floating perilously close to the infamous granite rocks.'

Count the number of times 'f' occurs in the above.

---

4. *Strategic blocks*: Similar to self-image blocks, where there is an over reliance on particular methods of problem solving, which can be termed methodological blocks, where those involved may consider there is one right way or only one correct strategy to pursue. Working from past experience or abilities with an approach, they may be less likely to question if it is the correct approach for the questions they want to ask and the situation in which they find themselves.

Perceptual blocks can be freed through careful observation and taking account of more than one person's views and opinions. Values are a more difficult problem, but creating an awareness of personal values in the individual and those of other people may offer some respite. Self-image blocks can profit from active management support to assist in developing the assertiveness of those experiencing the blocks. Strategic blocks can be challenged through creative problem solving training to allow the appreciation of how different and similar problems can and should be solved. By focusing effort upon breaking down these blocks it should be possible to develop the process of creativity.

4.2.2 Mindset

When stuck on a problem, managers and executives tend to follow their mindset, which is likely to be counter-productive. Mindset is often characterised by one-right-answer thinking, always looking for reasons why new or different approaches will not work and an over-regard for logical thinking. Past experience may have led one to believe that a particular way of dealing with a problem usually leads to a satisfactory solution. Constant

---

EXAMPLE 1

Ford Model 'T': the mindset of Henry Ford

Henry Ford's model 'T' remained unchanged for years while General Motors (Chevrolet) was making changes, often using new technology. Henry Ford said 'We'll give the customer any colour he wants as long as it is black.' It was an arrogant statement by an arrogant man who had been on top so long he thought nothing could dislodge him from the number one position. In the late 1920s Ford nearly went out of business because of this myopic approach. General Motors took over as number one in the US and Ford did not catch up until the late 1980s.

---

successful application of the approach, particular comfort or dexterity with a method may even give an impression there is only one available way, reinforcing the belief that this way is the correct way. When variations take place or new situations arise, the current approach may not be able to solve the problem, so those trying to find a solution who may only be able to answer questions from the past may become stuck.

Management problem solving often adopts a simple approach, over-emphasising previous experience, by selectively searching in areas close to where previous solutions have been found. For example, frequent absenteeism on the part of an employee is often associated with the employee's dissatisfaction with work. There is thus a tendency for managers to look for this kind of explanation whenever frequent absenteeism is noticed. By not looking deeper into the situation, such information does not necessarily help; with dissatisfaction potentially being caused by many other different aspects, giving such a reason does not give any assistance to resolving the problem. Absenteeism may even be a cause of the dissatisfaction, which gives even less insight into finding a solution.

4.3 THE POWER OF PICTURES

The key to creative problem solving is to have people in the organisation involved in the process regularly so they are able to build an understanding of the requirements of the process. As the complexity of the business environment increases, good communication and shared understanding among managers are vital; they need to be able to present increasing

Table 4.1   Cognitive functions

Cognitive Functions	Descriptions
Focuses attention	Allows managers to identify the areas of 'interest'
Triggers memory	Allows managers to make connections between past events
Shares thinking	Enables managers to share their thinking with colleagues quickly and effectively with less chance of misinterpretation
Stimulates thinking	Provides an invitation to view a situation in a way that may stimulate fresh thinking
Bridges missing information	Exploits the human visual system to extract information from incomplete data
Challenges self-imposed constraint (perception)	Enables managers to look at a problem in a new way by getting many personal views of a given situation

Source: Adapted from Platts and Tan (2003).

amounts of information to one another clearly and effectively. A good visual representation such as pictures or diagrams can convey instantly, and memorably, a relationship that would otherwise require a laborious and easily forgotten explanation. By including such an element within a problem solving approach it may be possible to create a common language for those involved in the process and the organisation as a whole.

Pictures could be seen as a 'visual' vehicle of thought in making decisions (McKim 1972). Pictures are an accessible form of knowledge representation that help to simplify complex data and ideas into a form that people can understand quickly. For example, visual representations such as maps and diagrams of business processes can provide managers with new ways of examining and improving managerial judgement in a problem solving process. Table 4.1 shows the cognitive function support that could be gained from applying visual presentation in a problem solving process.

4.3.1   Focuses Attention

Visual representations such as diagrams and graphs help to focus attention and identify areas of 'interest'. There are many situations in which data is available, and it could be in very large quantities, with managers being required to make sense of the data. By plotting a graph, greater quantities are depicted through the use of larger areas under the curve, longer lines, or some other visual dimension. A graph can help people to focus on or identify areas or points that could be of interest to them. Data can also be presented in specific ways to assist in making a particular point, and through the objective nature of the approach, extra weight can be given to inferences, compared with the opinion of a manager. For example, use of a fishbone/Ishikawa diagram (see Figure 4.1) to initiate ideas while collecting and categorising potential causes of lost orders can then be used to facilitate discussions to identify areas of further interest.

4.3.2 Triggers Memory

A picture is also useful for triggering memory. It allows managers to make connections between past events. An example of this is a mind map (Buzan 1982), which is based upon the effective use of key sketches and words linked together in such a way that they associate managers with past events and trigger further images. Figure 4.2 shows a simple lean management mind map.

4.3.3 Shares Thinking

Besides triggering memory, visual representation helps executives and managers to make sense of complexity. A diagram or chart illustrating business strategy can simplify ideas and develop an agreed set of causal links to facilitate the transmission of complex ideas from individual to individual and unit to unit. For example, a cognitive map can be used to share

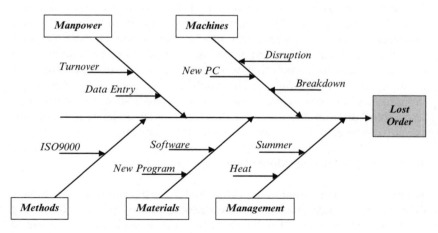

Figure 4.1   A fishbone diagram

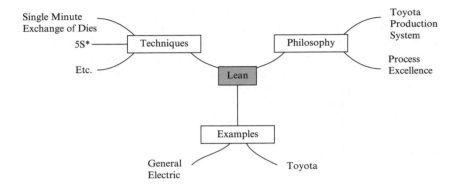

Notes: * 5S is an approach that aims to aid efficient working practice, by reducing clutter in the work place, translated roughly from the Japanese, they stand for Sort, Sift, Shine, Set in place, Stick at it (although other translations are often used). By following these steps, time wasted through searching for what is required is removed.

Figure 4.2   A simple mind map of lean

thoughts on the causes of congestion in a city. Most importantly, visual representation helps to divorce ideas from individual members of a group discussion, making the ideas more accessible to debate and modification (see Figure 4.3).

4.3.4   Stimulates Thinking

Visual representations can be a means of displaying graphically a firm's current strategic position, possibly constructed from how various observers interpret it. Developing a graphical representation from suitable members so that a suitably accurate and agreed upon picture can be created, input can be initiated to actions that will improve their current position. For example, climbing a career ladder could be represented by climbing a mountain, with those contributing to the system identifying potential 'crocodiles' or 'alternate routes' to develop a better understanding of how to get from where one is to where one wants to be (Figure 4.4).

4.3.5   Bridges Missing Information

We can exploit the visual system to extract information from incomplete data. A simple diagram, for example a prohibition sign, imposed across a cigarette with the word 'Lobby' underneath it, is sufficient for people to know that the diagram means no smoking in the lobby (Figure 4.5).

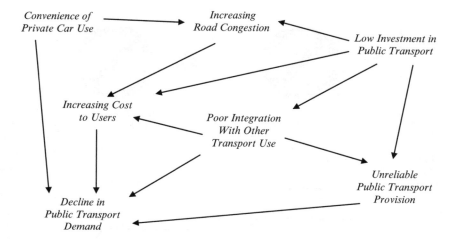

Figure 4.3   A cognitive map

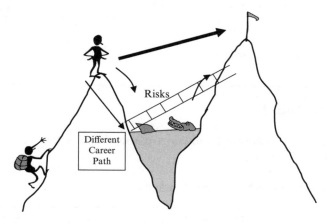

Figure 4.4   Risks associated with climbing a career ladder

4.3.6   Challenges Self-Imposed Constraint (Perception)

Diagrams also provide the function of challenging self-imposed constraint (perception). An appropriate use of diagrams can enable managers to look at a problem in a new way. Borrowing a simple example from geometry, the nature of the problem illustrated in Figure 4.6 is such that the area of a parallelogram (a) can be easily understood when diagram (b) is shown.

Similar activities could be carried out by rearranging how managers

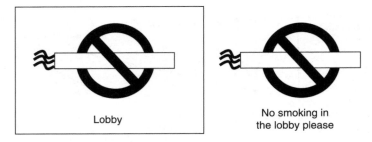

Figure 4.5   A no smoking sign

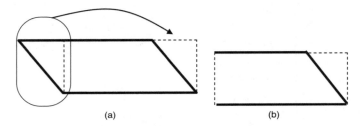

Figure 4.6   A parallelogram

EXERCISE 3

Use a single diagram to make a comparison of the evaluation results in Table 4.2.

Table 4.2   Project evaluation results

	Project A	Project B	Project C	Project D
Prioritisation score	15%	70%	35%	50%
Total cost	£20k	£65k	£150k	£100k
Risk assessment	35%	67%	25%	35%

Expressing this information visually can assist in gaining better understanding of the decision making process. Although the different aspects of the decision have been quantified, without combining them in a suitable way, choosing between the different projects in a logical manner is not possible.

visually represent an organisation. By representing the organisation in terms of services provided, rather than more traditionally hierarchical representations, it may be possible to begin viewing the organisation as the end user sees it. Viewing a situation in a different arrangement may assist in developing processes in a way that better reflects the strategic aims of the organisation.

4.4 OPERATIONAL FUNCTIONS

Pictures provide both cognitive and operational function support. Table 4.3 lists some of the operational functions.

4.4.1 Identifies Structure, Trends and Relationships

A key operational function of visualisation is that it can be used to identify structure, patterns, trends, anomalies and relationships in data. Strategy charting (Mills et al. 1998) is one of the visual representation techniques available that is designed to serve this purpose. It provides a simple-to-use visualisation tool which can capture activities and events that illustrate planned and emergent strategy, thereby giving managers a common understanding of past, present and future strategy within their organisation. The tool uses colour, text and organised space to record and display information in a readily understandable form. The basic chart is constructed on sheets of flipchart paper that are then attached to the wall with time represented along the horizontal axis. Moving from top to bottom of the display (Figure 4.7), the sheets are marked to show a decision/implementation hierarchy that describes the organisation under examination. The bottom two levels of the hierarchy are always 'strategy formulation' and 'strategy implementation'. Managers can use felt-tip pens or colour post-it notes to represent actions on the chart.

Representing business strategy as a pattern of actions appears to make

Table 4.3   Operational functions

Operational Functions	
Identifies structure, trends and relationships	Identifies structure, patterns, trends, anomalies and relationships in data
Displays multivariate performance	Enables managers to analyse complex performance
Highlights key factors	Allows managers to specify explicitly their views on the importance weighting of variables

Source: Platts and Tan (2003).

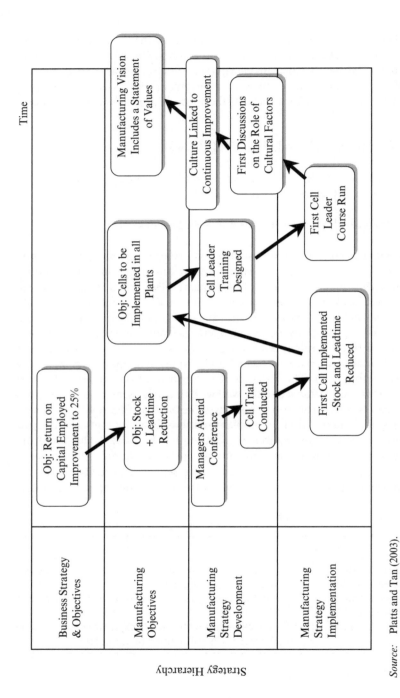

Source: Platts and Tan (2003).

Figure 4.7   An example of strategy charting

118

'strategy' an understandable and communicable concept for managers and the workforce. Although charts show parts of the content and process of a strategy, developing understanding of the process, the act of charting can be just as valuable. It can initiate understanding relating to the problems that may occur, helping build consensus about the path that is required. The act of charting can also provoke considerable discussion on how past strategies arose, how long they took to implement and which strategies failed and why. Thus, charting can be a small but important step in the direction of facilitating self-awareness, promoting sensitivity to an organisation's history and exploring the dynamics of its strategy development.

4.4.2 Displays Multivariate Performance

Visual representation can also be used to analyse complex decisions, such as assessing multivariate performance. In the early stage of a strategy process, it is usually vital for managers to identify and compare the market requirements and achieved performance of a range of products, often across a range of market segments. This requires multiple comparisons across a range of performance attributes, for example cost, quality and delivery. The aim of this is to enable managers to visualise the performance of these products (i.e. the achieved performance versus market requirements), assess the fit and identify the major gaps to begin understanding how developments need to direct the organisation. As described in Chapter 2, this makes up an important part of the Gregory–Platts procedure.

A profiling method can be utilised to display a comparative picture of this issue. Profiles of market requirements and achieved performance can be depicted in the manner shown in Figure 4.8. The profiling provides clear visual comparison, enabling managers to review the alignment that exists, that is, to test the correlation between market requirements and achieved performance. This graphic representation of those dimensions relevant to a business allows managers to recognise the issues, discuss any corrective action and determine particular areas of focus, allowing the prioritisation of action plans to be discussed.

4.4.3 Highlights Key Factors

Most strategic planning involves preparing thick documents filled with mountains of numbers. A diagram developed within a strategic planning process allows managers to specify their views on the importance weighting of variables. A 'strategy canvas' is a method to reveal a firm's strategic position. For example, a strategy canvas for two firms A and B competing in the on-line insurance market could be drawn as in Figure 4.9. The

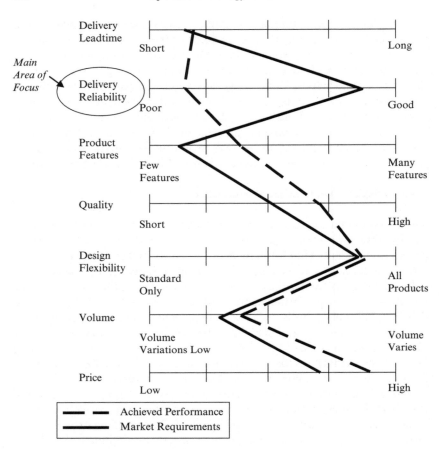

Figure 4.8   Performance profile

canvas provides a stark comparison, enabling managers to understand the gap in the factors of competition and identify those key factors that need attention. The specific relationships and composition of the different measures could be formulated within prior strategic discussions and mapping activities, which can help to give greater validity to the figures presented.

4.5   ADVICE FOR IMPLEMENTATION

We have encouraged managers to exploit the power of visual representations, arguing that managers possess more complex, subtle and useful

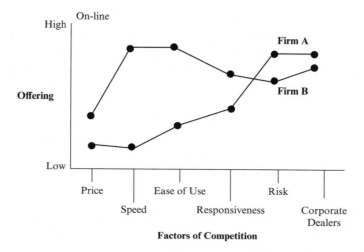

Figure 4.9   Strategy canvas

cognitive maps of their organisations than they can verbalise and than those higher up in the organisation. Those that work within the organisation are better able to understand the relationships that are present and the processes that take place. Visual representation can help managers to reap the benefits of experience by triggering their past experience. While these functions provide important tools for managing the decision process in organisations, each one has a dysfunctional side that needs to be guarded against. Table 4.4 highlights the function trade-offs of visualisation.

Too much focus leads to cave vision, while over-use of past experience leads to mechanistic perpetuation of past behaviour (Foil and Huff 1992). Excessive agreement or shared thinking will impose rigid views; too much stimulation will lead to groupthink; inappropriate application of information bridging could cause confusion; and too much challenge of perception inhibits teamwork and leads to alienation in a group.

Clearly, there are many benefits from using visual representation techniques to support strategic decision making and planning. However, the process of applying these techniques is clearly not prescriptive. It is likely to be very important for those carrying out the process to have a good understanding of the activities as well as where they are to be applied. Without appreciation of these elements that can greatly affect the process, incorporating them into the strategic planning routine may not always provide positive results.

Drawing from experience applying visual representation techniques for over a decade, we offer the following advice for managers:

Table 4.4   Function trade-offs

Under-use	Cognitive Functions	Overdo
Splatter-vision	Focuses attention	Cave vision
Inefficiency	Triggers memory	Mechanistic
Segmented	Shares thinking	Self-imposed
Individualistic	Stimulates thinking	Groupthink
Misrepresented	Bridges missing information	Confusion
Lackadaisical (languish)	Challenges self-imposed constraint (perception)	Alienation

1. *Graphic aptitude*: Not everyone displays an aptitude for working with graphic displays. Thus, existing visual techniques can carry a risk of over-generalising the responses of managers. To overcome this, attention should be paid to managers' freehand drawings. One should invite managers to draw pictures showing how they feel about a strategy before and after a new challenge. Foil and Huff (1992) point out that these drawings function as a catalyst, helping managers to articulate feelings that might be implicit but hard to define.
2. *Keeping it simple*: One should encourage managers to sketch out a strategy as simply as possible and avoid unnecessary decorations. It is important to ensure that users think about the substance of the data, but not the graphic.
3. *Different levels*: Data should be viewed at many different levels of detail. With these insights, managers will then have a broad overview of the data and, at the same time, it will allow them access to the detailed data that underlie the overview.
4. *Secondary components of visualisation*: Attention should be paid to secondary components of visualisation such as size (height, width, length), colour and density. For example, one should avoid the temptation to put too much information into a network diagram. A dense network will make reading and analysis difficult, thus defeating the purpose of visualisation.

4.6   APPRAISAL OF EXISTING TECHNIQUES

When setting out on the task of action planning, managers have available to them several existing techniques to generate and structure ideas in relation to the problems.

Idea generation techniques, such as brainstorming, are potential ways of broadening a manager's thinking platform to encourage more ideas to emerge. Van Gundy (1988) identifies 60 techniques of brainstorming and its variants for generating ideas in both group and individual settings. He points out that these techniques (such as 'brainwriting' and 'poolwriting') are based on free association, forced relationships or some combination of both. Various brainstorming software packages (Axon, IdeaFisher, etc.) are also available in the market. These packages use questions to prompt the user into taking new directions in their thought patterns and allow thoughts to be recorded.

Although such techniques might help managers to produce a lot of ideas, they are unfocused and hence inefficient. A lot of effort and time is needed to sort out the ideas generated and to identify those that are relevant and viable. What is required is a structuring and relating of these ideas to the objectives being pursued, not just the generation of ideas. Brainstorming may be adequate for naming a new game or new product, but it is too superficial to address complex strategic decisions because it fails to address the pattern elaboration stage in which one uncovers the complexities and subtleties inherent in the original thought (Weisberg 1986).

Thus, instead of just brainstorming ideas, managers need techniques to structure and analyse a particular problem in order to gain more understanding. Several causal mapping techniques are available allowing a manager to create a model and study the cause and effects of the situation. Notable among these techniques are fishbone (Ishikawa) diagrams, why/why diagrams, influence diagrams, mind mapping and cognitive mapping.

A fishbone diagram is probably the most widely known and used cause–effect diagram in operations management. It is a systematic technique for identifying the possible root causes of a problem by breaking it down into its components. The 'why/why' diagram serves the same purpose, generating a hierarchy of causes and sub-causes by continually asking the question 'why?' In other words, a fishbone diagram helps managers to map their perception of what collectively contributes to the problem, whereas the 'why/why' diagram helps them 'to explore the problem and contour the boundaries of their mindsets' (Newman 1995, p. 70).

An influence diagram is similar to Ishikawa and why/why diagrams but is different in that it attempts to show not just the causality, but also the direction of the effect. An influence diagram attempts to represent all causal relationships in a manner that is non-ambiguous and probabilistic.

Mind mapping and cognitive mapping are used to explore and structure problems. Mind mapping (Buzan 1982) emphasises the use of keywords and images to build a diagram around a single key issue. The images and keywords are an aid to memory and making intuitive associations. By contrast, cognitive mapping uses text only to build complex networks which may have several foci.

Could these techniques help managers sufficiently to identify a range of actions? In order for managers to generate a wide range of actions they need to identify the relevant variables within a problem situation, to develop an understanding of these variables and the linkages among them, to analyse these linkages and, hence, identify actions, tools and techniques that they can use. Finally, the alternatives need evaluating so that an action plan can be compiled for subsequent implementation.

From the understanding of the general purpose, mapping tools described above could be used for the first part of this task. They provide a way of scoping a problem and identifying relevant variables. However, because they are general purpose, they are not necessarily optimised for the action planning task. For example, cognitive mapping might result in overly complex models since it allows the development of multiple foci, whereas fishbone diagrams, created for specific problems with clear boundaries, might be too simplistic (see Table 4.5).

A range of commercially available software packages has been built around the techniques discussed above. These software tools (see Table 4.5) automate the application of the techniques and enhance information visualisation. However, they generally address a specific stage of the decision making process and do not provide comprehensive support through all the stages. This work aims to provide managers with a set of tools that can assist and support their analysis at every stage of the decision making process.

Figure 4.10 is an example of how tools that are aimed at developing creative thinking can be modified to assist in gaining better insight into problems and more relevant results. This diagram takes an inherently operational tool (the Ishikawa/fishbone diagram) and relates it to the organisation's strategy. The effect of this could be more than simply solving an operational problem, by helping the system to develop in line with higher-level goals. By understanding what particular tools are able to accomplish, it should be possible to combine them to meet the needs of specific problems and to develop appropriate solutions that appreciate how different elements of an organisation can contribute to solutions. For example, SWOT (Strengths, Weaknesses, Opportunities and Threats) analysis could be combined with Porter 5 Forces (Porter 1980), which is an approach that systematically considers the market forces external to an organisation. If a firm suffers from methodological blocks, they may consider that carrying out a SWOT or 5 Forces analysis constitutes a rigorous analysis of the problems an organisation may face when in fact they may restrict the creative process.

Table 4.5 *Comparison of causal mapping techniques*

Mapping Techniques	Characteristics	Strengths	Weaknesses	Useful Software
Fishbone	• Identifies root cause of a problem by breaking it down into its components	• Detailed analysis on specific narrow problems	• Narrowly focused • Difficult to analyse if the diagram becomes too complex	SmartDraw
Why/why	• Generates a hierarchy of causes and sub-causes by continually asking the question 'why?'	• Simple to apply, even verbally	• Tends to build a complex hierarchy as there is no boundary for asking the question 'why'	Autocad; Microsoft Office
Influence diagram	• Represents all causal relationships of a phenomenon in a manner that is non-ambiguous and probabilistic	• Quantitative analysis can be performed on the developed model	• May not be suitable to analyse complex problems which involve relationships that are qualitative in nature	Analytica

Table 4.5 (continued)

Mapping Techniques	Characteristics	Strengths	Weaknesses	Useful Software
Mind mapping	• Images and keywords are used as an aid to memory and making intuitive associations	• Personalised diagrams are easy to recall and associate	• Mainly for educational purposes	InfoMap
Cognitive mapping	• Uses statements to build complex networks for a problem. Allows multiple foci	• Easy to apply • Could build a network from any focus	• Could result in a very complex model • No structured approach for constructing a network	Decision Explorer

Source: Tan and Platts (2003a).

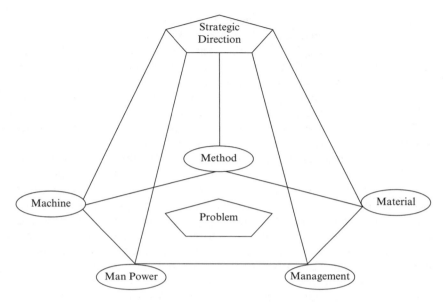

Figure 4.10   Combination of Ishikawa investigations with influence diagram to direct solutions to solve a problem while considering the overall aim

4.7   GENERATION OF ACTIONS: LINKING ACTIONS TO OPERATIONS OBJECTIVES

In today's competitive business environment, the level of complexity and extent of interrelations between causal factors have increased to an almost bewildering level. Any improvement actions for a manufacturing firm are likely to include decisions in both structural and infrastructural areas. Structural decisions concern capacity, facilities, technology and vertical integration, whereas infrastructural decisions relate to quality, production planning, organisation, workforce policies and performance measurement (Hayes and Wheelwright 1984). For example, with the objective to improve product quality, the actions could come from structural decision areas such as process technology or better process automation, or a combination of infrastructural decisions such as improving workers' skills or introducing statistical process control (SPC).

The large number of variables, and the complexity of the interrelationships, have made the generation of actions difficult. Managers rely on experience and intuition, combining these with their own mental models of

variable linkages. This creates the difficulties associated with idea generation already mentioned, even though the approach has the advantage of
swift decision making. However, the decisions made may be overly biased
by the managers' experience. Hammond, Keeney and Raiffa (1999) refer
to this as a 'business as usual' approach to problem solution, with many
decision problems appearing similar to others that have come before and
where choosing a tried alternative is the easy course.

The knowledge embodied in managers' experience is tacit, but ideally
managers should use an action planning tool that gives them a way of
eliciting and capturing this knowledge to allow its objective review. This
should be combined with a mechanism for retaining it and, if possible,
a way of providing a comprehensiveness check. A typical output could
be a formal explicit model of variable linkages, in contrast to managers'
previous tacit mental models, allowing greater involvement in otherwise
internal processes. By having an output of a formal, explicit model
of variable linkages, the process can be contributed to and ultimately
owned to a greater extent than the previously tacit mental models.

Once the variable linkages are understood, analysis is required to determine the potential impacts of changes being considered. An action planning tool that automates this analysis could allow managers to consider a
wider range of options in a short time. An evaluation of the options represents the final stage, which requires the consideration of many factors,
so some form of multi-attribute decision making is required. An action
planning tool should provide the appropriate level of functionality and
detail, yet be easy to use. In short, the requirements of a tool for action
planning are:

- *Sequential decision making* – supports managers through the entire
  process from identifying relevant variables to evaluating decisions.
- *Visualisation support* – provides visualisation support at each stage
  of the decision making process.
- *Integrated documentation* – captures information on variables and
  linkages for analysis or comparison.

4.8   CASE STUDY: JAPANESE CREATIVITY

Due to Japan's success in world trade and technical development, a lot of
people view the Japanese as being very creative. However, do Japanese
organisations with a high commitment to systematic processes produce
more creative research or products than Western organisations which
are more autonomous? Sarkis (1995) points out that American engineers

produce more creative research in the basic sciences but tend to be less productive in the process areas. Japanese organisations, on the other hand, appear to be less productive in basic science research but demonstrate high creativity in those areas related to process control and development. He further argues that group dynamics and the level of consensus in the decision processes appear to play an important role in this phenomenon.

A number of approaches to creativity emerged in Japan in the 1960s and 1970s, and were widely used in industries and governmental offices. These techniques constituted part of the basis for the quality control (QC) movements in Japan. For example, the 'NM Method' is a methodology developed by Masakazu Nakayama in the 1970s, and is well known because it is so called after the initials of his name. Nakayama emphasised his method as a training approach for activating the right half of the brain, and the NM Method consists of a five-step process for generating ideas (Nakamura 2003):

- *KW (Key Word)*: Define the function or the main feature of the required technical system in a short clause including a verb.
- *QA (Question Analogy)*: Look for an event that meets with the Key Word among natural phenomena and non-made systems.
- *QB (Question Background)*: Clarify the principles/mechanisms working in the analogous phenomena/systems.
- *QC (Question Conception)*: Generate ideas on the basis of the principles/mechanisms.
- *ABD (Abduction)*: Combine ideas and brush up into new concepts.

In point of fact, the NM approach has much in common with Synectics, where a word taken from the problem definition (or redefinition) is taken on an excursion into an imaginary world and treated in a similar way that is outlined above for the NM Method.

Other important techniques include the 'KJ Method' by Jiro Kawakita and Equivalent Transformal Thinking by Kikuya Ichikawa. Basically, these techniques place emphasis on the understanding of deep verbal meanings of phenomena/observations or analogies and on the understanding of mechanisms. However, translating these methodologies and examples from Japanese is so delicate that they have rarely been published in English by the developers and their associates. Hoshin Kanri (described in Chapter 2), the approach to strategy deployment, is an example of this: although it only consists of two words, it requires careful articulation to begin understanding its true meaning.

Many researchers (viz. Herbig and Jacobs 1996; Basadur 1992) have tried to shed light on Japanese creativity. Herbig and Jacobs (1996) argue that the Japanese are better at adaptive creativity, that is, refining ideas and technologies to create new products and markets, which is in contrast to the innovative style of the Westerners. Basadur (1992) points out that the Japanese place more emphasis on problem finding, that is, continuously identifying new and useful problems to be solved, and less emphasis on solving and implementation. This review has begun to investigate the differences between Japanese and Western approaches to creativity but does not help us to understand the different elements that are core to the perceived creativity of the Japanese.

4.8.1 Incrementalism

The incremental approach to creativity has its roots in the Japanese cultural background.[1] The Japanese do not believe in sudden change like Westerners, which is backed up by several proverbs that support this idea:

- Sit on the stone at least three years (to be matured).
- Wait for good things while you are sleeping.
- A thousand miles start from one first step.

This cultural background is also clearly rooted in the educational system. In the West, teachers do not suggest how to solve a problem directly to the children. There is a lot of freedom for children to think and innovate new approaches to solve their problems. However, in Japan, children imitate instead of being given freedom. They are taught to learn things well using three words (see Figure 4.11).

The first word, syu, means protect or keep; the second word, ha, stands for break, and the third word, ri, means leave or release. The point is that children can learn how to do things well from the experience of others. However, the disadvantage is that this process could block or even prevent creative insights. The core values central to this argument relate to incrementalism, which signals continuous improvement.

One can easily appreciate the side effects of such thinking – it means that the Japanese are good at the second step of creativity. This is echoed by many researchers who suggest that the Japanese are not good at coming up with brand new ideas (symbolically moving from 0 to 1), but can develop an idea or concept once it exists (symbolically they can advance from 1 to

守 (SYU)　破 (HA)　離 (RI)

Figure 4.11　Protect, break and leave

10, step by step). The Japanese always strive to improve things effectively, thereby producing small improvements little by little. Eventually the pile of small improvements becomes innovation as a consequence.

One example of this incremental paradigm is the so called Kaizen, an important element of the Toyota Production System. It assisted Toyota for many years to produce cars in one third of the time required by car manufacturers in the West. Other examples that benefited from Kaizen included the Walkman, an invention of SONY, where the incremental developments were focused on miniaturising products. The root of Japanese creativity comes from the heartfelt need to make others feel more comfortable. If we care for others, they argue, we will see what they need and what they require.

Incrementalism advocates moving not so much towards a goal as away from trouble; trying this or that small manoeuvre without any grand plan or sense of ultimate purpose. Such an approach has two attractive strengths. First, it eliminates the need for complete, encyclopaedic information by focusing on limited areas, those nearest to hand, one at a time. Second, it avoids the danger of grand policy decisions by not making any. Its main weakness is that it is highly 'conservative' (Etzioni 1989); it invariably chooses a direction close to the prevailing one. Grand new departures, radical changes in course, do not occur, however much they may be needed.

Theoretically, incremental improvements are either tentative or remedial – small steps taken in the 'right' direction whenever the present course proves to be wrong. But before small step improvements are suggested – in order to determine whether or not the present course is right – a broader guideline has to be established. Thus, this suggests that incremental progress needs the hallmark of grand, priori interrelated values and cultures to stay on course. One such value that is embedded in Japanese organisations is teamwork.

4.9 CONCLUSION

The aim of this chapter has been to develop an understanding of the creative thinking process at a fundamental, internal and practical level. With the appreciation of the different problems that are likely to be encountered, combined with an awareness of the different tools available to solve these problems, the reader should be better equipped to tackle the problems they face. By beginning the process of creative thinking with such a base, there is an improved likelihood of moving away from 'business as usual' solutions, with those involved in the process critically analysing the results.

With a set of criteria to analyse the decision making process against, rather than simply relying on the natural creativity of certain members of the group, the process can become more structured. This is not to say that the process should become prescriptive; instead, by undertaking the process in a methodical manner, experience of the creative process can be developed to be applied to other problems the organisation may face.

Understanding and formalising the creative process, through the education of those involved in creative thinking techniques, has the potential to develop a creative capability within the firm. Although within a Western setting this is important for the development of new ideas that give an organisation an innovative new direction, it will also be important within the Japanese setting outlined at the end of the chapter. By understanding the different approach taken by the Japanese to problem solving, an appreciation can be developed that creativity does not necessarily have to result in a step change. Viewing everyday activities and difficulties as new problems to be solved through innovative means can form the basis for bottom-up innovation, helping to draw together the different aspects of the business innovation process. However, ideas are not all that is required for the transformation of an organisation, and for this reason the next chapter introduces and outlines a visually based decision support tool called TAPS. Through its effective use with the ideas included within this chapter, the results should represent innovative action plans that are effectively and efficiently produced as a basis for transforming an organisation.

NOTE

1. In general, the incremental paradigm is just an approach to creativity in the West and it is not rooted in the cultural background.

5. Seeing the big picture

5.0 INTRODUCTION

As outlined in the previous chapter, it is extremely important for beginning to develop strategic objectives for an organisation to free oneself
of the self-imposed constraints of creativity. As already stated, without
a suitable array of alternatives, those responsible for selecting between
options are unable to use their ability and judgement, leaving the outcome
restrained within the confines of those charged with solution generation
(Drucker 1967). However, from this point, it is then the ability to generate
and identify appropriate action plans from the initial ideas that represents
an important part of managerial problem solving and decision making.
Professor David Garvin of Harvard Business School identified problems
associated with both these elements, where many managers do not spend
sufficient resources on developing enough alternatives. This results in the
'best choice' never even being considered, and not considering all the alternative actions that are available can have devastating consequences. This
chapter introduces an approach for the progression from the initial ideas
stage of strategic activities to the development of a variety of action plans
to allow the most appropriate to be selected.

Where the requirements of a suitable idea generation process are to
remove one's own internal blocks to creativity, as outlined in Chapter
3, the process for implementation can also be a very complex activity.
However, due to the need to introduce the ideas into an existing organisation, the relevance of a particular plan will have many constraints as to
whether or not it is appropriate for the organisation. Within the competitive business environment of today, the careful consideration of the competitive environment on its own can be a difficult activity. Combining this
with the level of complexity and extent to which elements of an organisation are causally connected, the process of creating an appropriate action
plan increases to an almost bewildering level. Within an improvement
activity, a well-balanced action plan is likely to include both structural
and infrastructural aspects that are effectively the harder and softer elements that make up an organisation. Structural decisions are concerned
with capacity, facilities, technology and vertical integration, whereas
infrastructural decisions relate to quality and performance (see Table 5.1).

Table 5.1   Structural and infrastructural areas

Decision Areas	Key Elements
Structural	Capacity
	Facilities
	Technology
	Vertical integration
Infrastructural	Quality
	Production planning
	New product development
	Performance measurement
	Organisation
	Workforce policies

As mentioned earlier, with an objective to improve product quality, the actions could come from structural decision areas such as process technology or better process automation, possibly in combination with infrastructural decisions such as improving workers' skills or introducing SPC. As stressed in Chapter 3 with the focus upon the development of a suitable implementation capability, to be effective, actions plans are likely to need the support of infrastructural developments to be effective and enable an organisation to develop.

With the extremely large number of variables, combined with the potential cobweb of interrelationships, simply understanding the effects of introducing new elements into the system can be difficult. The generation of new, innovative, appropriate action plans is likely to be considerably more difficult, due to the requirements of several levels of the organisation ranging from general manufacturing and management principles to details about specific technologies. With this being the case, is there a single member within an organisation with suitable understanding of the system to be able to consider all these elements of an organisation? If an organisation is fortunate enough to possess such a valuable resource, how are these elements able to develop alternative actions to choose from in order to achieve a particular objective?

5.1   SHORTCOMINGS OF EXISTING METHODS

Traditionally, managers have depended on the use of past experience and intuition, idea generation techniques (such as brainstorming) and seeking third party advisers, possibly combined with deployment techniques, to

Table 5.2   Summary of advantages and shortcomings of approaches

Approaches	Advantages	Shortcomings
Experience and intuition	Quick; easy to access	Bias; outdated
Brainstorming	Many ideas; vast areas covered	Irrelevance; time consuming to sort out ideas
Third party advisers	Reliable; quick; little effort	Costly; difficult to access; no learning from problem

assist them in making action generation and selection decisions. These approaches may not always give them the best decisions; the reasons for this are summarised in Table 5.2.

Using past experience and intuition, a manager has the advantage of making decisions swiftly, with what he or she feels comfortable with. However, the decision made could be overly biased towards the manager's own experience, and could easily exclude the latest operations management tools and techniques as well as other options which those involved may not have experienced or be aware of. It is very difficult for a manager to have learnt and kept up to date with all the developments in their field of expertise while also giving suitable consideration to other fields of expertise. Moreover, managers tend to fall into the trap of 'business as usual' and focus their actions on ideas with which they are familiar. For complex operational decisions, relying on experience alone is insufficient because it lacks objectivity, accuracy, repeatability and efficiency. Table 5.3 lists the common decision traps (frames) that hinder managers from making a decision objectively.

Most managers, in addition to experience will also hopefully use idea generation techniques such as brainstorming to help them broaden their thinking platform and to encourage more ideas to emerge. Although brainstorming can help managers to produce a number of ideas and cover vast areas and issues, it promises only little credibility in the ideas generated. A lot of effort and time is needed to sort out the ideas generated and to identify those that are relevant and viable. Without basing brainstorming activities within a suitable organisational context, with the complexity of operational problems, although solutions may potentially be innovative, they may not be what is required from the process. The idea generation process needs to be based within the confines of the current operating environment, so that the ideas relate to objectives and limitations of the development process such as time, cost and feasibility. Brainstorming may be appropriate for the development of superficial, unconstrained activities, such as naming activities; however, for operations decisions to be effective,

Table 5.3   Common decision traps[1]

Decision Traps	Descriptions
Framing	Setting out to solve the wrong problem because managers have created a mental framework for the decision; with little thought, they may overlook the best options or lose sight of important objectives
Short-sighted shortcuts	Relying inappropriately on 'rules of thumb' such as implicitly trusting the most readily available information or anchoring too much on convenient facts (looking for answers where they do not exist)
Overconfidence in judgement	Failing to collect key factual information because managers are too sure of their assumptions and opinions
Business as usual	Bias due to personal experience and knowledge

Source: Russo and Schoemaker (1989).

the idea generation process needs to be grounded upon the complexities and subtleties of the original situation. In technical and management professions, managers need to be able to think clearly, to be organised, to plan and to meet tight deadlines. As mentioned within the previous chapter, over-reliance on the fuzzy, magical elements of creativity is unlikely to be a foundation upon which long-term success can be built and, may even be deadly in certain contexts.

Alternatively, managers can seek advice from third parties such as consultants, superiors or academics who collaborate with the company. The advantage of this approach is that a reliable answer can be obtained quickly, and without much effort from the manager. However, the cost of hiring a third party can be very high and, for a company with limited resources, access to third parties is difficult. One of the biggest downsides of this approach is that managers do not learn much from the process. What the managers get is a solution, but not the skills and know-how to address the problem. Without grounding activities within the confines of the host organisation, the ideas may not be appropriate or may be too difficult to integrate with existing processes. As outlined in Chapter 3, without the development of understanding of business processes that represents an implementation capability, the long-term benefits of such activities to an organisation may be reduced. This is notwithstanding the considerable cost of the approach: if organisations must use such approaches regularly their business performance may even be affected by the approach.

5.2 REQUIREMENTS OF AN ACTION PLANNING PROCESS

In order for a manager to generate actions the following activities are required. The manager must:

- identify the relevant variables within a problem situation;
- develop an understanding of these variables;
- identify actions, tools and techniques that may be appropriate;
- evaluate the alternatives and compile an action plan.

As mentioned in Chapter 4, managers often hold this knowledge in an unstructured form based on previous experience, but rather than restricting those involved in the process, it should be effectively combined with the above elements, allowing systematic comparison with similarly structured information from other managers. Within the decision making process, managers should have a way of eliciting and capturing this knowledge, a mechanism for retaining it and, if possible, a way of checking its comprehensiveness.

Every manager brings to a problem a set of tools consisting of knowledge, understanding and experience of the problem situation which is unique to that individual. A good decision making process should have additional tools with the functionality to elicit that understanding, and a mechanism to achieve a consensus view, by producing a model that has been able to build on the abilities of those present.

5.3 THE TAPS APPROACH

TAPS (Tool for Action Plan Selection) is an approach developed to address the shortcomings of existing methods. It provides managers with a complete decision making process from problem understanding to evaluation.

TAPS is the result of a three year research project that utilised previously developed approaches to problem solutions with practical applications of the approaches. The TAPS approach is built on the foundation of a set of powerful tools to support managers in the generation and evaluation of actions (see Figure 5.1). TAPS utilises the connectance concept (Burbidge 1984) and the Analytic Hierarchy Process (AHP) approach (Saaty 1987). The connectance concept is used to assist managers in building up a variable network to visualise the interrelationships between objectives, variables, actions and management tools. The original approach was based

TAPS Process   **Process and Analytical Tools**

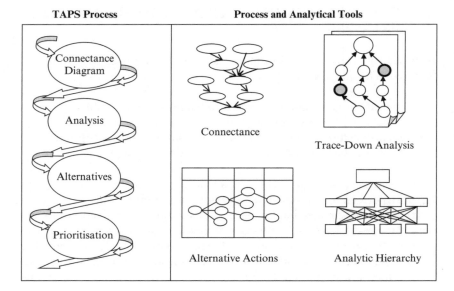

Source: Tan and Platts (2003b).

Figure 5.1   The TAPS approach

on empirical data from manufacturing studies that enabled the development of fact-based relationships between different variables, assisting in
increasing the objectivity and validity of results. The AHP process allows
the merits of the identified actions to be assessed. The approach taken
to TAPS in this chapter is to develop an understanding of the approach
and its concepts; it is supported by a software tool. This assists in further
increasing the objectivity of the approach to action plan development,
giving support to those responsible for the activity. The reason for not
including the software is that the true value of the approach flows from
the personal involvement with the TAPS process; the software tool simply
supports the process. The value specifically comes from the communication and insight into their organisational processes that managers gain
that are developed from undertaking the process. The software tool also
helps in automating analysis, facilitating effective communication and
providing documentation of the process.

The benefits generated from using a TAPS approach are:

- *Collective understanding*: The variable network building process
  enables everyone to have their knowledge brought into the open

and their assumptions challenged. Managers with experience of the process agreed that this process was useful to enhance their understanding of an issue, as well as to facilitate organisational learning. Moreover, the TAPS process assists in avoiding individual 'experience bias' in making decisions by discussing assumptions in an open, fact-driven environment. The Chief Executive Officer (CEO) of an instrumentation manufacturer commented that, 'TAPS encourages people to take a broader view and also helps them understand the implications and effects one variable can have on another.'

- *Decision support*: The three stages of the TAPS process – a) model building, b) action generation, and c) action evaluation and prioritisation – support managers in making decisions right from problem framing and understanding to making decision choices. The analytical processes in TAPS help managers to decompose the complexity of strategy deployment into manageable steps, and help them to crystallise thoughts and reduce inconsistencies at each step of the process.
- *Facilitate discussion*: The variable network helps managers to increase both the depth and breadth of participation in the discussion of action generation and selection. The TAPS approach recognises the importance of assisting the evolution of the managers' ability to deal with the problems, confronting them through increasing their understanding of the relevant variables. It provides models of the environment from which a manager can develop insights into the effects of his or her decisions on progress towards the goals that he or she wishes to achieve.
- *Knowledge management*: The building of a variable network allows information to be passed, assessed and quantified, so that the ideas and beliefs contained within the model can be altered or modified at will.

5.4   SEE-THE-BIG-PICTURE APPROACH

From the TAPS research, we are able to identify that there are three generic steps when it comes to visualising and translating strategy into actions, namely a) building a connectance visual diagram; b) generating actions, and c) evaluating and prioritising actions. These steps may be carried out in the form of workshops involving those affected by the process. The workshops need to involve particularly important members of the process, such as a process champion to gain support for upper management, and a facilitator, who acts as a TAPS process expert and possibly project manager as well, to assist in maintaining progress. This section outlines the process from start to finish.[2]

1. *Workshop 1 – Building a Connectance Visual Diagram*: Different aspects of an objective are identified. Relevant variables that have an impact on each aspect of the objective are discussed and determined. This process is continued until it is possible to identify the management tools and techniques that can contribute to addressing the different aspects of the objective, which is represented as a connectance diagram. Using this diagram it is possible to identify the important elements that affect and contribute to achieving the objective.

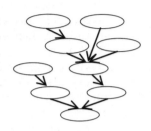

2. *Workshop 2 – Generating Alternative Actions*: From the connectance diagrams alternative actions are identified for achieving the objective. Diagrams with different levels of detail may be created to enable participants to study in depth the connectance between objective and variables. This will help to ensure that the analysis of potential actions will be based upon comprehensive analysis of the relationships that are present within the organisation. This step can also be used to begin identifying elements that have a particular effect on achieving the object; these are known as key drivers.

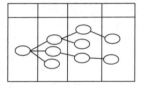

3. *Workshop 3 – Evaluating and Prioritising*: The criteria for assessing the merits of the different actions are identified. By carrying out pair-wise comparisons between the different actions, which are then prioritised, and following this activity with sensitivity analysis of each action, the robustness can then be quantified. This allows the key drivers to be systematically identified, to allow plans for the next steps to be considered.

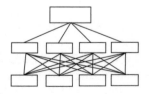

5.4.1 Workshop 1: Preparation for the Building of a Connectance Diagram

With the aim of the workshop being to systematically develop a representation of the processes that are present within an organisation that forms the basis for subsequent activities to be developed upon, suitable planning and support for the step is important. Without allocating the appropriate resources (time and personnel) to the step, results of the process will suffer, which in turn will affect the chances of smooth and successful implementation of the process. In the preparation phase, the following steps need to be taken:

- Agreeing on an objective as the focus for the process.
- Planning time scales.
- Getting a project champion (possibly a managing director or CEO).
- Selecting a facilitator (an expert with the TAPS process).
- Forming a team and appointing a project manager (if the facilitator is not taking the role).

Agreeing on a focus objective
Action planning is about translating objectives into actions; that is, identifying what actions will achieve a given objective. The first step therefore is to specify clearly the objective that the process aims to achieve. This must be done carefully: the clearer the definition of the objective, the easier the subsequent steps will be. As stated earlier, simple objectives such as quality, flexibility or even capacity are too highly aggregated to be able to represent the aims of a development activity, for example an objective of improving capacity would have many different connotations. Depending on the level – machine, cell, department or factory – the associated action plan may be very different, which is without including other areas of an organisation that are affected by capacity, such as administrative functions. Once this has been defined, the possibility of the process producing a relevant action plan should be greatly improved, by knowing the question it is expected to answer.

Aims
- Discuss and identify the different aspects of the objective.
- Identify and discuss the relevant variables that have an impact on the objective.
- Build a connectance diagram interactively during a group discussion.
- Summarise the outputs from the workshop and discuss areas for further work.

Step 1: identify different objective aspects
- Participants are asked to identify the different aspects of the objective. This allows the disaggregation of the objective to enable more focused analysis.
- The different aspects are mapped, which can involve using the special TAPS software. Participants should ensure that all the key aspects are covered. For example, an improvement in manufacturing flexibility could be achieved from the aspects of System, Labour, Process, Control, and so on. (See Table 5.4 for some examples of the different aspects for objectives.)

Step 2: identify and discuss the relevant variables
- Starting with the objective and focusing on one aspect at a time, participants are asked to generate a list of variables that have an impact on the objective.

Step 3: building a connectance diagram
- Step by step, variables in the network are broken down to finer detail.
- For each variable in the middle of the connectance diagram, the potential actions that can be taken to change its value are identified.
- For each action, ask participants to contribute, based on their knowledge and experience, the appropriate management tools that could be utilised.
- Thus, the final connectance diagram should have five basic levels. The bottom level displays the objective or the variable on which analysis is to be performed. In level two, the objective is broken into its different aspects. For example, 'flexibility' is broken into four resource aspects: System flexibility, Labour flexibility, Process flexibility and Control flexibility. In level three, the relevant cause–effect variables for each aspect are displayed. The fourth level displays the actions that could be taken to address the variables. For example, the variables affecting Labour flexibility could be training and working hours. One of the actions that could be taken to address 'working hours' is overtime (see Figure 5.2). Level five consists of the tools that have been identified as being able to address the particular actions or variables identified.
- In building the network diagram, the following guidelines need to be followed:
  1. *Focus on one variable at a time*: Participants are advised to focus on one variable at a time and work systematically to determine

Table 5.4   Key objectives such as quality, cost, time and flexibility can be defined in various different ways

Objectives	Aspects
Quality	• Performance – the primary operating characteristics • Features – optional extras • Reliability – likelihood of breakdown • Conformance – conformance to specification • Technical durability – length of time before the product becomes obsolete • Serviceability – ease of service • Aesthetics – look, smell, feel, taste • Perceived quality – reputation • Value for money • Durability (time between failures)
Flexibility	• Process – the range of activities of which the process is capable • Labour – the range of activities of which each person is capable • Supply system – the range of supply potential, both in terms of quantity and type, of materials, labour or any other input resources • Control system – the range of states for which the system can effectively respond • Product – the range of products which the company has the design, purchasing and manufacturing capability to produce • Mix flexibility – the range of products which the company can produce within a given time period • Volume flexibility – the absolute level of aggregated output which the company can achieve for a given product mix • Delivery flexibility – the extent to which delivery dates can be changed
Price and cost	• Manufacturing cost • Value added • Selling price • Running cost – cost of keeping the product in production • Service cost – cost of servicing the product • Profit • Total lifetime cost for the customer • Perceived value
Time	• Manufacturing leadtime • Rate of product introduction • Delivery leadtime • Frequency of delivery • Speed of quotation • Keeping promises (dependability) • Due date performance

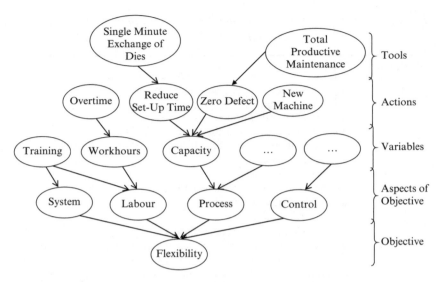

Figure 5.2   Structure of the network diagram for flexibility

its linkages, based on the network structures described in 'building a connectance diagram'.

2. *Consider only 'first order' relationships*: Participants should identify only direct cause–effect relationships. For example, the variable 'Pre-setting' (CV) has an effect on 'Set-up time' (V1) and 'Work centre capacity' (V2). The effect on Set-up time is direct, a first order relationship, whereas the effect on 'Work centre capacity' (V2) is indirect, a lower order relationship. Thus a cause–effect diagram as in Figure 5.3a is incorrect. Note that if 'Set-up time' (V1) is fixed, then a change in 'Pre-setting' (CV) will have no effect on V2. A change in CV can only directly affect V1. The correct representation is therefore as shown in Figure 5.3b.

3. *Loop*: If a 'loop' or 'triangle' appears in the network, it might indicate an error in the logic. The participants are asked to check the reasoning.

- This process is repeated for all variables so that a hierarchical variable network is created. Within the network, the variables at the bottom of the hierarchy have a direct impact on the objective, whereas actions at the top of the hierarchy have an indirect impact on the objective.

- The facilitator should encourage a process in which participants interactively move back and forth among the different levels of the

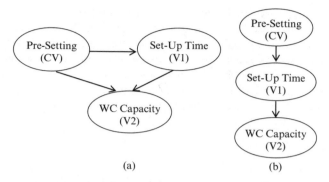

Figure 5.3 An example for establishing a 'first order' relationship

network. Individuals initially form their own networks through separate analyses of the problem variables. Within the process of generating the final network, the process promotes the continual identification of new variables or factors to be included within the discussions. The facilitator should also allow participants to go back and modify their own networks, so that the resulting final network considers the views of all involved in the process, assisting in developing consensus for the process and the outcome.

- In forming the cause–effect network, it is important that participants agree on a set of definitions for the variables. These represent a commonly agreed terminology. If new variables surface during the process, developing consensus of the participants on their definition must be achieved. Without this, the participants may in fact be agreeing to different networks, effectively meaning the consensus is actually an illusion.

Post-workshop actions

The developed connectance diagram is stored within a database associated with the development activity, with copies left with all of the participants to promote further, personal deliberations on the resulting network. This element can allow the logic of the network to be double checked by those involved in preparation for the next workshop.

5.4.2 Workshop 2: Generating Actions

Following a quick review of the current connectance diagram, allowing for the inclusion of the corrections or additions following the personal analysis, the second workshop focuses on the generation of a range of actions. Before this can begin, the variables and their connectances are categorised. To allow for the categorisation of variables and their relationships within the connectance diagram, the strengths of the variables and their connectances need to be collectively assessed, to allow those variables that are considered key for success in the process to be identified: key drivers. With consideration of the operating constraints of the development process, feasible actions are identified with the potential to address the key drivers that have been identified.

Aims
- Review the outputs from Workshop 1.
- Collectively analyse the network to identify key drivers for success.
- Identify a range of feasible actions that have the potential to address the key drivers.
- Summarise the outputs from the workshop and discuss areas for further work.

Step 1: review the outputs from Workshop 1
- Collectively and interactively review the connectance diagram to ensure there is still consensus regarding the network being a realistic representation of the connections that are present within the organisation. By discussing additional suggestions for the network, it is possible to keep it a live representation that can be easily changed to account for the continual learning the whole process initiates.

Step 2: network analysis for key driver identification
- The participants are asked to discuss, and gather information from, existing production records in order to decide on the key variables. For example, the monthly production records will indicate how much production time was utilised on set-up, breakdown and idle time. Variables that contribute to a high percentage of production downtime will be the ones needing attention. To facilitate discussion, a form is used to record the key drivers and the reasons or data for making the choices (see Table 5.5). This may allow quantitative

Table 5.5   Key drivers record form

Key Drivers	Evidence/Reasons	Remarks

data to be added to the connectance diagram, assisting in determining which elements, if changed, will have the greatest effect on the objective.

- This process is conducted interactively, starting with the objective or focus of the analysis, where a number of key drivers are identified. From each of the key drivers, the process is repeated and a further five or six variables are identified. In the model, these key drivers are highlighted using different colours.

Step 3: action generation
- By focusing on those high impact key drivers identified in the previous step, participants are asked to identify the potential actions that could be taken to address them. To stimulate thinking, for each key variable the facilitator should ask participants to look at the corresponding variables, actions and suitable management tools.
- As the process's interactive nature is such an important part of the process, the participants need to discuss and propose actions based upon their knowledge and experience.

Step 4: summarise progress
- The identified actions are then recorded on the Alternative Generation Form (see Table 5.6).
- At the end of the workshop, the outputs including the actions identified should be summarised and integrated with the summary from Workshop 1. This summary should be distributed to participants for review prior to Workshop 3.
- Before the final workshop, a process coordination meeting to discuss progress may help to cement current understanding of the activity within the major stakeholders, such as the project champion

Table 5.6   Alternative Generation Form

Drivers	Actions	Remarks

and/or business owner; this should be conducted by the facilitator or project manager. This has been found to be a useful opportunity to confirm the current direction of work that satisfies those with investments in the process.

BOX 5.1   THE ROLE OF FACILITATOR WITHIN ACTION GENERATION

The role of facilitator within the activity is likely to be critical in determining success; it is their role to initiate, support and when acting as project manager as well, to communicate progress to those within the organisation. For this reason, the following is important when determining who within an organisation should be given the role of facilitator within a TAPS activity. Within the action generation steps, they are essential for creating a supportive group dynamic that is necessary for promoting innovative thinking.

The facilitator should make the idea generation process as much fun as possible, creating an idea-friendly atmosphere, by:

- *Attention to etiquette.* Ideas in early stages need to be nurtured until they can be fully explored and developed. The facilitator should use appropriate questions to help develop ideas, such as: ' Tell me more about the ideas', 'That's a really different approach. Let's see what we can do with it' and 'Let's talk about how we can take care of some concerns I see with this.'
- *Suspending judgement.* Emphasise that quality will come later and recognise and reward the number of ideas that are collected. It may be useful to set quantitative idea generation goals at the outset of an idea workout. This encourages the participants to keep working until reaching their goal and it gives everyone a sense of accomplishment.
- *Humour and playfulness.* Creating a relaxing and fun atmosphere throughout the workshop. Laughter and humour will help participants to challenge the rules and stimulate new seeds for ideas.
- *Good knowledge of idea generation techniques.* By being competent in the ideas discussed within Chapter 4, the facilitator should be able to conduct the activity to promote innovative ideas in an efficient manner.

5.4.3   Workshop 3: Evaluating and Prioritising

Having identified a range of actions that could contribute to the attainment of the objective, this workshop is concerned with evaluating and selecting the most appropriate actions. The decision is complex due to the evaluation process requiring assessment against multiple criteria. A formal decision making technique, the AHP approach, is used. AHP allows a decision maker to structure a multiple attribute decision problem visually in the form of an attribute hierarchy. The AHP evaluation process involves the following stages: a) setting criteria; b) pairwise comparison of criteria; c) pairwise comparison of alternatives; d) synthesis of results; and e) sensitivity analysis.

Aims
- Review outputs from previous workshops.
- Identify a set of criteria to assess the merits of the identified actions.
- Discuss and prioritise the actions using the AHP approach.
- Perform sensitivity analysis to check robustness of the decisions made.
- Identify gaps in knowledge.

Step 1: workshop preparation
- As before, the workshop is introduced by summarising and discussing the outputs from Workshops 1 and 2, specifically the current make-up of the connectance diagram, key drivers and proposed actions. It is important to update them with the additional information and understanding that has been made available since the last workshop.
- The aims and content for Workshop 3 are presented.

Step 2: setting the criteria
- Participants start by establishing a set of criteria for assessing and comparing the identified actions, listing them within a suitable table with appropriate definitions.
- The participants are asked to debate and select those criteria that are most appropriate, a range of criteria of between three and six has been found to be appropriate. Examples include:
  - Time effectiveness – minimising the amount of time required to produce results.
  - Cost effectiveness – minimising the amount of capital expenditure needed for implementation.
  - Sustainability – maximising the ongoing impact of the action.

- Integration – minimising the amount of disturbance caused by the changes.
- The identified criteria are then keyed into the AHP function in the software tool.

Step 3: pairwise comparison of criteria

- Having established the criteria and the range of actions for evaluation, the next step involves the pairwise comparison of the criteria. For each pair of criteria, the participants are required to make pairwise comparisons showing their relative importance. Responses are gathered in verbal form and subsequently codified on a nine-point intensity scale (Table 5.7), which is integrated into the software tool.
- If there are n alternative actions under consideration, the participants need only make $n(n-1)/2$ comparisons, since the comparisons are assumed to be reciprocal. Thus if the solution to the problem is to be judged against three criteria and there are six possible solutions, then there are $[3 \times (6 \times 5)]/2 = 45$ comparisons to be made.

Table 5.7   Fundamental scale

Intensity of Importance on an Absolute Scale	Definition	Explanation
1	Equally important	Two activities contribute equally to the objective
3	Moderate importance of one over another	Experience and judgement moderately favour one activity over another
5	Essential or strong importance	Experience and judgement moderately favour one activity over another
7	Very strong importance	An activity is strongly favoured and its dominance demonstrated in practice
9	Extremely important	The evidence favouring one activity over another is of the highest possible order of affirmation
2, 4, 6, 8	Intermediate values between two adjacent judgements	When compromise is needed

Source: Saaty (1987).

The formula used to determine the number of comparisons is [$k \times n(n-1)$]/2, where k is the number of criteria and n is the number of potential actions.

- Each criterion is compared with every other criterion and the results of the comparison are arranged in a matrix. For each comparison, the participants discuss the most appropriate rating. For example, when creating an important ranking of the criteria 'sustainability' and 'effort', the following question is asked: 'With the objective of cost reduction, which is more important when selecting an action, "sustainability" or "effort"?'

- If there is any disagreement on the input, a geometric mean of the inputs is sought. The geometric mean is an appropriate rule for the combining of individual ratings to obtain the group rating for each pairwise comparison. For example, if there are four participants each with different ratings of 2, 5, 6 and 6, the geometric mean for the comparison will be $(2 \times 5 \times 6 \times 6)^{(1/4)} = 4.35$. Alternatively, through a process such as the Delphi technique, the reasons for each participant choosing each particular figure could be discussed to determine the reasons for the differences. Following this, the reassigned ratings may be closer together; if consensus is not possible, the geometric mean could still be taken.

$$\text{Geometric mean} = (a_1 \times a_2 \times a_3 \times \ldots \ldots a_k)^{(1/k)}$$

Note: a is the input from each participant and k is number of participants.

- The entire AHP computation process is automated by the software although it can be relatively easily included within a spreadsheet to assist with carrying out the process live while participating in the workshop. The result will be an importance ranking of the different criteria.

Step 4: pairwise comparison of alternatives

- The next step of the evaluation process is to perform pairwise comparisons of the chosen actions by referring to each criterion in turn.
- For example, if the objective of the analysis is cost reduction, using the criterion of 'sustainability', the pairwise comparison of the actions A, B and C, the following questions are posed: 'Based on the objective of cost reduction, will action A be more sustainable than action B?'; 'Based on the objective of cost reduction, will action B be more sustainable than action C?'; 'Based on the objective of cost reduction, will action A be more sustainable than action C?'

Step 5: synthesis of results
- Once the pairwise comparison for each of the actions has been conducted, the results are combined to give the overall importance ranking for each action.

Step 6: sensitivity analysis
- Sensitivity analysis is used to investigate whether the decisions will change if there is a shift in emphasis on the criteria. The process is straightforward as long as the effort is put in by the software tool or a relatively able spreadsheet manipulator versed in Excel Solver, for example.
- From this, it is possible to determine the range where the solutions given remain valid and how sensitive results are to changes in inputs.

Step 7: post-workshop analysis
- After the workshop, the outputs including the AHP evaluation results are summarised and integrated with the summary from Workshops 1 and 2. This summary should be distributed to participants.

Step 8: Prioritisation
- The results of the AHP activity are overall ratings for the proposed actions to achieve the objectives.
- The ratings are also broken down into the different criteria, allowing the prioritisation of activities to be selected on the most appropriate for a given situation, such as starting the process with low resource and time requirements of implementation to assist in gaining support for the implementation activity.
- Present within a decision matrix.

5.5   WINNING SUPPORT FOR THE DECISION

Having identified the appropriate action plan, this needs to be widely 'sold' to ensure successful implementation. Acceptance begins with understanding developed from justifying decisions to the affected parties as comprehensively and objectively as possible, which is vital to win their support and to assist with successful implementation. A guideline for producing reports for decision justification is given below. The proposed format is useful for communicating the reasons for the decision to upper management as well as other parties affected by the proposed activities.

5.5.1 Executive Summary

The summary should describe the problem, recommend the course of action and justify the action. The executive summary should be short and concise, no more than one page long. Although important as separate documents to support subsequent activities, the executive summary may include a number of the following elements:

Problem statement
- Describe the nature and scope of the problem.
- Provide the history of the problem, including its cause and the result of any previous attempts to solve the problem.

Objective statement
- Describe each objective.
- Briefly explain the aims.

Connectance diagram
- Present the developed connectance diagram and briefly explain its contents.

Key drivers and alternative actions
- Present the key drivers identified and the reasons for them being described as such.
- List the alternative actions and indicate how comprehensive the list is, if possible.
- Describe each alternative action.

Criteria/measures
- Describe each criterion and explain why it is appropriate.
- Explain the relative importance of each criterion.

Evaluation and selection
- Present the decision matrices.
- Explain which alternative is 'best' and why.
- Outline the drawbacks of each of the other alternative actions.

Follow-up plan
- Prepare an implementation plan, a monitoring plan and a performance measurement plan.

5.6   ADVICE FOR IMPLEMENTATION

Managers who develop a TAPS connectance network will be the first to agree that establishing and evaluating causal relationships between variables are not straightforward tasks. Often a company cannot develop a complete model with full connectance information in the initial exercise. Based on the knowledge and experience gained from TAPS application in industry, the following advice is given:

- *Managers must be committed to the process*: Senior managers must consistently support the process of identifying and measuring causal relationships. They could demonstrate its importance by asking about the progress in monthly operating reviews, for example.
- *Start by building a partial model focused on one objective*: Customising or building a model involves significant management time, analytical effort and internal communication. It may not be worth spending too much time building a complete model in one go. A partial model, one that features only a single manufacturing objective, may be a good starting point. It can be expanded later as managers get used to the process.
- *Keep it simple*: The model should have an intuitive and commonsense basis so that the rest of the organisation can readily understand it.
- *Articulate and communicate the model*: Managers should communicate the model throughout the ranks of the operations function and actively encourage its use to support decision making. The simpler the model, the easier that will be.

5.7   CONCLUSION

As stressed in Chapter 3, the reason for operations strategy implementation being so difficult is the need to develop a capability that effectively combines different elements of an organisation. The capability, whether it is a quality management system or a Balanced Score Card, allows an organisation to understand how focusing developments in a particular area can affect overall performance. The problem with these approaches is that often they require considerable amounts of resources to be allocated to them before the connections within an organisation can be effectively identified. By basing the TAPS process around a stepwise approach that involves many members of an organisation who understand the processes, it is possible to focus direct attention on the development of the relationships and connections that are present within the organisation. The position of the facilitator represents the strategic capability for carrying out this activity that organises workshops to develop the understanding of the system within the different functional elements of the organisation.

Although not necessary, combining the process with the use of software can allow the automation of many of the steps and can assist in giving those charged with the position of facilitator confidence, especially if they are new to the process. Within the later portion of the TAPS process, it is possible for those involved to remain objective, systematically working through potential solutions to the problems they face and choosing the action plans that best meet the needs of the system. Although similar in some respects to strategy charting (Mills et al. 1998) or strategy maps (Kaplan and Norton 2004), the systematic, continually improving nature of the process may allow greater input from those affected. Keeping the process focused around the operations function, the high-level strategic decisions do not need including, allowing those involved to focus on what they are able to affect. The process also allows greater openness of the strategy process that may not be possible if carried out within closed meetings. This is further assisted by the amount of documentation that the process produces which can assist in getting the rest of the system involved and enthused about the activity.

By opening up the strategy process to those within the firm, TAPS allows the organisation to take ownership and actively contribute to all elements if they have information that could help. Although the facilitator may be critical within the initiation stages of the process, as the approach becomes established within the organisation, discussions on developments are possible throughout the organisation to consider novel solutions or investigate proposed connections within the system for testing. Importantly, the aim of the approach is to produce action plans that are relevant to the organisation. However, and although it should be possible to implement them, TAPS is not itself a tool for strategy implementation. For this reason, we move to our concluding chapter on a project management approach to operations strategy implementation. This offers a means of moving forward from an action plan to a process that changes how operations function. The TAPS approach has the potential to give an organisation the strategic capability for developing understanding related to the organisation and to create suitable action plans. In contrast, project management will be outlined as a complementary strategic capability that gives those within an organisation the tools and confidence to begin working on developing their organisation themselves.

NOTES

1. For more discussion on common decision traps, please see Russo and Schoemaker (1989).
2. The original TAPS approach (Tan and Platts 2003b) consists of four main steps. In this book, we simplify the TAPS approach into three steps. Readers are encouraged to read the book *Winning Decisions: Translating Business Strategy into Winning Action Plans* for a full description of the four main steps.

6. Operations strategy implementation through effective project management

6.0 INTRODUCTION

On the critical analysis of the implementation of an operations strategy, the similarities between the activity and a generic project are striking. Both are likely to be complex activities that cannot be effectively accommodated by the main business processes present within an organisation, meaning it is necessary to apply specific attention and resources to facilitate their completion. Another common feature that may be overlooked is that both projects and strategy implementation activities are unique. Even if the strategic activity is the same (lean, the introduction of a standard ERP system or even building a house), the processes required to complete the activity effectively will be unique. Due to numerous forces acting on the activity, modifications will be required to the standard processes and unless they are suitable may even create further problems (Love 2002). For this reason, the use of project management within the sphere of strategy implementation has almost been an inevitable progression, especially when the processes are sometimes considered to have a specific beginning and end. Taking a finite approach to project management with businesses that may not be broken down into specific packages of work, there may also be a need to consider how to integrate the activities into the organisation as a whole (Slack and Lewis 2008).

Within other business fields that utilise projects as a means of effectively and efficiently delivering complex products, considering projects in a finite way may be appropriate, especially if they result in more tangible outputs such as new products, pieces of software or a new facility. However, within fields where the activities may require careful integration with current processes, the efficiency of carrying out the processes within specific departments or teams may be forfeited if introduction is difficult. This is likely to be the reason why this element was included within Platt's 5Ps approach, but it also needs considering within more project-oriented organisations. To assist with this as well as enabling more complex activities, organisations may choose to break large projects down into a number of smaller projects. The 'programme of projects' approach may also be beneficial as it reduces the complexity and time frame of projects, helping to improve control and promote effective completion. Managers realise that project management is a way for them to manage their organisation effectively, that when combined with the ability to terminate poorly performing projects assists in giving them control of the process as a whole (Meredith and Mantel 2006).

By developing their project experience, managers may consider that developing their understanding of specific project management tools can improve their project management ability, assisting with strategy implementation. Unfortunately, by taking an operational view of project management they may overlook how project-focused business sectors effectively achieve their strategy. The strategy within these organisations is not the result of a particular project, or the result of a number of projects; instead it is the 'consistency of actions' (Mintzberg 1978). For example, is Apple Computers' strategy accomplished by the launch of the latest branded product, or the result of all innovations combined with its ability to continue innovating? Although a central part of achieving a strategy, unless it is appreciated that project management tools only assist in the process, additional project management understanding may be necessary to focus projects in a strategic manner. Further problems begin to arise when there is considerable focus on particular tools that make up project management as a subject, rather than how the specific tools assist in the organisation's transformation process. In such cases, organisations may consider themselves competent project managers, but may find it difficult to demonstrate how project management directly assists in achieving their operations strategy.

Another issue related to project management that is similar is how their experience can potentially restrict managers from thinking in a creative manner. This may be present when firms carry out a large number of similar projects and focus on efficiently exploiting their current knowledge and overlook important learning opportunities. In such a situation, managers may even mistake their experience with these projects as ability in project management. With all projects being unique, even with extensive experience of similar projects, managers must appreciate that the activity has never been undertaken before, and should use their experience to prepare rather than plan. If this is not done, the fluid, 'consensual' nature of strategy (Maylor 2005) is less possible, as those involved try to make a project into a repetitive process, losing an important aspect of the approach. They also consider their experience to be what allows them to be able to complete projects, rather than their ability to effectively configure,

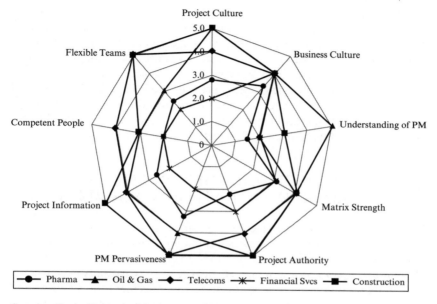

Source: Cooke-Davies and Arzymanow (2003).

Figure 6.1 *Preliminary trial results of the prototype instrument*

coordinate and manage teams consisting of numerous professional skills. This is demonstrated in the abilities of different industries to manage projects in an effective, mature manner that is not necessarily determined by how much of an industry's work is carried out as projects (Cooke-Davies and Arzymanow 2003) (Figure 6.1). Even with similar levels of project maturity, construction projects are still notorious for overrunning and not being completed within the budget (Love 2002).

Taking an approach where experience takes priority over project management as to how organisations achieve their strategy may be why some organisations do not consider project management a strategic capability (Maylor 2005). If this was true, the most innovative organisations, able to efficiently achieve their organisational goals, would potentially be those with the longest serving boards, which firmly disagrees with certain eminent writers (Drucker 1955; Hamel and Prahalad 1994). Maylor (2005) commented that project management not being considered a strategic capability may be founded on simple misconceptions; if an organisation considers project management to be the use of a Gantt chart, it is likely it will not be using the capability effectively. In this type of situation, where projects are simply planned and monitored using a particular tool, can the activity be called project management or simply project planning? Mintzberg, Ahlstrand and Lampel (1998) commented on the planning school having fallen out of favour within the area of strategy due to its lacking scope, making such approaches to project management seem outdated. Interestingly, the Gantt chart was a tool included by Slack and Lewis (2008), which in such a difficult an area of project management as strategy implementation may even seem misplaced, due to its limited ability to contribute to project management.

6.1 CAN PROJECT MANAGEMENT BE CONSIDERED A STRATEGIC CAPABILITY?

If one considers project management to consist simply of a Gantt chart, it is very difficult to consider it a strategic capability; on its own it is little more than a tool for communicating progress. From this perspective, it may be difficult to consider project management a strategic capability even when it is a combination of any number of project management tools (White and Fortune 2002). The same can also be said of previously mentioned strategic capabilities, such as SPC or accounting; it is not what a particular function consists of, it is how it allows different elements of the business to work together more effectively. For this reason, it becomes more important for the different tools of project management to be managed correctly, which requires considerable knowledge and understanding of them. If the use of project tools such as Microsoft Project is promoted without understanding of how the tools should be related to and assist with other activities within the project, it is unlikely their inclusion will noticeably contribute to the process, simply adding extra administrative elements.

Unless the subject of project management is appreciated at a much deeper level, the introduction of additional aspects of project management is less likely to contribute to the project by improving performance. As views of project management develop, considering project management as anything but a strategic capability becomes more difficult to conceive. Meredith and Mantel (2006) approach strategy implementation through project management from two distinct perspectives, both making use of its ability to be considered a strategic capability, which reflects the two main approaches taken in the literature. The first is a more traditional approach to implementation, where the ability to effectively manage and control a project is used to effectively complete particular strategic activities, such as those described by Alexander (1985). The second approach is where the strategy of the project management function is aligned with that of the organisation, which is the necessary approach for more project-oriented organisations.

The first approach, which may consist of one or a number of projects that aim to improve the organisation's capabilities that relate to one or a number of important performance metrics, takes a relatively finite approach. The strategy may consist of a strategic decision as listed by Alexander (1985), but could also be the implementation of a new operating system such as a quality management system or lean manufacturing. By using a relatively competent project management capability, it will be able to move away from an ad hoc, unstructured approach to the project and be able to appreciate how the organisation is able to learn as the project progresses (Remy 1997). Compared with a more traditional approach to introducing new operating systems that roll the system out to the entire company as one activity, a project management approach may choose to take a more systematic approach. By understanding that the project management capability as well as those needed by the new operating system could be developed throughout the implementation process, improvements could be made on two fronts. Through structured assessment of completed processes, the ability to effectively complete upcoming, more complex projects should increase as the overall programme progresses. Whereas an unstructured approach to implementation may lose steam as the enormity of the process becomes apparent, understanding of the current performance of implementation activities may help maintain motivation (Figure 3.4(b)). Such an approach could be considered similar to Wheelwright's and Hayes's (1985) stage 2, where manufacturing ideas are identified in other organisations and implemented within. The benefit of this approach is that with an internal implementation capability, the 'point of entry' may assist with the introduction of activities that depart from current approaches, helping increase the level of 'participation' (Slack and Lewis 2008).

Apple Computers could be considered an example of the second approach, where although the results of each of the individual projects are important for the organisation, they do not represent its development strategy. The definition of strategy as 'consistency of actions' is considerably more relevant in this situation, where the elements of the strategy require aligning with the corporate goals, with the individual end products being even less important to the whole strategy. The project management function in such a situation needs to develop in line with the projects within the system, to be able to effectively manage them even though each project could be a type of project that has not been worked on before. The project management capability allows the effective coordination of increasingly complex activities, which should have the risk of non completion reduced by the skills that are present such as risk management that help to identify, reduce and eliminate problems even before they occur. Through effectively focusing on the development of project management skills that are aligned with overall corporate aims, the organisation can develop a tailored approach to projects that effectively utilises and further develops its internal capabilities. Similar in many respects to Wheelwright's and Hayes's (1985) stages 3 and 4, those within the system are able to focus on what they are best at, in the knowledge there is a function available to effectively develop their innovations into tangible results.

The first approach could be appropriate for organisations present within relatively stable environments, and require step changes in the organisation's performance. Although the project management ability allows them to effectively complete strategic activities, the development of the ability does not represent their own strategy. Their own strategy may be more focused around the continued improvement of their main business functions, possibly through continual improvement activities. The second approach to project management may be more appropriate for more progressive consultancies, which tailor their approach to activities to a specific client. Here, the project management capabilities will be considered more critical and their ability to apply the skills effectively to their clients will be what defines them within the market place. For such a consultancy, it is likely its corporate aim will be customer oriented, focused on providing them with optimised solutions to difficult problems and developing long-term working relationships. To achieve the consultancy's strategy, it is likely to require the continued improvement of the project management capability that allows it to continually improve its abilities to effectively meet and exceed the client's requirements.

6.2   PROJECT MANAGEMENT AS A TOOL OF STRATEGY IMPLEMENTATION

Although appreciating the significance of a project management approach to work is important, including its appropriate integration into the existing organisational structure, project management 'content' cannot be overlooked. Where project management is different from the other strategic capabilities described earlier in the book, is that it is focused directly on achieving goals rather than as a by-product of other functional activities. The problem this may cause is that it could be considered to be an additional function that does not directly contribute to the main business processes, giving weight to an argument of it being a form of unstructured diversification (Hamel and Prahalad 1994). At the same time it could also be considered an additional business function that is focused directly on improving the processes that affect the customer. Through the creation and management of teams of numerous business functions to improve customer satisfaction in every area of the business it may be possible to consider an effective project management function as a true strategic capability.

What project management has to offer strategy implementation is the array of tools that are available, which like value stream mapping in lean, could be considered meta-tools (Bicheno 2004). The tools do not directly assist or enable elements in the strategy process, but help to improve the knowledge within the system, and sometimes promote creativity. Although a number of tools may seem focused on assisting in planning and controlling projects, an important non-planning, creative tool is the work breakdown structure (Burke 2006). The work–breakdown structure uses a systematic approach to problem definition that decomposes the proposed end product into elements of a manageable size. Similar to some of the ideas proposed in Chapter 4, the approach promotes creative thinking while ensuring that all important elements are included. Originally devised for project management of complex military projects, the approach can allow those involved in estimating to systematically build up total projects from 'work packages' that are of a comprehensible size, allowing moderately accurate estimates of time or other relevant resources. Figure 6.2 shows the simple example of a chair; different approaches can be taken to break down the finished item that reflect the specific area of focus – the approach taken below is to divide into the different departments that are involved. Alternatively, the finished item could be divided into components or the personnel involved in completing different activities. The same example will be followed through to show how the different project management tools are applied to different stages of the project process.

After the original problem definition, it is likely the next step will be to build up the project network that represents the interconnections between all the work packages graphically, allowing estimates to be prepared for how long the whole activity will take to complete. By connecting all units together in a manner that accounts for the specific orders and priorities of the activities, it is possible to determine the shortest possible time a project will take to complete, as the network of interlinked work packages will not take the sum of all the work packages to complete, unless the activities are carried out sequentially. Table 6.1 and Figure 6.3 demonstrate this, with the shortest time required through the network highlighted in Figure 6.3; this is known as the Critical Path Method (CPM) to managing projects. Following on from this, by introducing estimates into a network to reflect that it is not possible to be certain of the time required to finish them,

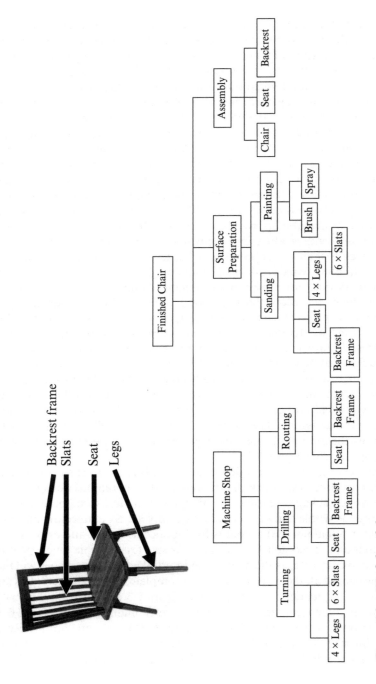

Figure 6.2 Work breakdown structure

Table 6.1   Work package information (no. of hours)

Assemblies	Turning	Drilling	Routing	Sanding	Painting	Assembly	Total
(0) Chair						0.3	0.3
(1) Seat						0.25	0.25
(2) Seat		0.3	0.2	0.2	0.1		0.8
(2) Legs (4)	0.2	0.0	0.0	0.1	0.1		1.6
(1) Backrest						0.25	0.25
(2) Slats (6)	0.1			0.07	0.1		1.62
(2) Backrest frame		0.1	0.2		0.1		0.4
Total	1.4	0.4	0.4	1.02	1.2	0.8	5.22

it is possible to estimate the possibility of completing the project within a certain time frame (Meredith and Mantel 2006). Due to uncertainty with the completion time of unique project activities, this process can be important for determining if additional time should be allocated to assist completion to a predefined schedule. Appreciating that the shortest possible time through the network is only possible if all activities finish on time allows project managers to focus on specific activities that have the potential to make a project run late. Although these activities are likely to be located on the critical path, other elements that are close to the critical path may also need careful monitoring to ensure any delays are within an acceptable range.

As mentioned in Chapter 2, the effective scheduling of resources in project management can be an extremely important activity, which has led to the development of a project management technique to account for this: critical chain (Goldratt 1997). The approach builds upon the Theory of Constraints, where it was appreciated that bottlenecks are what restrict an organisation's ability to improve performance (Goldratt and Cox 1992). The concepts were applied to project management by identifying inherent problems with the Critical Path Method that Goldratt stated was destined to perform badly, simply because of human nature (Goldratt 1997). Understanding that there is generally one constraining resource within a project system, all other activities within the system should be arranged in a manner that supports the bottleneck to ensure that it produces at its highest capacity. Other approaches to organising project processes do not require resources to be considered in this way, meaning that it may be impossible to complete a particular project within the time originally quoted, due to critical resources being scheduled twice (see Figure 6.4, where different shading represents different types of resources). Within

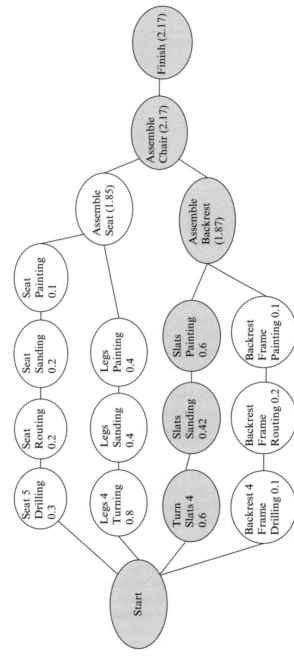

Figure 6.3 Critical path network for manufacturing a wooden chair

Figure 6.4   Resource requirements for the Critical Path Method

projects there are also issues, such as the agency problem[1] (Eisenhardt 1989), Parkinson's law[2] (Parkinson 1957; Gutierrez and Kouvelis 1991), splitting priorities between tasks and the difficulty of rescheduling activities that have been prescheduled to benefit schedules if an activity finishes early (Williams 2004). The network in Figure 6.5 shows the focus around the critical resources (turning, sanding and assembly), understanding that it is certain resources that determine progress; by applying Theory of Constraints concepts to the resources, the performance of the project as a whole can be systematically improved (Goldratt and Cox 1992). Compared with the CPM method, the smoothing of the resources is clearly visible.

By focusing on the critical resources and planning activities to support them, it is possible to increase control of project progress due to the reduced variation in resource requirements that is promoted by the technique. The result is that the network and the scheduling are simplified, reducing the possibility of total project delays by the knock-on effects caused by activities with numerous subsequent tasks being delayed. The critical chain takes into account that tasks can be late and allows for this with a buffer, whose size is dependent on the estimates of the tasks. If the process goes as expected, the buffer is likely to be used up at approximately the same rate as the critical chain progresses, meaning that when the project is complete, the buffer will be used and the project will be finished on time. The use and management of the buffer have an added benefit in that they allow the project manager to gauge the progress against the schedule, so that it can be determined early in the project's life if it is likely to be late, or if estimates were too generous and the project is likely to finish early. Unlike other measures of progress, such as earned value (Meredith and Mantel 2006), critical chain progress is not open to manipulation through representing non critical activities within the measure of progress. Earned value is an important tool to measure progress that can assist in the control of projects, but the simpler nature of the buffer management approach has the potential to be a more powerful communication tool, as it is a simpler, truer measure of progress that accounts for the need to reschedule upcoming activities.

The use of just this small array of project management tools has the

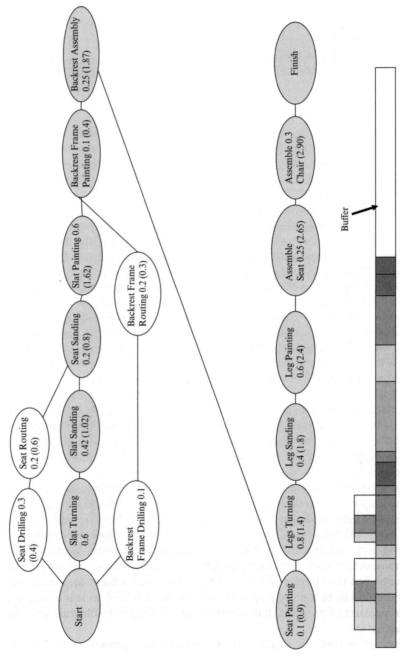

Figure 6.5   Critical chain network diagram and revised resource requirements with buffer

potential to improve visualisation of the activity as a whole as well as assisting in approaching activities using novel approaches. Within a strategy implementation setting, these visualisation and control tools allow those involved to begin viewing implementation as a process that is more similar to their everyday activities. Introducing processes of control and a constructive team dynamic can then facilitate the modification of subsequent activities to take account of what has been learnt from the project since its beginning. Combining this with making up the project out of relatively manageable work packages, assessing progress should be a relatively simple activity, which then means a strategic control system is already present within a project management-based operations strategy implementation activity (Hrebiniak and Joyce 1984; Goold and Quinn 1990). Unfortunately, this is something that can potentially be overlooked within strategy implementation and project management. Unless the tools are used to aid understanding and promoting learning to proactively account for what has been learnt during the process, the benefits of a project management capability may not be exploited. If this situation is present, project management will not be acting as a strategic capability, representing no progression from Mintzberg's, Ahlstrand's and Lampel's (1998) planning school. Without organisations changing their perception of project management, it may be unlikely they will consider project management in a strategic manner; in this case it may not be project management, but experience affecting an organisation's perception of project management (Somerville 2007).

6.3 AS A SYSTEMATIC APPROACH TO CONSISTENCY

With the approach described earlier of an organisation's strategy consisting of its ability to complete projects of a particular type consistently, although the ability to complete activities is critical, the projects themselves need to be able to contribute to the organisation's strategy. The projects need to have consistency between them, reflecting Mintzberg's (1978) consistency of actions and Meredith and Mantel (2006), who stated that project selection needs to be consistent with strategic goals, effectively meaning that in project management, each project represents a strategic action. Maylor (2005) stated that strategy should be more consensual, growing alongside the major activities carried out by the organisation to further establish the approach to operations strategy implementation through project management. Understanding how specific projects can contribute to the strategy can allow those within the system to self-select projects on which to work (Saam 2007). Unfortunately, although this will allow the empowerment of those within the system to take responsibility for the strategy process, it may also allow them to act in a manner that directs the organisation in a direction that is not in line with the organisational vision (Bourgeois and Brodwin 1984; Jenkins, Ambrosini and Collier 2007).

However, if upper management are able to appreciate the benefits of autonomous project managers, who are able to pursue activities they have chosen themselves, the situation does not need to be associated with the same risks that are associated with localised decision making. An important element of project management, that is likely to be of particular relevance to operations strategy as a whole, is the use of management science for decision support, enabling more systematic consistency (Ghasemzadeh and Archer 2000; Balakrishnan, Render and Stair 2006; Meredith and Mantel 2006). Rather than simply relying on culture to define how those within the system work, Meredith and Mantel (2006) outline that quantifying elements of the selection process can help remove intuition from important decisions, which Drucker stated should not be a requirement to be a good manager (Drucker 1955). This could simply be a means of gauging if a particular project is financially viable (a cost-based model), although such a model, as with financial means of controlling an organisation's strategy, does not give sufficient control to the process. However, if the model is created to carefully consider the elements of a project the company deems important strategically, projects that are selected by the model will match with the organisation's development requirements (Meredith and Mantel 2006). For example, the model could consider the current utilisation of staff, if the organisation wants to smooth the flow of projects through the company. A model could also look at the skills required to complete a given project; if the skills that could be developed by undertaking the project were consistent with the organisation's strategy, the profitability of the project may be considered less important.

Meredith and Mantel (2006) spoke of how over time those involved in selecting projects would understand the requirements of selection and actively pursue strategically relevant projects, effectively creating consistency and possibly a culture that is strategically minded. The development of further commitment to the selection and completion of strategically relevant activities could be supported by the introduction of a remuneration system that is suitably aligned with the selection process (Guth and Macmillan 1986). The resulting goal and system congruence should assist in reducing principal risk where it may not be possible to have all information about the agent's activities (Eisenhardt 1989). Although project management tools can assist in monitoring the system through

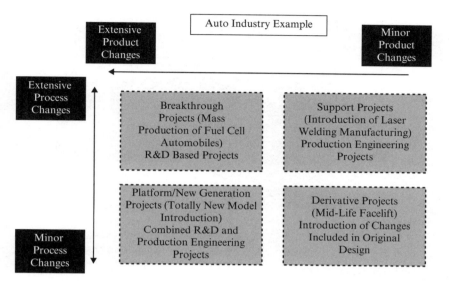

Figure 6.6   Project portfolio process types

the introduction of tools that allow systematic communication of relevant project information, it may not be possible to have all information about a project manager's actions. However, the use of project management approaches could actively reduce the agency problem, potentially offering greater improvements in performance than simply imposing control on the system. These elements can be used to actively remove the risks of agent opportunism where they carry out activities that may adversely affect other actors within the system, while simultaneously improving performance and reducing cost.

An extension of a project selection model is the project portfolio process (PPP) (Wheelwright and Hayes 1992; Hayes et al. 2005; Meredith and Mantel 2006). Rather than having a single selection criterion that may allow appropriate projects to be selected, PPP appreciates that an effective strategic trajectory should be made up of a number of distinct types of projects (Figure 6.6). Irrespective of how appealing particular project opportunities may be, it will only select them if they fit in with the other projects currently in the system. By dividing projects into four areas, Support/enhancement, Derivative, Platform/new generation and Breakthrough, projects of a similar type are always compared, meaning for example that the profitability of a Breakthrough project will not be compared with another type. Although the support projects may have a relatively high return on investment and a quick payback period, because

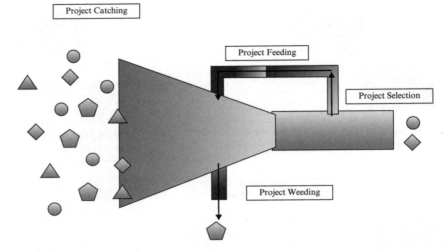

Source: Hayes et al. (2005).

Figure 6.7   Project selection funnel

they require only small, incremental developments in product or process, they do not assist in preparing the organisation for future markets. On the other hand, the Breakthrough projects may not give a return on investment for a number of years, if at all, but the research and design involved in them may be considered important for the contributions the knowledge developed during them can offer the organisation as a whole.

Through the careful construction of a selection model and determining how the portfolio should be made up to reflect the organisation's strategy, an organisation should be able to develop in a structured manner that gives suitable focus to short- and long-term goals. In addition to this, by using an appropriate project selection process, it may be possible to consider a large number of potential projects against selection criteria. Those that may not be appropriate at a particular time can be discarded, kept for future consideration or even have resources allocated to develop them further by carrying out small investigation projects on them. Through this process of weeding and feeding (Figure 6.7) (Hayes et al. 2005) it is possible to develop understanding of projects before committing to them, allowing project selection to be further fine-tuned to the organisation's strategy. In addition to this, the results of completed projects can be assessed against the original selection criteria and the composition of the portfolio to determine if they are directing the organisation in the appropriate direction. If, for example, the current approach is affecting profitability due to market conditions, it may be appropriate to increase the number of short-term projects, until a time when there are resources available to focus on organisational innovation.

When considering project management as a strategic capability, it is possible to consider most project management tools in a strategic manner. One tool that is of particular relevance is system dynamics (Rodrigues and Bowers 1996; Rodrigues and Williams 1998), which is a means of understanding and controlling what happens to a project when changes are made. It helps to explain some of the problems that are witnessed with projects, such as running longer than expected or costing more than originally budgeted. As mentioned earlier, although project management's ability to view the whole project and learn from current activities are important benefits of project management, a careful balance needs striking between current conditions and the original plan. Systems dynamics appreciates that changes are necessary, but the effect of its introduction needs considering in relation to getting the project completed. Appreciation of this led Burke (2006) away from the use of contingencies within a particular project to a programme approach, that was not just to assist in complex projects but also to account for changing conditions. By taking such an approach it may be more appropriate to finish one project and then begin another project, rather than taking into account the changes required, which could help reduce the effects of scope creep (Meredith and Mantel 2006; Young 2007), where it can become very difficult to complete a project. This approach to projects also needs careful control, to allow the customer to receive a product that strikes a balance between meeting current requirements and meeting a schedule (Figure 6.8).

6.4   SUPPORTING ELEMENTS OF PROJECT MANAGEMENT

When introducing a project management function into a traditional organisational structure, although it may cause issues regarding responsibility for project and functional work (Meredith and Mantel 2006; Slack and Lewis 2008), other elements of the approach give considerable structural and organisational benefits. The first of these is related to the structure of the organisation, which although it has become considered difficult to use to implement strategies due to the constraints it puts on the process (Mintzberg, Ahlstrand and Lampel 1998) is considered from a different angle with regards to project management. Relatively early when the implementation of strategy began to be considered, the links between strategy and structure were commented upon (Chandler 1962; Galbraith

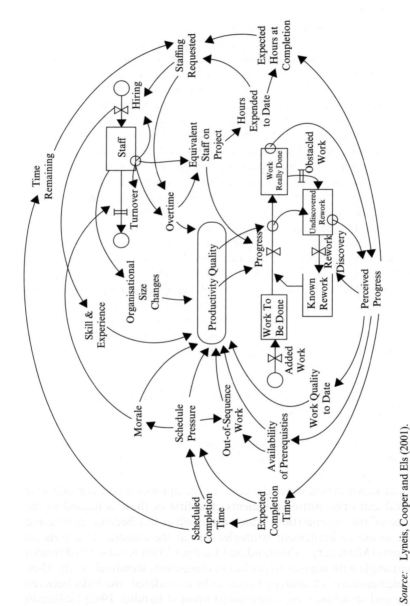

Source: Lyneis, Cooper and Els (2001).

Figure 6.8 Effects of project dynamics

and Nathanson 1978; Bourgeois and Brodwin 1984). However, due to the difficulty and expense of changing the structure, this has sometimes been done as a last resort, only when the original structure has become too inefficient to continue (Galbraith and Nathanson 1978). Although it is beneficial for structure to lead strategy, it is not always realistic, due to the expense required to change, especially if there is uncertainty that a particular strategy is in fact the correct approach for the organisation.

For this reason, the structure approach to strategy's appeal decreased, as although it was significant, as with 'belling the cat' (Jacobs 2002), it was difficult or impossible to implement. However, with the increasing significance and importance of project and supply chain management activities, including such activities as the Japanese Keiretsu (Peng, Lee and Tan 2001), the ability to modify structures easily has become apparent. In these situations, the relationships are more fluid and have the potential to form when the need arises while not disrupting the more traditional functional structure that may be more difficult to change. From project to project or product to product, it is possible within these networks to bring together those elements of a system that are best able to carry out a specific activity, whether it is a person or an entire company. By developing understanding of such an approach to work, Noble (1999) spoke of moving all operations to project-based work, removing the obstacles that are associated with effective cross-functional activities, such as power and leadership. Although only touched upon by Slack and Lewis (2008), the careful consideration of informal networks available to members of a team could be used to improve effectiveness by altering the way the team interacts with the organisation as a whole (Noble 1999).

Noble (1999) spoke mainly of the importance of creating an implementation network within an organisation and using this as a basis for carrying out all organisational activities as projects. Jenkins, Ambrosini and Collier (2007) spoke of this in a more general sense, where the ability to create teams made up of the most able people assisted in creating a competitive advantage. By taking this further, brokering specific connections within the network could take place to bring specific skills into a project team that may not even be present within the boundaries of the firm (Jenkins, Ambrosini and Collier 2007). The approach lends itself to the e-enablement of product development (Bal and Swift 2002), where all network connections may be brokered by a third party, allowing products to be developed by virtual companies with no base or costs associated with operations. Starkey, Barnatt and Tempest (2000) took this further by appreciating the importance of not simply considering single connections within the network, but particular groups that reform over time, giving the efficiency of hierarchy without associated costs. Within a project structure, reoccurring teams may be able to develop specific project capabilities, assisting in the completion of particular types of work or working with particular clients.

The third area that should receive focus to assist in improving project management effectiveness is experience. Although experience has already been mentioned on a number of occasions as having some negative effects, restricting those involved in effectively analysing situations based on facts rather than hunches, it is now referred to in a different context. Within a project management setting, the term 'experience' can have a number of different meanings. In the traditional sense of the word, it could mean experience of a particular type of project, which like functional experience may assist in adding consistency and increasing confidence in completion, but may also lead to reductions in adaptability. In a different way, the experience developed could be purely project management based, where there may be very little consistency between the different types of projects on which the project managers work. In this situation, traditional experience is even potentially replaced by problem solving ability and the understanding of effective approaches to completing projects as what is considered important for completing activities. With the majority of project teams being unique, having the ability to add confidence about completing a project that no one within the team has worked on before is likely to be of considerable benefit. Taking a lead role within the team that may not be based on subject knowledge should assist in effectively working with the team as a facilitator, promoting an effective team dynamic. Although it may not seem as possible working within a specific company, by appreciating the importance of separating project management and sector knowledge, the project management ability could remain the important element within project activities.

The above elements of project management that assist in the careful selection, structuring and control of projects to realise a strategy aim to outline the greater abilities project management has rather than simply planning or tracking the strategic activities. Pfeffer and Sutton (2000) and Bossidy and Charan (2002) both spoke of the difficulties companies have in accomplishing their strategic goals; although the development of subject- or process-based knowledge may not be difficult, the problems occur when it comes to applying this knowledge to the organisation. Potential problems are listed by Beer and Eisenstat (2000), which all affect how the ideas are integrated into an organisation, but there may simply not be suitably confident people within an organisation able to effectively lead the activities. With a project management approach to work that is focused on the completion of complex activities, their position within the organisation forms a direct link between the activity and top management. Using their position, project managers are able to form strong links directly between frontline activities and top management's vision. The ability of the project management capability to act as a function that supports and involves all within the organisation in the process should assist in gaining bottom-up support for the strategy (Akao 1991). The practical approach taken requires those involved to participate in the strategy process, promoting learning by doing rather than by reading or seeing (Pfeffer and Sutton 2000), with project management translating ideas into the process of getting things done (Bossidy and Charan 2002).

6.5 ELEMENTS REQUIRED FOR CONSIDERING PROJECT MANAGEMENT IN THIS WAY

Unfortunately, poor appreciation of project management as an approach to working is not the only possible cause for project management not being considered as a strategic capability. Participation and Point of Entry (Slack and Lewis 2008) are both important elements of project management that affect how an organisation is able to use its capability to implement strategy. When speaking of these elements Meredith and Mantel (2006) commented that if the project management function does not integrate suitably with the organisation, creating synergy between business and project activities may be difficult. There may be issues with split responsibilities: if they have not been defined, functional staff may not be fully committed to activities that take them away from their line activities that need completing for their direct superior. However, a considerable benefit of project management is that it is able to operate outside or around potentially restricting organisational structures; to reduce possible resistance, it may be necessary to carefully define the aims of the project. By understanding that the development activities are in the best interests of the organisation it may be possible to reconcile relationships between functional and project managers.

Although Meredith and Mantel (2006) spoke of this being a potential issue within an organisation, Drucker (1955), in his argument against 'line and staff' employees, stated how this problem should never exist if all activities are directed in an appropriate manner, such as satisfying the customer. Resolving this issue does not necessarily require the creation of official lines of command and procedures listing where responsibilities lie; instead it requires all involved to take responsibility for strategic activities. Drucker (1955), Akao (1991) and Bossidy and Charan (2002) spoke of the amount of time top managers should be required to spend on long-range strategic work, which infers that functional managers should almost be responsible to those carrying out the strategic activities, the project managers. With the project managers being directly responsible for strategic activities, functional staff, where possible, need to be focused on achieving the aims of the project, which should represent the aims of the organisation as a whole. Such a departure from a traditional structure by altering clear lines of responsibility may be difficult for members of an organisation restricted by experience and mindset, but to refuse such an approach effectively represents refusing to answer to the customer.

6.6   APPROACHES TO A DEVELOPMENT STRATEGY

As with an inefficient company structure, even if an organisation may not be actively pursuing a development strategy, there may arrive a time and situation when a need to change may seem essential to remain competitive within the market place. As mentioned in Chapter 3, this may be done through the employment of a consultancy to carry out analysis of the operating system and propose an effective plan to solve the situation they have found themselves in. In some cases, this may even involve active participation within the process to allow the activity to be completed within a certain period of time. Unfortunately, as Bourgeois and Brodwin (1984) comment, although the approach can be effective, it can also be costly and if inappropriate, even with assistance, may be difficult or impossible to implement (Wheelwright and Hayes 1985). If development is necessary in today's 'hypercompetitive environment' (Pryor et al. 2007, p. 3) just to continue operating, would it not be advisable to develop such capabilities within the organisation that allow changes to happen continually? Or at least, would it not be beneficial to employ the consultant on a regular basis to allow more gradual changes to minimise the instability the change process creates?

As stressed in earlier chapters, the development of internal capabilities that allow the implementation of strategies is likely to be beneficial compared with regularly employing consultancies to reinvent an organisation. However, there may be times when the activities that need carrying out are unrelated to the development strategy or the organisation's operating focus. For this reason, employing an external capability may be a necessity, and not reflect badly on the organisation, that there are no adequate capabilities in the organisation to implement its own strategy. The following section investigates how different development strategies can be approached and how a project management function may relate to them. The main aim of the second half of the chapter is to establish how the ideas related to project-oriented companies may be relevant to more traditionally structured organisations. As mentioned earlier, the structural transformation of a firm may only be considered appropriate as a last resort, so to propose a need to change the entire organisational structure would be considered inappropriate and outdated. For this reason, the following begins from a point where an organisation appreciates the need for change and may already employ an external consultancy or simply outsource certain elements of its work. From this point, the relevance of the situation will be linked to an organisation's own internal activities to establish how project management can be applied onto the existing organisation, to complement, not necessarily change, the organisational structure already present.

6.7 EMPLOYMENT OF AN EXTERNAL CONSULTANCY

The appreciation of the above elements of project management is likely to be important to improve the effectiveness with which a project management function can operate within or with an organisation, but may not be essential. If an organisation appreciates the need to develop in a way that requires capabilities or resources that are not currently present within the firm, it is likely that some form of consultancy will need to be employed. Examples of this could be financial auditing, training or third party accreditation. The example that will be used to explain the different scenarios is a construction project, due to the project-oriented nature of the work and increased complexity of the situation, but the ideas can be applied to other types of externally focused activities. Other types of external consultancies are likely to have some similar features, although there may be fewer external consultants, such as the situation investigated by Akdere and Azevedo (2006). Figure 6.9 outlines the difficulties that can be created even with a single external consultant introduced into an organisation and how the complexity of the interactions can be reduced with internal consultants. However, if the development of skills present in the consultancy is not consistent with those required by the overall strategy, developing an appropriate capability in house may not maintain consistency.

If there is more than one external consultant, each interaction will need carefully controlling to prevent the number of separate interactions making the project team unworkable. As outlined by Slack and Lewis (2008), the effective integration of the strategic activity with the main operation is likely to affect the end results. In a construction setting this may

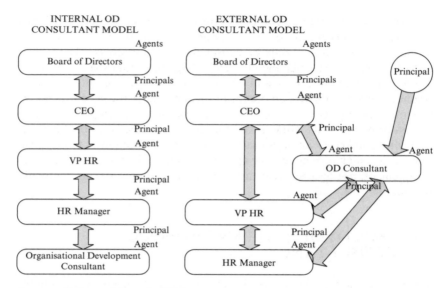

Source: Akdere and Azevedo (2005).

Figure 6.9 *An internal and external model of the organisation and the OD consultant*

be less likely, due to the interactions between the parties mainly taking place at a board level, but effective consideration of end user requirements is still likely to improve end product performance. Although the need to consider integration into the main operations may potentially be less in a construction setting, or indeed consultancy activities that may not have an end product that affects the main operating activity, managing the situation is still important. Even if the interactions are only between the top management and a consultant, careful control of the interactions has the potential to greatly affect project performance, as outlined in the following project coordinator approach.

6.7.1 Project Coordinator

Without suitable understanding of the importance of an effective project management capability to aid the effective completion of strategically significant activities, it is unlikely this will be a selection criterion of a client. Without an appreciation of how a project management capability can add tangible value to a project, the need to gauge ability and possibly contract more expensive consultancy services may not be appreciated. Focusing on price and experience of the firm, the client may tend to select a project management function with considerable experience, while not fully appreciating how an effective project management capability can allow some firms to charge considerably more for their services. In this situation, there is likely to be a legal requirement for competency and certain accreditation, giving the client confidence all activities will be carried out to the required standard, without exposing them to undue financial or legal risks. However, in this situation, without appreciating how project management is able to draw different functions together or understanding the specific aspects of the project, it is unlikely that the value they add to the project is noticeably more than the sum of the constituent parts. If the project management capability does not noticeably contribute to the outcome of the project, it is unlikely specific focus will be given to its development. For this reason, to develop the profitability of the organisation, there may be a tendency to add other functions to increase the value of the contract. Alternatively, they may aim to improve efficiency by controlling the amount of time a project manager engages in a particular activity, so a single manager is able to work on more projects.

In this situation, although the project coordinator may have experience in the general business sector, they may not have client-specific knowledge. This may make it difficult to form a close working relationship with the client and require the client to take an active involvement in the project to ensure the project progress is to suitable standards. The situation could possibly be improved by socialisation activities within the client's firm (Johnson and Medcof 2007), allowing the project manager to build better empathy with the client from first hand experience. However, this could represent the project manager spending time and resources on activities that are not in line with their own development strategy as it could not be transferred to other clients. However, if this was not done the client's involvement with the project is likely to create a negative situation within the project team, where the original scope changes, affecting subsequent activities as well as activities that may have already been planned, resulting in schedule creep (Rodrigues and Bowers 1996). Without an appropriate understanding of project management concepts, the coordinator will neither be able to take a central role within the team nor will they be able to effectively manage the changes requested by the client (Figure 6.10). The result of this may be a degradation of relations within the team, as each element pursues their own goals rather than focusing on the client's end product due to a lack of project unity and focus.

Unless the project management element takes a proactive role within the team, it is unlikely the client will be able to notice improvements

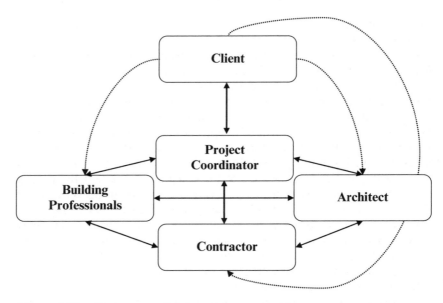

Figure 6.10   Project coordinator project network

between projects that may be present if project managers are willing to take a more experimental approach to working (Wheelwright and Hayes 1985). Without being active within the team, the need to act differently between projects may not be immediately apparent, reducing the perceived value of a critical post project completion review that has direct input from the client. If this does not take place, even though there is a relatively high level of interaction with the client, there may not be a process present to determine and align success factors with those of the client, meaning internally successful projects may not satisfy the client. If the information available within the system is not appropriately used, although there may be an organisational aim, unless work is critically reviewed, developments may be uncoordinated and ad hoc (Remy 1997). The lack of improvement activities can also have repercussions outside the project management function that result from them not taking a strong position with the project team. If they are unable to effectively influence contractors within the team, it is unlikely they will be able to resolve contractor issues from previous projects. This may allow contractors to continue to pursue their own goals that do not reflect the goals of the client's project, resulting in sub-optimal results and low client satisfaction that may all be directed towards the project management function.

Client strategy

Although the above situation may not seem appropriate for many complex strategies that require effective management for completion, the approach will be more appropriate for standard activities that may be less complex. If the client requires an external contractor to carry out specific activities whose performance of the tasks will not greatly affect the outcome, the savings in fees that are possible with the approach will make it suitable. Within the building industry, this may mean the construction of a large number of simple elements where, over time, client standards can be learnt and experience will allow problems to be effectively resolved. The situation will mean savings in fees will be increased due to the number of projects; however, due to them still being projects and in some respects unique, it will be important for the client to ensure consistency when there is a need to account for localised requirements. In this situation the lack of project management ability may still be a hindrance if they are unable to effectively manage conditions that arise during a project. For this reason, it is likely that increasing the level of project management ability, if only slightly, could have a noticeable effect on performance, allowing them to complete activities with more certainty and develop confidence with the client that if unforeseen problems occur they will not need to get directly involved.

6.7.2 True Project Managers and Project Leaders

With the appreciation of the importance of an appropriate project management capability combined with the need to optimise a particular aspect of the development strategy, a client may have very different selection criteria for a project management capability. In this situation the presence of industry accreditation within the firm is likely to be assumed as a base requirement for market presence. The criteria that are important for the client is whether they will be able to work well together, if they will be able to manage the project team effectively and whether they have the ability to produce an optimised solution. The cost aspect of the service is likely to be considered in a long-term perspective, where although the upfront fees may be higher, the confidence in there being no delays combined with extra earning potential associated with an optimised solution will offset the extra initial expense. The project manager needs to be able to convey to the client from an early stage in their relations that although the projects they will be working on are unique, they have produced similar projects, are aware of potential problems and know how to actively manage them.

To be able to actively manage projects, the presence of good, subject- rather than experience-based knowledge of project management is likely

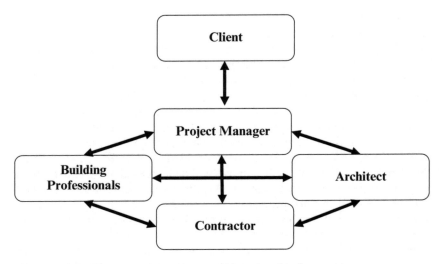

Figure 6.11   True project manager and project leader

to be necessary. With confidence in their project management ability, they are able to take a strong role within the project team, bringing together unique teams that may not have a history of working together, but by representing the client can align the goals of the activity (Figure 6.11). The strong position within the team combined with client focus assist in the team being more responsive to client input that may alter previously approved plans. Appreciation that the client's ultimate satisfaction is what is important, the team is able to alter plans to account for changes in the most effective manner. Critically analysing how contractors affect the project outcome may direct them towards developing long-term relations with certain critical suppliers. By appreciating the need for supply chain management and effective contracting, better working relations can be fostered with the critical contractors that may otherwise have the potential to disrupt team dynamics. Within the building industry context, the building contractor is such an example, where experience of being self-managed may mean they tend towards business-as-usual practices and may resent having to alter the way they work.

Building a project management capability upon industry knowledge ensures standards will be met, with the effective project management capability allowing stronger bonds to be created within the project team. The result of this should be a client that is more confident in project progress and may also be combined with more confidence in working standards due to a general greater level of control in the project process. For this reason, the client will be less likely to communicate directly with the other contractors, unless it is within a more formal setting, where proposed changes are discussed with the team and potential solutions are decided upon, preventing problems of system dynamics. With the true project manager, they may be involved in the early stages of the design process, assisting in reducing oversights and changes in subsequent project processes. The true project manager may not have specific client-based knowledge; for this reason it will be important for them to be able to actively manage client initiated project changes to take account of developments in the client's business sector during the project's life.

The project leader or interim development management position builds an additional capability on top of project management to allow them to effectively take a position on the board of the client and take full responsibility for the external activities. To be able to take up such a position, it is necessary for the project manager to have sector-specific knowledge that allows them to form close working relations, promoting the development of client-specific solutions. The close interaction allows the solution to be specifically tailored in a way that may not be possible if the client is unable to relate the sector knowledge to the project. In addition to project management-focused personal development, the project leader may also participate in sector-specific learning, to appreciate how industry and sector knowledge relate to each other. From this, the project leader may even be able to educate the client who may be inwardly focused on their operations and not appreciate what represents the industry's cutting edge. By combining all these elements, it is possible for the client to be presented with solutions that may be better than they are able to imagine, they are completed on time and should be actively managed to account for changes during the project process.

For the two different types of project management organisation, the true project manager and the project leader, there is an important difference between the types of work they carry out. To be able to offer the client an in-depth appreciation of the client's area of business, considerable time and resources will need diverting to the creation of an appropriate knowledge base. Although this allows the project leader to take a position of leadership and take development responsibility from the client, it also restricts the types of projects for which they are able to offer such a total service. Unless they are able to use their knowledge effectively on a project, it is unlikely the client will be able to benefit suitably from the skills present, reducing the long-term benefit they receive from employing a more expensive consultancy. The same is also true, but to a lesser extent, with the true project manager, who may not be required to use all their project management ability on very simple projects. This reflects Hayes's

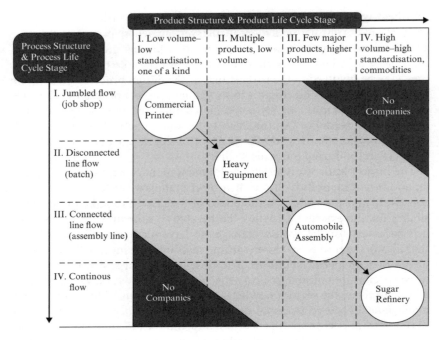

Source: Adapted from Hayes and Wheelwright (1979).

Figure 6.12   *Product–process matrix: matching major stages of product
and process life cycles*

and Wheelwright's (1979) product/process matrix (Figure 6.12), where it
is important to match the capabilities present with the requirements of the
product or service. Whereas the project leader is likely to be restricted to
higher flexibility, lower volume markets, the true project management firm
may be able to offer a broader range of products or services. In addition to
being able to offer non sector-specific services, by varying the amount of
involvement with the client, they may be able to work on projects that are
highly specialised, but also more standard projects. Increasing their target
market and number of potential clients should allow them to offer a lower
cost service by generally having less involvement with the client but also
reducing business risk associated with having limited market appeal.

Client strategy
The client's strategy is likely to be quite different for these two approaches
to project management. The significant relation within the network is

that between the project manager and the client. With the true project manager, apart from socialisation or experience developed from past projects with a client or similar clients, it is less likely they will have a deep understanding of the client's field of business. For this reason, the majority of what they will be bringing to the relationship will be industry knowledge, and it is the responsibility of the client to address the majority of sector development aspects of the project. Unlike the project coordinator, changes and requirements should be actively managed, but there is an unknown for the client as to the amount of involvement that will be required on a given project, that may restrict the rate of the developments. The type of strategy for which the approach is likely to be appropriate is unique, tailored projects that reflect the client's own internal development strategy. The ability to develop the main business process is likely to be considered core to what the client adds to the development strategy, and the ability of the project manager to effectively include these into the process while still completing projects to schedule is important. Due to the continually developing nature of the projects and the strategy, the optimisation of a single project is not paramount, but rather that the projects are continually evolving to reflect the client's main business capabilities.

With the strong relationship that is created with the project leader approach and greater responsibility for the outcomes, the consultancy fees are likely to be considerably higher than a non sector-specific true project manager. The responsibility taken on in the role is likely to reduce the direct involvement of the client, allowing them to focus on their main business processes. In this situation, it may be the running of the business processes that is of primary importance, meaning the receipt of an optimised solution will give the best return on investment over the operating life cycle. The extra invested in a project management capability should result in increased earnings that depending on the life of the project may make the interim development manager the lowest total cost solution (Kaplan and Norton 2004). If the client's development strategy is not of a finite length, the extra costs associated with the consultant could potentially be better spent on developing an internal capability. In addition to this, there may be another potential problem that if the strategy is not finite, the project leader may be able to develop and direct the client's strategy in a way they see fit. Although it may be considered preferable to relinquish an element of the business that may not be core, the project leader may be able to develop their position on the board, creating an increasingly dependent client. By effectively locking the customer into future contracts, the board may become increasingly dependent on their services, allowing them to further increase fees (Kaplan and Norton 2004).

6.7.3   Project Team

Elements of both the above approaches can be identified in the third approach, by combining the multiple disciplines that may be present within a project coordinator firm but focusing them around project management. In this situation, rather than diversifying skills within a firm to increase profitability, additional skills are brought in depending on how well they complement skills already present. The focus of how they complement is importantly directed towards the client and how bringing additional capabilities into the firm will directly improve the service they receive. Rather than focusing on the additional function in isolation, the value added to the project can be considered in regard to every additional interaction the function has with the team that would not be possible with an external function. Rather than simply added, the profit associated with a particular function, and value associated with introducing the function into the organisation, is a product of the team as a whole and the standard of the end product.

Taking a similar position in regards to the client as a true project manager, there remains a specific need for input from the client, although as many of the functions are present within a single firm, the client can easily work directly with the team. All business functions will continue to contribute their constituent parts to the project, but as all functions are located within a single organisation a concurrent engineering approach can be taken. Concurrent engineering is an approach that considers the whole process at once to allow the design stage to take account of subsequent processes, helping to reduce the need for mid process changes, or a designed part that cannot be produced within the real world. Rather than problems arising in particular areas of the project and a meeting of the project team being called, all those involved can quickly discuss the issue and prepare solutions. In this way problems can be discussed effectively much sooner than the previously discussed project management arrangements. The client does not need to be consulted until issues have been discussed internally, allowing them to present a number of potential solutions with professional advice much sooner than even the project leader. Although a project leader may have a broad knowledge, it is unlikely they will have the in-depth knowledge of the professionals that make up the team. Importantly, by involving the client in this way in all important elements, the personal responsibility of the project manager may be reduced, assisting in reducing the cost of the service.

With the client interacting with the team, although general communications is focused through a project manager, it allows all within the team to be directly responsible to the client (Figure 6.13). With the other

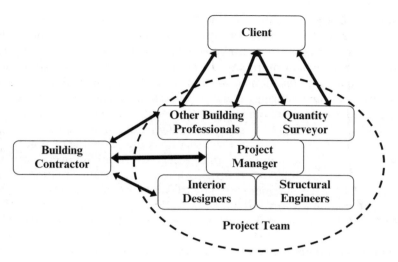

Figure 6.13 Project team

arrangements, less creative professionals, doing more standard work, may not consider the importance of their work in relation to the client. Being directly responsible to the client means if there is a certain issue with the project, the team member most able to handle the issue is able to contact the client directly. This also means that with the large amounts of communication that are present within a project, as the project manager is not the single point of contact, they should not represent a communication bottleneck, as they might if all information is expected to be passed via them. If the project manager no longer has to act as a proxy for the client when communicating with professionals or vice versa, the project group allows those present to better utilise skills while simultaneously reducing risks of miscommunication. If the project leader or coordinator must discuss technical issues with other members of the team for communication with the client, it may be necessary to have a broad working knowledge of all functions within the project team. What this could represent within the project leader team is doubling up of skills that may be reflected in the fees but may not add significantly to the project output. In the project team, it could be said that the project manager does not need to know, they simply need to know who to ask or call upon.

Although the project manager may only have the same level of project management competency as a true project manager, there is potential for them to take a stronger role with the external contractor that results from the team acting as a single unit. The project team can act as a single project element that has all skills available to it and can modify the skill sets to meet the needs of a particular project by acting as a network node within a larger organisation. In addition to the improvements in team dynamics that the arrangement promotes, the structure can allow more structured channels of communication between the team, client and external contractors. Rather than requiring official channels to be in place to exert control, the external contractors can appreciate the knowledge and ability that are available to them. In addition to promoting regular dialogues between all team members and the client, the structure could allow the external contractors to be included in the team to a degree, promoting overall project integration of the different elements. Although in certain situations there may still be a need to remain separate (possibly for legal reasons), by promoting communications and integrations the 'us and them' mentality that may be present within the project coordinator arrangement is likely to be reduced.

Due to the number of project-related activities present within the organisation, the project team approach is more akin to project-oriented organisations, carrying out the majority of their work as projects. Even though the clients are external, the project management function is likely to face some of the same problems and obstacles as those experienced when working within a larger organisation. If there are numerous teams operating within the firm, it will be possible to arrange project teams to make the best use of available skills to best meet project requirements. Using a project portfolio process, possibly with a member utilisation selection element, the formulation of project teams could be aligned to reflect these elements. Through carefully controlling the process, the formulation of project teams could reflect the organisation's strategy to allow for a global optimal rather than maximising the output of a single project while other projects do not have appropriate resources available that may reduce the performance of other projects within the system.

Client strategy
Due to the abilities of the project team being relatively similar to the 'true project manager' it is likely that the client's strategy will be similar. However, the firm where the project team was observed was created as an architect partnership, which adds another element for consideration. Due to the increased prominence of the architect within the project team compared with the other project management arrangements, it is likely the resulting projects will develop in a way that reflects the architect's developing appreciation of the client's requirements. With all elements of the project team being focused around optimising design, while simultaneously considering all relevant business functions, the design quality should

improve. By effectively integrating the client requirements into initial designs, there is potential to consider all elements of the process from the start, appreciating how decisions made early on will have to be managed by them later in the process. For this reason, the client strategy may have a greater focus on development, due to the ability to effectively integrate ideas throughout the process. For project types other than construction, although there may not need to be a particular area of focus for the project manager, other than project management, a particular area of focus may allow the approach to be tailored to the specific needs of the client. Due to the greater involvement of the client in the early stages, the level of in-process alterations may be lower than with the 'true project manager' approach, helping to build greater confidence in the client that the project team will inform them of all relevant issues. This may even reduce the level of general involvement with the client, allowing for a greater rate of expansion than the true project manager while allowing greater tailoring to the solution to meet their needs.

6.7.4 In-House Project Management Capability

As mentioned with the employment of a consultancy for internal process development, not carrying out the activity internally has the potential of forfeiting important learning processes that may assist with future developments. Although in the case of capital expansion, through the construction of additional facilities, the employment of external capabilities may be necessary, the decision to take project management in house may ultimately need considering against the overall strategy. Where the project leader approach is appropriate for a strategy that focuses on business performance, the learning process of the project leader does not reflect the client's own strategy. Similarly, with the project group or true project manager approach the client's learning is carried out in parallel with the development strategy, reflecting the continual development of the client. The problem with this situation is that as the number of projects increases, the commitment of the board to continually track and develop the product may create a bottleneck. A potential solution for such a situation would be to employ an additional member of the top management team who is responsible for development activities.

By working closely with the board, it may be possible to develop a clear understanding of the organisation's strategy and effectively integrate this information into the project team (Figure 6.14). With the development responsibilities being focused externally, the development manager will be able to take a similar position to a project leader within a team. Although it may be considered appropriate to develop industry capabilities in house,

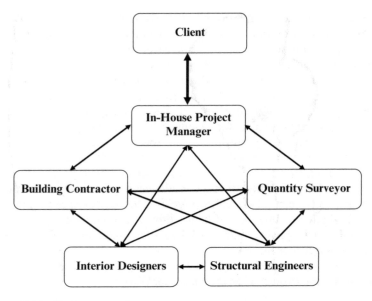

Figure 6.14   In-house project manager

this may represent unstructured diversification if they do not make use of other capabilities present within the firm (Hamel and Prahalad 1994). For this reason, the internal development manager may choose to employ a project coordinator to ensure legal requirements are met. This would also ensure that there were appropriate supporting capabilities present within the team. In this situation, the development manager would bring project management and sector information to the team. By approaching the development activity as a long-term activity, through focused development of the product design, the strategic trajectory can be specifically tailored. The fact that the project manager may not operate within the industry may make taking a strong position of leadership slightly more difficult, but by focusing on good leadership skills, project management and customer-focused project goals, the creation of an appropriate team dynamic should still be possible.

Depending on the specific requirements of the client's development strategy, the issue of team leadership could be resolved by recruiting a project manager from the industry in question and carrying out a process of socialisation (Johnson and Medcof 2007). Alternatively, a client employee could develop their understanding of project management and begin working with current projects to develop a suitable position within the project team combined with subject-based project management training.

Taking this approach is in line with Drucker (1955), where giving those within an organisation the opportunity to develop while effectively using their business function knowledge was considered important to improving the performance of an organisation as a whole. Both of these options are likely to require considerable time and resources directed to a capability that may not be the core of the client's business. The cost of this project management development will need careful consideration against the potential product development aspect as well as the cost savings realised from not employing more expensive external project management capabilities. For the client, the approach does have considerable risks attached, as with the project leader restricting their customer base, the client is restricting their development strategy to one of expansion. There may also be an additional element that the project manager may have considerable responsibility placed on them for project and strategic success, which may lead to over-involvement in the project team. Unless their involvement is carefully controlled to prevent smothering with unwanted or unneeded attention, this may even lead to a weakening of the project bonds, resulting in a reduction in project performance.

Client strategy
In a similar way to the project coordinator, the client's strategy is likely to be one that focuses on increasing the size of the organisation. Unlike the project coordinator, it is important for the product development to reflect concerted internal learning that takes place continually. This is possibly initiated by a board that sees the process of developing their products as what defines them within the market place and reflects their long-range vision within which they do not want to involve external entities. The added costs involved with employing the more expensive project management capabilities may be considered more effectively deployed on focused internal product development. An extreme of this approach could be a property developer, whose ability to carry out the activity defines their whole business and continued development of the products allows them to maintain their position in the market. Within other businesses, the strategy could possibly consist of both increasing the size of the organisation, but also increasing the value of the organisation as a whole.

6.8   INTERNALISING PROJECT MANAGEMENT

One of the first steps of the strategy process is building an understanding within the organisation that the current approach to business, even if it may be successful at the moment, will not guarantee success in the future

(Hamel and Prahalad 1994). This means that for a company that is pursuing a development strategy, the top management either appreciate this or may realise there are entrepreneurial opportunities within the market place they are able to exploit (Drucker 1955). As already mentioned, to pursue a development strategy it may be inevitable that at least elements of project management will be involved at some point, especially if external firms employed carry out a large portion of work in this manner. These will be important aspects of a development strategy, especially one of capital expansion, which is why the above focuses on the external elements of such a strategy. However, unless the development strategy is that of a property developer, it will be necessary for the activities carried out by the project management firm to be effectively integrated into the firm's core business processes.

For this reason, even if they do not fully appreciate it, they may already be carrying out their own internal portion of the development strategy as projects. The success of a particular project that makes up the client's development strategy not only depends on the success of the external elements, but requires suitable integration with internal elements. If the two projects are not suitably coordinated with each other, there may be considerable financial penalties, as well as benefits of one successful project being unrealised. For this reason, the introduction of a suitable, possibly administratively focused project management capability may be beneficial not only to assist in improving coordination between the two projects but to allow for improvements in internal performance. Appreciating how project management is applicable to different areas of business other than where it was originally applied could allow top management to realise that an in-house project management capability could focus their development activities inwards.

Understanding that the external development strategy is the total of a number of projects, the same ideas could be applied to internal developments. Most organisations are likely to have a corporate or company mission statement, whether it is to conform to a quality control standard or to aid the development of the company. Although the creation of a suitable, relevant statement requires careful consideration to reflect the needs of the business and market, success is generally determined in a subjective manner rather than from results. By beginning to take a project management view to strategy, rather than defining the strategy out of broad, potentially meaningless, top-down targets, strategic activities can begin on a small directed scale. Possibly using a selection model, or simply critically assessing the expected outcome of the project against the vision, project management could assist in selecting suitable projects. The finite nature of the projects also means that on completion the results can be critically assessed to aid systematic process development to improve sub-sequent project performance. Post completion reviews carried out with the project team act as an important stage, allowing the analysis of the selection criteria, but also aiding personal development of those involved with the team to improve project capabilities in general. Compared with more general approaches, that may set board targets without firm dates, the focused nature of the project approach should assist in preventing the loss of interest in the latest management drive (Drucker 1955, pp. 110–11).

With the continued assessment of projects, post completion, combined with subject-based knowledge of project management, it should be pos-sible to create a capability that can be deployed within the organisation. By involving frontline staff, the capability will form a direct link between them and the organisation's vision, assisting in giving support to frontline creativity that may not be possible to realise without suitable support. Through promoting and empowering frontline staff, the culture created could make frontline staff confident in developing their work to account for localised or dynamic environments (Johnson and Medcof 2007). In addition to this, functional managers who may be involved in work with frontline staff and project managers may develop their own project man-agement skills and begin carrying out improvement projects themselves. The project management capability may also be used to assist the top management team to carry out particularly innovative elements of their strategy that may not be possible without a systematic and structured approach to complex activities. The objective feedback from the project teams regarding progress and performance may also assist in developing top management's future plans for development, possibly inspiring and directing capability development throughout the firm.

Within today's hypercompetitive business environment (Pryor et al. 2007), developing a capability that allows the company to drive the stra-tegic process from all levels of the company could be considered essential. However, what is especially important when pursuing such a strategy of development is to remain focused on what is considered the company's core activity, which is often the element that is considered most impor-tant to the end user. For this reason, when pursuing such an approach, the abilities and knowledge of the members charged with such activities need to be suitable for the specific company. As mentioned earlier, devel-oping such capabilities from within the organisation may be beneficial, as it ensures those involved have a deep understanding of the core busi-ness process. As with the different approaches described to organising a project management firm, having different types of knowledge built upon one another may be essentially the same with internally based project

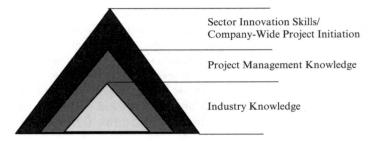

Figure 6.15   Project management skills sandcone

management capabilities. With the project leader, the third level is sector-specific knowledge and innovation; with the internalised capability this may not need to be present. In this situation, the innovation may come from the organisation as a whole (Figure 6.15) and feed into the different projects that have been proposed by empowered, enabled frontline staff, possibly waiting for selection (Hayes et al. 2005) (see Figure 6.7). This has the potential to drive the organisation in a new direction, while continually considering the mission to ensure consistency is maintained. If this is not considered sufficient, further innovation could be promoted within the project management function, possibly through consideration of concepts such as core competences (Hamel and Prahalad 1990), Blue Ocean Strategy (Kim and Maubourgne 2005) or general process improvement techniques that may not currently be used within the industry.

6.8.1   A Hybrid Structure

The main problems with the above approaches to arranging a project team are performance (coordinator), cost (project leader) and time (in-house project manager). Although the true project management and project team approaches are able to reduce the problems, they may not drive performance in any of the areas that are caused by the need to trade off different aspects of performance. For the true project manager or project team to produce results that truly match with the client's strategy, that may be continually changing in line with the service they provide, there will need to be considerable input from the top management team, which may become a constraint. Top management should concern themselves with long-range development (Akao 1991), which will suffer if they are required to focus on process-level developments whether it is within the project or business process setting. For this reason, it may be beneficial to combine these approaches with the 'internalised project manager', to reduce top management's responsibility for process and product-related

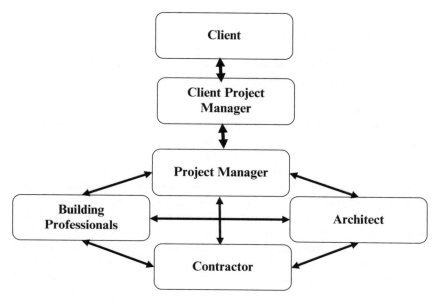

Figure 6.16   Hybrid structure

learning and development. Within the project team itself, unlike the 'in-house project manager', the role is that of client/top management surrogate, to direct activities in a way that reflects developments as well as the client's overall strategy (Figure 6.16).

By taking an advisory role within the project team, the client project manager should not have to allocate the amount of time that is deemed appropriate if all project management activities are their responsibility. By combining the function with a competent external project management firm (true project manager or project team), the need to monitor and control contractor activity should be removed, combined with the benefits associated with well-established supplier relations. The reduction in time requirements within the project team allows the hybrid project manager to concentrate a considerable amount of time on internally focused project management activities. Alternatively, if the firm carries out a large number of projects simultaneously, the hybrid project manager could allocate a greater amount of time to external aspects of the development strategy, which could be reflected in the firm's project portfolio. Although the hybrid project manager is likely to be a practical role, positioning the role close to the board is likely to be beneficial, allowing them to openly discuss business sensitive issues with the board that may not be possible with an external entity. Discussions such as the particular make-up of the project portfolio should be assisted by the close relationship and allow it to effectively match the whole strategy. By determining the correct mix of external, expansion elements with internal, improvement elements, the function may even be able to take direct responsibility for a large proportion of the strategic activities carried out by the firm.

Client strategy
Due to the hybrid structure allowing a degree of flexibility with the level of interaction with the external contractors, it allows the greatest level of flexibility in client strategy. Without the need to employ a project leader, the costs can be kept down, but with the variable interaction with the project team, it is also possible for the client to pursue a programme of rapid expansion. If projects are particularly standard it may even be possible to employ a project coordinator, to further reduce costs, while assisting in increasing the level of control present within the system. Although it is unlikely that this approach will initially be able to produce the optimised solutions of the project leader by assigning a greater amount of the manager's time to a particular project, it may be possible to develop the best possible outcome in relation to current internal capabilities. The overall strategy is likely to be focused on the development of the organisation as a whole, enabling the company to define itself within its market space or even create uncontested markets, through innovation of the value offered to the customer (Kim and Maubourgne 2005).

Due to the ability of the approach to be tailored relatively easily to the market requirements and environmental conditions, it has the potential to satisfy the needs of managers favouring retrenchment as well as entrepreneurial activities (Reed and Buckley 1988). Even if the approach is fully focused on internal improvements and the size of the organisation does not change, the operations would be developing, improving the value of the organisation as a whole. For example, in a situation where environmental conditions were particularly unfavourable, such a situation would allow the organisation to streamline processes in such a way that when the market improved, systems would be in place to allow rapid expansion. Even though it may be possible to view this approach as a compromise, that may not satisfy anyone; it could be considered the approach that is able to promote the highest level of innovation and performance in all areas. Although the approach does require an additional management capability to be developed within the organisation, the focus on adding value to the major elements of the development process allows it not to be seen as just another management function. Importantly, the approach can also engage and enable those within the organisation that otherwise may not have direct involvement with capital expansion or internal improvement activities. As well as promoting their creative ideas regarding innovative work practices the organisation is undertaking in a way similar to Hoshin Kanri, the process could be seen as a means of connecting important workers with the strategy process (Scarbrough 1999).

6.9 CREATING AND SUPPORTING A PROJECT MANAGEMENT-BASED OPERATIONS STRATEGY IMPLEMENTATION STRUCTURE

The organisational structure that is developed with the internalised approach to project management is relatively similar to work on new organisational forms such as networks and latent organisations. Work on these approaches seems to have been largely observational, with less focus on how the ideas proposed may relate to more traditionally structured organisations. The ideas outlined above begin to address these issues, as a means of creating a network while carrying out focused strategic activities within projects. In addition to those being involved in projects developing experience of project management, and connecting them to the organisation's strategy process, the relationships developed between the team members represent another important aspect of the process. They represent the connections within a network structure that if suitably supported following the completion of a particular project may remain within a hierarchically structured organisation. Their presence can then assist in the formation of future project teams that, as with latent organisations, will already have good working relationships established.

The difficulty that is likely to arise is that within such an organisation there will be numerous other activities taking place that may mean maintaining and developing relationships that are not part of everyday work will have relatively low priority. For this reason, there may need to be elements of the organisation specifically responsible for the activity that, as Jenkins, Ambrosini and Collier (2007) stated, could represent a significant competitive advantage. With a capability such as a hybrid project manager taking responsibility for the practical aspects of the strategy implementation process, this may give functional elements of the organisation additional resources to direct on to the maintenance of such a network. In such situations, upper management may actively manage the network to develop it in a way that meets the requirements of the strategy, possibly through brokering connections by initiating projects that involve particular elements of the organisation.

With strategic activities being undertaken within visibly cross-functional, well-supported projects, functional management should be able to develop an understanding of their relation with the process. Appreciating that they are able to support the processes directly through functional development of their capabilities and with suitable allocation of functional resources to the process, their functional aims can be suitably aligned with the strategy. Arranging the functional work in a manner that effectively supports the main business process, management of the functions can take a role described by Drucker (1955) with the management of the professional employee. Rather than being present to motivate and guide those within the business process, management's function is similar to a human resource function, where they focus on the personal development of those within particular departments. With a good understanding of the activities of the project management function, it should be possible to effectively align the development with the needs of the strategy, effectively developing the resources that will be applied to the project. This may also apply, to a degree, to those working on the main business processes, where although the managers need to be focused on getting the best possible performance out of the system, human resource elements may still have a place. By allocating suitable resources from within the main business process to the strategic activities, the skills developed within the project setting can be applied to the main business process, which may also give 'line' employees greater empathy towards 'staff' employees.

Although not the most important element of the system, as all elements should contribute to the process, it is the project management function that enables the system. With upper and general management focused upon the maintenance and development of the networks that promote cross-functional relationships and the functional management focusing on developing the resources necessary to complete the activities, the strategic activities themselves are effectively the responsibility of the project managers. With suitable input from all within the organisation to determine the requirements of the customer and the organisation as a whole, the project manager needs to combine the resources in a way that will develop the organisation to better meet the customer's needs. Drucker (1955) stated how management need to be a resource to enable the worker to perform better. In the project management organisation, the different types of manager are present to support different types of activities. The general managers are responsible for the effective running of the main business process and the functional manager supports the professional employee to ensure their specialised skills are appropriately developed to meet the needs of the system, with both supporting the network. It is then the project manager's responsibility to effectively combine the resources to solve outwards facing issues.

Within a traditional organisational structure (Figure 6.17), there may

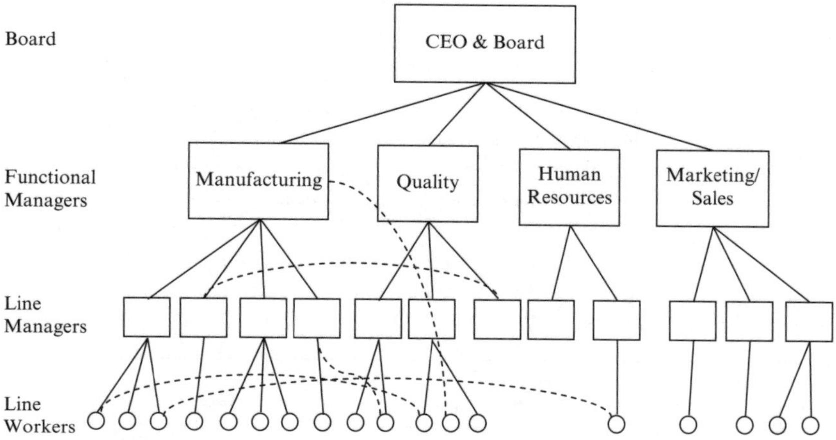

Figure 6.17   Hierarchically structured organisation, with some informal relationships

only be a small number of connections outside official channels; this means that within business-as-usual activities, the system may be slow to react to difficulties, due to the number of connections to inform other parts of the organisation. With the initiation of project-based activities (Figure 6.18), the number of connections within the organisation increases significantly, which in turn connects all involved with a strategic capability that is working closely with the board. Following the completion of the project, as well as the maintenance of the connections being important, the development of project management skills could also assist the system. If smaller projects are initiated by functional managers, with the support of the project management function, the number of connections within the organisation will increase rapidly. This could represent a human resource aspect of the project management function, who, as well as carrying out projects directly, would also assist in supporting the development of capabilities within the organisation.

Even without the initiation of projects within the organisation, by selecting projects that involve certain functions within the organisation, the network can be tailored to give focus to the needs of the strategy (Figure 6.19). In addition to the connections that are formed within the projects helping with subsequent projects, they allow each member to consider different elements of the organisation in their everyday activities. As with the project team, by considering activities from a different perspective, it should be possible to identify new problems and new solutions to the processes with which they work. By suitably supporting the

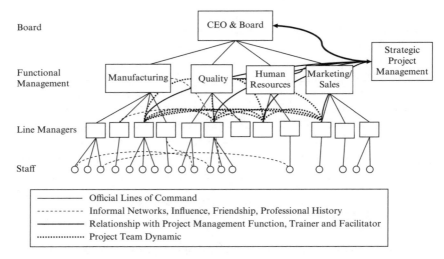

Figure 6.18   Initiation of project-based activities

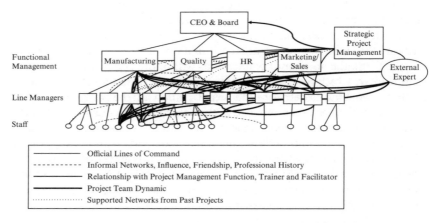

Figure 6.19   Further development of a project management network

previously made connections with the allocation of resources to maintain them, this may give those within the process the ability to investigate problems within other departments. Using connections in this way, potential projects could even be identified and investigated within a team setting even before management are aware of an issue. In such situations, these projects may even involve the project management function in an informal manner to develop understanding of the problem, and possibly secure additional resources for further investigations. Within the above system, although the maintenance of the system may be seen as additional resources being allocated to the process that do not contribute to the strategy process directly, it needs to be thought of in a different way. Rather than simply maintaining, it could be thought of as supporting a culture of strategic activities. If the organisation only allocates resources towards large scale projects, the bottom-up understanding and knowledge may be overlooked. The above situation where frontline staff identify and investigate potential issues that are not actively controlled or monitored is considered preferable when trying to motivate innovation (Johnson and Medcof 2007).

6.10   CONCLUSION

With the number of high profile, overrun and over-budget projects in the world today (Love 2002), it is not surprising that the cause of the problems may be laid at the feet of project management. If project management was created to effectively manage complex unique activities, surely it should assist in solving these problems. Such problems are not surprising if one takes a view of project management as simply being planning or the use of a Gantt chart (Maylor 2005). Then one begins to ask if it is the perception of project management as a whole that may be the problem; it is not the tools that are available but instead the human element that is able to cast judgement and make decisions in a situation that determines performance (Drucker 1955). The term 'project leader' came from a project management firm and was later confirmed by a coordinator, that managers may not be what is required in these difficult situations, where doing things right may not be appropriate and they should focus instead on doing the right things (Drucker 1955). Unless there is someone within a group of people that is able to take responsibility, create a team dynamic, it may be difficult for a selection of individuals who may not have met each other before to be expected to produce unique complex outputs. For this reason it is likely that in the selection of an effective project manager, character and drive are likely to be considerably more important than how well they use the currently fashionable project management techniques (Cicmil et al. 2006). Being able to take a position of leadership within the team and align team member goals with those of the client must be more important for improving project performance.

By taking project management as a starting point for a modified approach to strategy implementation, the aim of this chapter has been to develop a broader understanding of what the approach has to offer a difficult subject. Although it does assist in the planning stages of the implementation process with tools that assist idea generation and communication of the process, this is not the extent of what project management has to offer. Project management considers strategy in a different way from other approaches, while also making the process seem more accessible to those within the organisation. It may also be an effective tool to developing a culture within an organisation that is focused on 'getting things done' (Bossidy and Charan 2002), that through relatively systematic control can effectively manage achieving long-term goals. Compared with some approaches that allow strategy realisation through the promotion of ideas from within the organisation (Bourgeois and Brodwin 1984; Johnson and Medcof 2007), project management is both able to initiate the situation and control the process in a less haphazard way, without over-reliance on cultural aspects. Through the use of post completion project reviews as well as a suitable selection process, an organisation is able to set in place systems that allow control to be maintained; combining this with a suitable reward structure, the goal congruence should assist in the systematic creation of strategic consensus throughout the firm.

The above configurations of project management teams were devised after discussing project management issues with a number of project management firms. By subsequently discussing the findings with a client of one of the firms, the ideas proposed within this chapter were formulated. Where Mills, Platts and Gregory (1995) used project management as the element of the 5P approach to get the activities completed, this approach aims to expand its importance. Project management literature stresses how project management firms are able to implement their operations strategy without having to allocate specific resources to the process (Maylor 2005). During business as usual, they are able to achieve unique strategies by simply selecting, reviewing and improving their business processes. If the same were possible for other non project-oriented companies, the implementation process would no longer be as difficult as it often seems. It may also be considerably easier to alter a strategy than traditional approaches that require whole systems to be discarded when new strategic directions are taken. Within a project management system, the strategy is defined by the projects that are taken on and how they are completed. By assessing projects within the system to determine if they should be terminated in regards to the new strategy, changing the selection process and changing success criteria of projects, the strategic development can effectively be altered. Importantly within a project management firm or consultancy, the main business processes are the capabilities present within the organisation rather than process technology, which is likely to mean it is considerably easier to change strategies without capital investment.

For this and other reasons, organisations that are not project oriented, due to the main business processes representing previous operational systems and processes, may have difficulty in pursuing vastly different strategy. However, with strategy representing a path rather than a destination, the starting position may not be critical. With decision theory-based strategy selection tools (Balakrishnan, Render and Stair 2006; Meredith and Mantel 2006), it may be possible to quickly educate those within the system of the new strategy, possibly by articulating how selection criteria have changed. If the project management function is relatively well established within the firm, the amount of project experience in the organisation should be significant, with numerous competent function project managers. If the new strategy requires considerable changes to take place, it may be possible for the project management function to act as a coordinator over a number of projects that are directly managed by functional managers who have developed project management skills. Compared with the development of other improvement functions within an organisation (such as a continuous improvement department), the analytical, subject-based approach of project management allows those who participate in projects to become actively involved. For this reason it may even be less beneficial to develop a project team configuration within the firm that may prevent other functions from taking key positions within the team. The project manager may train those within the team in particular project-related activities that can be developed through the life of the project and then deployed on future projects.

In this way, the development of a project management capability within an organisation has the potential to transform its abilities at carrying out strategic activities. With a basis around a top management initiative to expand or develop the organisation, it has the potential to affect all within a firm, ideally through direct involvement in project activities. Rather than the other strategic capabilities described earlier in the book, project management is not function specific, allowing it to be more applicable to certain administrative or service activities. Combined with the requirement for working in cross-functional teams, it allows the creation of many new connections within the organisation that may not form under normal circumstances. Through effectively brokering network connections throughout the organisation, it may be possible to reduce the effective size of the organisation. Reducing the number of connections necessary to communicate with different people in the organisation may allow quick responses even if the organisation is large. With other approaches, although the empowerment of specific divisions allows localised conditions to be accounted for, these approaches may require controlling and may even distance themselves from the organisation as a whole. If divisions are able to identify global changes and are not suitably connected with the organisation as a whole, they may leave other divisions unprepared when they experience the conditions directly. Through the effective brokerage of connections throughout the organisation, the ability to sense change and effectively inform the organisation will be improved. Combined with an organisation with an integrated project management capability, it should be able to drive change from within the organisation at all levels, allowing the organisation as a whole to take account of new conditions or exploit new opportunities.

6.11   END REMARKS

The aim of this book has been to give a view of operations strategy as it is seen by the authors. Compared with the fragmented view of the subject that is sometimes presented, that keeps divisions between process and content with implementation simply included as an after-thought, we have tried to offer a view with more cohesion. We feel that without taking such a view, the subject has potential to be over-facing to those charged with the activity, which may make them take refuge within the comfortable surroundings of their function of origin. However, operations strategy is not the multi head hydra that some may see and although the first half of the book was focused upon the current approaches, this was not meant to dissuade future process champions. Instead it aimed to give an understanding of the elements that should be considered and if appropriate studied further to develop specific areas of operations to meet the needs of those the organisation is serving. None of the elements should be totally disregarded, and as with the operations functions as a whole, it is how all the different elements operate together that determines performance, so if outstanding performance in one area is required, the other areas should at least be able to support.

The second part of the book was to introduce the reader to approaches that the authors consider are able to offer assistance to the difficult activity of operations strategy implementation. Splitting this into three elements, our aim has been to guide the reader through the elements that are considered important to begin developing an organisation that can meet the needs of the modern competitive business environment. Rather than dividing process and content, we have taken a logical path from developing ideas, to developing an organisational understanding of need and proposing means of achieving the organisational goals. Although focused upon a practical approach to operations strategy, the book has deliberately steered away from attempting to be a textbook with all the answers or a workbook listing all the steps. Instead, we have aimed at giving a moderately broad and manageable overview of the subject complemented by accessible approaches to converting this understanding into organisational development activities. We appreciate that experience with any of the elements included in the second half of the book will assist; however, we hope that what we have provided should be enough to begin building confidence. If further content of these approaches is required, there are focused books, but we hope to have provided a foundation to show how these elements can be combined to enable the development of an operations strategy that is tailored to the needs of the organisation and its environment.

NOTES

1. The agency problem occurs when ownership and management of an organisation are separated. The owner must employ an agent to carry out the running of the organisation, who will invariably have more information about the organisation than the owner. Problems arise when the agent may have an opportunity to do something that is not in the best interests of the principal (or shareholder). This can be reduced by employing means of monitoring and controlling the agent, but this tends to increase the cost of the arrangement, which is known as the agency cost.
2. Parkinson's law is when work will invariably increase in size to fill that which is available; the same principle has also been found to apply to other resources, such as space within a facility planning setting.

References

Adams, J.L. (1986). *The Care and Feeding of Ideas*. London, Penguin.

Akao, Y. (1991). *Hoshin Kanri: Policy Deployment for Successful TQM*. Portland, OR, Productivity Press.

Akdere, M. and Azevedo, R.E. (2005). 'Agency theory from the perspective of human resource development.' *International Journal of Human Resources Development and Management* 5(3): 318–32.

Akdere, M. and Azevedo, R.E. (2006). 'Agency theory implications for efficient contracts in organisation development.' *Organisation Development Journal* 24(2): 43–54.

Alexander, L.D. (1985). 'Successfully implementing strategic decisions.' *Long Range Planning* 18(3): 91–7.

Amabile, T.M., Conti, R., Coon, H., Lazenby, J. and Herron, M. (1996). 'Assessing the work environment for creativity.' *Academy of Management Journal* 39(5).

Anderson, J.G., Cleveland, G. and Schroeder, R.G. (1989). 'Operations strategy: a literature review.' *Journal of Operations Management* 8(2): 133–58.

Arnold, J.E. (1962). 'Education for innovation.' In S.J. Parnes and H.F. Harding (eds), *A Sourcebook for Creative Thinking*. New York, Scribners.

Bal, J. and Swift, M. (2002). 'Supporting SMEs through e-business.' *Manufacturing Engineer* 81(5): 219–24.

Balakrishnan, N., Render, B. and Stair, R.M. (2006). *Managerial Decision Modelling with Spreadsheets*. London, Prentice Hall.

Barney, J. (1991). 'Firm resources and sustained competitive advantage.' *Journal of Management* 17(1): 99–120.

Basadur, M. (1992). 'Managing creativity: a Japanese model.' *Academy of Management Executive* 6(2): 29–41.

Beckman, S.L. and Rosenfield, D.B. (2008). *Operations Strategy: Competing in the 21st Century*. New York, NY, McGraw-Hill Irwin.

Beer, M. and Eisenstat, R.A. (2000). 'The silent killers of strategy implementation and learning.' *Sloan Management Review* 41(4): 29–40.

Beer, M. and Eisenstat, R.A. (2004). 'How to have an honest conversation about business strategy.' *Harvard Business Review* Feb.: 82–9.

Berry, W.L., Hill, T.J. and Klompmaker, J.E. (1995). 'Customer-driven manufacturing.' *International Journal of Operations & Production Management* **15**(3): 4–15.

Bhimani, A. and Langfield-Smith, K. (2007). 'Structure, formality and the importance of financial and non-financial information in strategy development and implementation.' *Management Accounting Research* **18**(1): 3–31.

Bicheno, J. (2004). *The New Lean Toolbox: Towards Fast, Flexible Flow.* Buckingham, UK, Picsie Books.

Bossidy, L. and Charan, R. (2002). *Execution: The Discipline of Getting Things Done.* New York, NY, Crown Business.

Bourgeois, L.J. and Brodwin, D.R. (1984). 'Strategic implementation: five approaches to an elusive phenomenon.' *Strategic Management Journal* **5**: 241–64.

Braganza, A. and Korac-Kakabadse, N. (2000). 'Towards a function and process orientation: challenges for business leaders in the new millennium.' *Strategic Change* **9**(1): 45–53.

Burbidge, J.L. (1984). 'A classification of production system variables.' In H. Hubner (ed.), *IFIP Production Management Systems: Strategies and Tools for Design.* Amsterdam, Elsevier Science Publishers/North Holland.

Burke, R. (2006). *Project Management: Planning and Control Techniques.* Hoboken, NJ, John Wiley & Sons.

Buzan, T. (1982). *Use Your Head.* London, BBC/Ariel Books.

Callon, M. (1993). *Social Ordering.* Urbana Champaign, IL, University of Illinois.

Chandler, A.D. (1962). *Strategy and Structure.* Cambridge, MA, MIT Press.

Cicmil, S., William, T., Thomas, J. and Hodgson, D. (2006). 'Rethinking project management: researching the actuality of projects.' *International Journal of Project Management* **24**: 675–86.

Cooke-Davies, T.J. and Arzymanow, A. (2003). 'The maturity of project management in different industries: an investigation into variations between project management models.' *International Journal of Project Management* **21**: 471–8.

Cravens, D.W. (1998). 'Implementation strategies in the market-driven strategy era.' *Academy of Marketing Science Journal* **31**(11/12): 237–41.

Dale, B.D. (2003). *Managing Quality.* Oxford, Blackwell Publishing Ltd.

Drucker, P.F. (1955). *The Practice of Management.* Oxford, Butterworth-Heinemann.

Drucker, P.F. (1967). *The Effective Executive.* New York, Harper & Row.

Eisenhardt, K.M. (1989). 'Agency theory: an assessment and review.' *Academy of Management Review* **14**(1): 57–74.

Etzioni, A. (1989). 'Humble decision making.' *Harvard Business Review* July/August: 122–6.

Ferdows, K. and De Meyer, A. (1990). 'Lasting improvements in manufacturing performance: in search of a new theory.' *Journal of Operations Management* **9**(2): 168–84.

Floyd, S.W. and Wooldridge, B. (1992). 'Managing strategic consensus: the foundation of effective implementation.' *Academy of Management Executive* **6**(4): 27–39.

Foil, C.M. and Huff, A.S. (1992). 'Maps for managers: where are we? Where do we go from here?' *Journal of Management Studies* **29**(3): 267–85.

Galbraith, J.R. and Nathanson, D.A. (1978). *Strategy Implementation: The Role of Structure and Process*. St Paul, MI, West Publishing Co.

Garvin, D.A. (1993). 'Manufacturing strategic planning.' *California Management Review* **35**(4): 85–106.

Garvin, D.A. and Roberto, M.A. (2001). 'What you don't know about making decisions.' *Harvard Business Review* September: 108–16.

Ghasemzadeh, F. and Archer, N.P. (2000). 'Project portfolio selection through decision support.' *Decision Support Systems* **29**(1): 73–88.

Gilliam, T.K. (1993). 'Managing the power of creativity.' *Bank Marketing* **25**, 12 (Dec.): 14–19.

Goldratt, E.M. (1997). *Critical Chain*. Great Barrington, MA, North River.

Goldratt, E.M. and Cox, J. (1992). *The Goal: A Process of Ongoing Improvement*. Great Barrington, MA, North River.

Goodwin, P. and Wright, G. (1998). *Decision Analysis for Management Judgement*. Chichester, Wiley, 2nd edition.

Goold, M. and Quinn, J.J. (1990). 'The paradox of strategic control.' *Strategic Management Journal* **11**: 43–57.

Guth, W.D. and Macmillan, I.C. (1986). 'Strategy implementation versus middle management self-interest.' *Strategic Management Journal* **7**(4): 313–27.

Gutierrez, G. and Kouvelis, P. (1991). 'Parkinson's law and its implications in project management.' *Management Science* **37**(8): 990–1001.

Hamel, G. and Prahalad, C.K. (1990). 'The core competence of the corporation.' *Harvard Business Review* **68**(3): 79–91.

Hamel, G. and Prahalad, C.K. (1994). *Competing for the Future*. Boston, MA, Harvard Business School Press.

Hammond, J.S., Keeney, R.L. and Raiffa, H. (1999). *Smart Choices: A Practical Guide to Making Better Decisions*. Boston, MA, Harvard Business School Press.

Harrison, E.F. (1999). *The Managerial Decision-Making Process.* Boston, MA, Houghton Mifflin Company, 5th edition.

Hart, S.L. (1992). 'An integrative framework for strategy making processes.' *Academy of Management Review* **17**(2): 327–51.

Hayes, R.H. and Wheelwright, S.C. (1979). 'Link manufacturing process and product life cycles.' *Harvard Business Review* **57**(1): 133–40.

Hayes, R.H. and Wheelwright, S.C. (1984). *Restoring Our Competitive Edge: Competing Through Manufacturing.* New York, John Wiley and Sons.

Hayes, R., Pisano, G., Upton, D. and Wheelwright, S. (2005). *Operations, Strategy and Technology: Pursuing the Competitive Edge.* Hoboken, NJ, John Wiley & Sons.

Herbig, P. and Jacobs, L. (1996). 'Creative problem solving styles in the USA and Japan.' *International Marketing Review* **13**(2): 63–71.

Hill, T. (1985). *Manufacturing Strategy.* London, Macmillan.

Hill, T. (1993). *Manufacturing Strategy: The Strategic Management of the Manufacturing Function.* Basingstoke, UK, Macmillan.

Hill, T. (1995). *Manufacturing Strategy, Text and Cases.* Houndmills, UK, Macmillan Press Ltd.

Hrebiniak, L.G. (2006). 'Obstacles to effective strategy implementation.' *Organisational Dynamics* **35**(1): 12–31.

Hrebiniak, L.G. and Joyce, W.F. (1984). *Implementing Strategy.* New York, NY, Macmillan.

Humphreys, J. (2004). 'The vision thing.' *Sloan Management Review* **45**(4): 96.

Jacobs, J. (2002). *The Fables of Aesop*, Mineola, NJ, Dover Evergreen Classics.

Jenkins, M., Ambrosini, V. and Collier, N. (2007). *Advanced Strategic Management: A Multiple Perspective Approach.* Basingstoke, UK, Palgrave Macmillan.

Johnsen, A. (2001). 'Balanced scorecard: theoretical perspectives and public management implications.' *Managerial Auditing Journal* **16**(6): 319–30.

Johnson, H.T. and Kaplan, R.S. (1987). *Relevance Lost: The Rise and Fall of Management Accounting.* Boston, MA, Harvard Business School Press.

Johnson, W.H.A. and Medcof, J.W. (2007). 'Motivating proactive subsidiary innovation: agent-based theory and socialization models in global R&D.' *Journal of International Management* **13**: 472–89.

Kaplan, R. and Norton, D. (1992). The balanced scorecard: measures that drive performance. *Harvard Business Review* **70**(1): 71–9.

Kaplan, R. and Norton, D. (1996). 'The balanced scorecard: translating strategy into action.' *Harvard Business Review* **74**: 75–85.

Kaplan, R. and Norton, D. (2001). *The Strategy Focused Organisation: How the Balanced Scorecard Companies Thrive in the New Business Environment.* Boston, MA, Harvard Business School Press.

Kaplan, R.S. and Norton, D.P. (2004). *Strategy Maps: Converting Intangible Assets into Tangible Outcomes.* Boston, MA, Harvard Business School Press.

Kelly, G.A. (1955). *The Psychology of Personal Constructs.* New York, Norton.

Kim, J.S. and Arnold, P. (1996). 'Operationalising manufacturing strategy.' *International Journal of Operations and Production Management* **16**(12): 45–73.

Kim, W.C. and Maubourgne, R. (2005). *Blue Ocean Strategy: How to Create Uncontested Market Space and Make the Competition Irrelevant.* Boston, MA, Harvard Business School Press.

Koestler, A. (1964). *The Act of Creation.* London, Hutchinson.

Lewy, C. and Du Mee, L. (1998). 'The ten commandments of balanced scorecard implementation.' *Management Control and Accounting,* (April): 34–6.

Love, P.E.D. (2002). 'Influence of project type and procurement method on rework costs in building construction projects.' *Journal of Construction Engineering and Management* **128**(1): 18–29.

Lyneis, J.M., Cooper, K.G. and Els, S.A. (2001). 'Strategic management of complex projects: a case study using system dynamics.' *System Dynamics Review* **17**(3): 237–60.

MacCrimmon, K.R. and Wagner, C. (1994). 'Stimulating ideas through creativity software.' *Management Science* **40**(11): 1514–32.

Manor, P. (2002). Introduction to 'Development of Inventive Thinking' According to the SIT (SIT – Structured Inventive Thinking), http://www.osakagu.ac.jp/php/nakagawa/TRIZ/eTRIZ/epapers/e2002Papers/eManor020721.htm.

Maylor, H. (2005). *Project Management.* Harlow, UK, Financial Times/ Prentice Hall.

McFadzean, E.S. (1998a). 'Enhancing creative thinking within organisations.' *Management Decision* **36**(5): 309–15.

McFadzean, E.S. (1998b). 'The creativity continuum: towards a classification of creative problem solving techniques.' *Creativity and Innovation Management* **7**(3): 131–9.

McFadzean, E.S. (1998c). *The Creativity Tool Box: A Practical Guide for Facilitating Creative Problem Solving Sessions.* Milton Keynes, UK, TeamTalk Consulting.

McKim, R.H. (1972). *Experiences In Visual Thinking.* Monterey, California, Wadsworth Publishing.

Meredith, J.R., Jr and Mantel, S.J. (2006). *Project Management: A Managerial Approach*, Hoboken, NJ, John Wiley & Sons.

Mills, J., Platts, K. and Gregory, M. (1995). 'A framework for the design of manufacturing strategy processes: a contingency approach.' *International Journal of Operations & Production Management* **15**(4): 17–49.

Mills, J., Neely, A., Platts, K. and Gregory, M. (1998). 'Manufacturing strategy: a pictorial representation.' *International Journal of Operations and Production* **18**(11): 1067–85.

Mills, J.F., Platts, K.W., Neely, A.D., Richards, A.H. and Bourne, M.C.S. (2002). *Creating a Winning Business Formula*. Cambridge, Cambridge University Press.

Mintzberg, H. (1978). 'Patterns in strategy formulation.' *Management Science* **24**(9): 934–48.

Mintzberg, H., Ahlstrand, B. and Lampel, J. (1998). *Strategy Safari: A Guided Tour through the Wilds of Strategic Management*. London, Prentice-Hall.

Morgan, G. (1989). *Riding the Waves of Change – Developing Managerial Competencies for a Turbulent World*. San Francisco, Jossey-Bass Publishers.

Nakamura, Y. (2003). 'Combination of ARIZ92 and NM method for the 5-th level problems.' *Proceedings of TRIZCON2003*, Altshuller Institute for TRIZ Studies.

Newman, V. (1995). *Made to Measure Problem Solving*. Aldershot, UK, Gower Publishing.

Noble, C.H. (1999). 'Building the strategy implementation network.' *Business Horizons* **42**(6), 19–28.

Parkinson, C.N. (1957). *Parkinson's Law*. Cambridge, UK, The Riverside Press.

Peng, M.W., Lee, S.H. and Tan, J.J. (2001). 'The *keiretsu* in Asia: implications for multilevel theories of competitive advantage.' *Journal of International Management* **7**: 253–76.

Pfeffer, J. and Sutton, R.I. (2000). *The Knowing–Doing Gap: How Smart Companies Turn Knowledge Into Action*. Boston, MA, Harvard Business School Press.

Platts, K.W. (1993). 'A process approach to researching manufacturing strategy.' *International Journal of Operations and Production Management* **13**(8): 4–17.

Platts, K.W. (1994). 'Characteristics of Methodologies for Manufacturing Strategy formulation.' *Computer Integrated Manufacturing Systems* **7**(2): 93–9.

Platts, K.W. and Gregory, M. (1989). *Competitive Manufacturing: A*

Practical Approach to the Development of a Manufacturing Strategy. Bedford, IFS.

Platts, K. and Tan, K.H. (2003). 'Strategy visualisation: knowing, understanding, and formulating.' *Management Decisions* **42**(5): 667–76.

Porter, M.E. (1980). *Competitive Strategy.* New York, NY, The Free Press.

Porter, M.E. (1985). *Competitive Advantage.* New York, NY, The Free Press.

Proctor, T. (1995). *The Essence of Management Creativity.* London, Prentice-Hall.

Pryor, M.G., Anderson, D.M. and Toombs, L.A. (1998). *Strategic Quality Management: A Strategic Systems Approach to Continuous Improvement.* Mason, OH, Thompson Learning.

Pryor, M.G., Anderson, D.M., Toombs, L.A. and Humphreys, J.H. (2007). 'Strategy implementation as a core competency: the 5P's model.' *Journal of Management Research* **7**(1): 3–17.

Ranchhod, A. and Gurau, C. (2007). *Marketing Strategies: A Contemporary Approach.* Harlow, UK, Prentice Hall/Financial Times.

Reed, R. and Buckley, M.R. (1988). 'Strategy in action – techniques for implementing strategy.' *Long Range Planning* **21**(3): 67–74.

Remy, R. (1997). 'Adding focus to improvement efforts with PM3.' *PM Network* **11**(7): 43–7.

Rickards, T. (1985). *Stimulating Innovation: A Systems Approach.* London, Frances Pinter.

Rickards, T. (1988). 'Creativity and innovation: a transatlantic perspective.' *Creativity and Innovation Year-Book.* Manchester, Manchester Business School.

Robins, J.A. (1993), 'Organisation as strategy: restructuring production in the film industry', *Strategic Management Journal*, **14**, 103–18.

Rodrigues, A. and Bowers, J. (1996). 'The role of system dynamics in project management.' *International Journal of Project Management* **14**(4): 213–20.

Rodrigues, A.G. and Williams, T.M. (1998). 'Systems dynamics in project management: assessing the impact of client behaviour on project performance.' *Journal of the Operational Research Society* **49**: 2–15.

Rogers, C. (1954). 'Towards a theory of creativity.' *A Review of General Semantics* **11**: 249–60. (Reprinted in P.E. Vernon (ed.), *Creativity*, Penguin, 1975.)

Russo, J.E. and Schoemaker, P.J.H. (1989). *Confident Decision Making.* London, Piatkus.

Saam, N.J. (2007). 'Asymmetry in information versus asymmetry in power: implicit assumptions of agency theory?' *Journal of Socio-Economics* **36**: 825–40.

Saaty, T.L. (1987). 'The AHP – what it is and how it is used.' *Math Modelling* **9**(3–5): 161–76.

Sarkis, J. (1995). *Proceedings of the 1995 ASEM National Conference.* Arlington, Virginia, American Society for Engineering Management.

Scarbrough, H. (1999). 'Knowledge as work: conflicts in the management of knowledge workers.' *Technology Analysis & Strategic Management* **11**(1): 5–16.

Skinner, W. (1966). 'Production under pressure.' *Harvard Business Review* **44**(6): 139–45.

Slack, N. and Lewis, M. (2001). *Operations Strategy.* Harlow, UK, Prentice Hall.

Slack, N. and Lewis, M. (2008). *Operations Strategy.* Harlow, UK, Prentice Hall, Financial Times.

Slack, N., Chambers, S. and Johnston, R. (2007). *Operations Management.* London, UK, Prentice Hall/Financial Times.

Somerville, I. (2007). 'Agency versus identity: actor-network theory meets public relations.' *Corporate Communications: An International Journal* **4**(1): 6–13.

Starkey, K., Barnatt, C. and Tempest, S. (2000). 'Beyond networks and hierarchies: latent organisations in the U.K. television industry.' *Organization Science* **11**(3): 299–305.

Swink, M. and Way, H.M. (1995). 'Manufacturing strategy: propositions, current research, Renewed Directions.' *International Journal of Operation and Management* **15**(7): 4–26.

Tan, K.H. and Platts, K. (2003a). 'Linking objectives to action plans: a decision support approach based on the connectance concept.' *Decision Sciences Journal* **34**(3): 569–93.

Tan, K.H. and Platts, K. (2003b). *Winning Decisions: Translating Business Strategy into Action Plans.* Institute for Manufacturing, Mill Lane, Cambridge, University of Cambridge.

Thorpe, E.R. and Morgan, R.E. (2006). 'In pursuit of the "ideal approach" to successful marketing strategy implementation.' *European Journal of Marketing* **41**(5/6): 659–77.

Tompkins, J.A., White, J.A., Bozer, Y.A. and Tanchoco, J.M.A. (2003). *Facilities Planning.* New York, NY, John Wiley & Sons.

Van Gundy, A.B. (1988). *Techniques of Structured Problem Solving.* New York, Van Nostrand Reinhold Co.

Weinman, C. (1991). 'It's not art but marketing research can be creative.' *Marketing News* **25**(8) (15 April): 9–24.

Weisberg, R.W. (1986). *Creativity, Genius and Other Myths*. New York, W.H. Freeman.

Wertheimer, M. ([1945] 1959). *Productive Thinking*. New York, Harper and Row.

Wheelwright, S.C. and Hayes, R.H. (1985). 'Competing through manufacturing.' *Harvard Business Review* **63**(1): 99–109.

Wheelwright, S.C. and Hayes, R.H. (1992). 'Creating project plans to focus product development.' *Harvard Business Review* **70**(2): 70–82.

White, D. and Fortune, J. (2002). 'Current practice in project management – an empirical study.' *International Journal of Project Management* **20**: 1–11.

Williams, J. (2004). 'Why Monte Carlo simulations of project networks can mislead.' *Project Management Journal* **35**(3): 53–61.

Young, T.L. (2007). *The Handbook of Project Management*, London, UK, Kogan Page Limited.

Index

academics 136
accountancy 95
action generation 127–8
action planning 122, 127–8, 133–4, 137
  requirements for process 137
  see-the-big-picture approach 139–40
    Workshop 1: building connectance
      visual diagram 140, 141–5
    Workshop 2: generating
      alternative actions 140, 145–8
    Workshop 3: evaluating and
      prioritising 140, 149–52
  shortcomings of existing methods
    134–6
  Tool for Action Plan Selection
    (TAPS) approach 137–9, 154–5
    advice for implementation 154
  winning support for decision 152
  executive summary 153
Adams, J.L. 109
agency problem 167
Ahlstrand, B. 87, 160, 169
Akao, Y. 98, 177
Akdere, M. 179
Alexander, L.D. 160, 161
alternative generation 103–4
  see-the-big-picture approach 140,
    145–8
Ambrosini, V. 175, 199
Analytic Hierarchy Process (AHP) 137
Anderson, D.M. 87
Apple Computers 158, 161
Arnold, J.E. 109
auditing 98
Azevedo, R.E. 179

Balanced Score Card (BSC) 22, 23, 81,
  91–3
Barnett, C. 175
Basadur, M. 130
Beer, M. 47, 176
Bhimani, A. 95

blocks to creativity 108–10, 133
Bossidy, L. 46, 47, 49, 77, 79, 176, 177
bottom-up approaches 15, 24–5, 30, 98
Bourgeois, L.J. 178
brainstorming 107, 123, 135
branding 65
Brodwin, D.R. 178
business as usual approach 128, 131,
  135, 204
business school approach to strategy
  implementation 89–94

capabilities 2, 41
  capability development 56–7
  project management and 160–62,
    178
capacity strategy 34–6
catchball approach 48–9, 65
causal mapping techniques 123
Chandler, A.D. 44
change 106
  paradigm shifts 106–7
Charan, R. 46, 47, 49, 77, 79, 176, 177
charting strategy 117
cognitive mapping 123–4
Collier, N. 175, 199
competition 106
connectance concept 137
  building connectance diagram 140,
    141–5
consistency 52, 158
  project management as systematic
    approach to 169–73
constraints
  blocks on creativity 108–10, 133
  challenging self-imposed constraints
    115–17
  Theory of Constraints (TOC) 19–20,
    28, 165, 167
consultants 95–6, 97–9, 136
  project management and 178,
    179–80

217